ABOUT

The ordinary bus
or train can take
exploration of land
beaten track. Convenient, cheap,
roomy, with over-the-hedge views:
what better way to explore the real
England away from the tourist-packed
centres? This book describes many
such journeys taken by the author in
spring, early summer or autumn, some
day tours and some mini-holidays. She
also recommends dozens of other
scenic routes for joy-riding by bus.

ABOUT THE AUTHOR

Elizabeth Gundrey, well known for her
books on consumer affairs and on activities for children, is also a writer on
travel in England. Her sense of place,
and her eye for small, wayside details –
the extraordinary that's to be found in
the ordinary – turns any bus-ride into
an exploration. She is married to a
psychiatrist and has a 16-year-old son.

ABOUT THE
'DAY EXPLORER' TICKET

In conjunction with the publication of
this book, National Bus Company has
launched dozens of special Explorer
programmes of interesting bus trips
from centres of population and resorts
up and down the country. Readers of
this book can purchase their first two
Explorer tickets (for use on *any* of these
trips) at half price using the vouchers
printed on the last page.

*Cover photographs and chapter illustrations
courtesy of National Bus Company*

Dedicated to Andrew Cockburn.

Of many and unceasing Virtues,
Affectionate and Gentle,
Benevolent to All.
He shared my Journeys with Enthusiasm
Or bore my Absences with Fortitude.
Well done, thou Good and Faithful
Husband!

ENGLAND BY BUS

Elizabeth Gundrey

Hamlyn Paperbacks

ENGLAND BY BUS

ISBN 0 600 20253 4

First published in Great Britain 1981
by Hamlyn Paperbacks
Reprinted 1981
Copyright © 1981 by Elizabeth Gundrey

The author would like to thank a number of people who
have helped her in the writing of this book, and in
particular Annette Brown of the English Tourist
Board, Sally Varlow of the South East England Tourist
Board and Peter Stonham of the National Bus
Company.

Hamlyn Paperbacks are published by
The Hamlyn Publishing Group Ltd,
Astronaut House,
Feltham,
Middlesex, England

(Paperback Division: Hamlyn Paperbacks,
Banda House, Cambridge Grove,
Hammersmith, London W6 oLE)

Printed and bound in Great Britain by
Cox & Wyman Ltd., Reading

FOREWORD

If it is true, as is often said, that it is 'better to travel than to arrive', then what more pleasant way than by bus? Bussing clearly allows a closer look and more route variations than are possible with more tightly organized forms of transport. And considering the cost of petrol and the difficulties with parking, it can be cheaper and more convenient than travelling by private car. If you can 'hop on a bus' in London or other cities, so equally can you hop off a bus in the countryside or a small village.

At first the thought of travelling round by local buses may be surprising. But if friends told you that they were going to tour England's canals on a leisurely boat trip you wouldn't raise an eyebrow, and venturing out by bus produces the same combination of the planned with the unexpected. Exploring England by bus is a splendid idea which tourists of every age, adventure-minded or not, cannot help but enjoy.

The highways and byways of this country are full of unexpected pleasures. They are also full of bargains, whether in overnight accommodation or genuine home-made English products. Bussing is an ideal way to discover the attractions that can be found off the beaten track.

Elizabeth Gundrey has written a marvellous and much-needed guide to bussing around England that provides information and inspiration for both British and overseas visitors. Who knows – her book may turn out to be the first spark in a travel revolution!

Michael Montague
Chairman,
English Tourist Board

CONTENTS

INTRODUCTION

WHY GO BY BUS?

*'A fast road and a wise traveller
don't go together'*

Local buses are alive and well. Despite cuts in services, some 20,000 are on the roads of England – trundling through hills, villages and dales at a tranquil 20 miles an hour or less. They are one of the best ways to see England and one of the last undiscovered resources for the traveller.

Pick up any guidebook or tourist brochure and it will tell you about car routes, parking sites, perhaps even where to hire a car if you haven't got one. It will tell you about the railways. It probably lists coach services. It may even tell you where to hire a cycle, a horse-drawn caravan or a motor boat. But the humble buses rarely get a mention, despite all their virtues.

Buses are comfortable. Except at rush hours, they are half empty. You can spread out and move about. They have space for baggage, big windows for the view and sometimes open tops.

The buses are easy. They take you into the centres of towns (rail stations and car parks are often on the perimeter) and off the beaten tracks of motorways and main roads. You can alight and get on again at will. You don't have to book ahead. There is no parking problem.

The buses are for everyone. For students and other young people, they offer a low-cost, free-and-easy way to get about – and they have the same attractions for pensioners (who can often travel half-price). Their possibilities for the disabled are described on page 25. Children enjoy them (see page 16) with or without parents in tow – what safer way to let them go exploring on their own when school holidays start to bore? Bus riding can be educational: spotting-games are a natural (monarchs on inn signs, types of church spire, tree identification, farm machines, breeds of cattle and sheep), as is collecting a scrapbook full of bus tickets, picture postcards, pressed leaves and so on. Courting couples, I notice, favour the back seats of buses on Sundays – but not for the view!

Taking a short break of two or three days on her own may be an ideal tonic for a housewife who normally gets a holiday only when her husband is free. And even on family holidays it can be refreshing to abandon the car for a while and spend a day on the buses – a relief for both the car driver and the children cooped up in the back, and often an economy, for according to the AA it now costs nearly 20p a mile to run an ordinary car (allowing for depreciation).

For overseas visitors who want to reach the parts of England unknown to those who troop round the overcrowded 'sights', this is a good way of seeing a slice of country life. England has a better local bus service than any country in Europe and perhaps in all the world. In Spain you may be obliged to rise at dawn to catch the only bus of the day, and in Norway you could easily spend £100 on fares within three or four days.

It is extraordinary that buses (ordinarily so familiar a sight) suddenly become invisible when touring for pleasure is the objective. In the information office of a bus station one summer day I heard a couple ask to book for a round-trip excursion. When they learned that no seats were available for a week, they walked out disappointed and vanished. Yet right outside the door an ordinary bus going to the same destination stood waiting, with plenty of empty seats. On an excursion every seat is filled, the coach belts along, stops are few, and one gets off with the crowd and on again when the driver dictates. It is amazing that anyone could prefer that to the airy, easy-going bus! Perhaps it is because city buses are tedious (all stop-start-stop, and queueing at bus stops) that country buses are ignored, but they are a very different species and far pleasanter to use.

Although in some areas more services are available in summer than in winter, most buses keep going throughout the year; so for a short out-of-season break in spring or autumn they are ideal (and warm when the weather turns chilly), particularly if a midweek break is possible. At off-peak times accommodation is often much cheaper, and English scenery can be at its most beautiful when the first blossoms and the fresh greens of spring appear, or when autumn colours glow.

My ideal bus journey involves finding attractive routes (for the journey is the object, not the destination) and linking up a number of different bus services in the course of a day. An hour or so at a time spent relaxing on a bus between pottering in a country town, visiting a rural museum or sitting in the sun on a cliff top or river bank makes a pleasant alternation of activities. There's a lucky-dip element in bussing around, for often one's halts are dictated by the routes and times of the buses – and sometimes this has led me to discover something unexpected. But above all, bussing is to do with enjoying landscapes and countryside.

Not for me the record-beating efforts of, for example, the four schoolboys who covered 280 miles in one day using the £1 day-tickets issued by a Kent bus company. They started before 5 am and it was nearly midnight when they returned home; at about ¼p per mile they certainly proved bus travel can be cheap. But for me the big attraction of the buses is their relaxing, leisurely pace, and I deliberately average only about 70 miles a day with plenty of opportunities to 'stand and stare'. Studying maps and timetables, I avoid built-up areas and busy roads – my chosen routes lead to lanes sometimes so narrow that two vehicles (a rare encounter) cannot easily pass each other, and which arrive at villages 'unknown to grandeur and unknown to fame'.

I like bussing about mainly because I feel both free and relaxed. Free because it's easy and cheap to get away by this means for a day or two: it's so simple to give oneself a few days' holiday, perhaps at the end of a business trip or after a visit to relatives, by hopping on a handy bus. For such brief breaks I can travel light, with no need to lug a suitcase about – just a small nylon holdall weighing only a few ounces. I feel relaxed because of the slow speed (average 15 mph), and at this pace one sees far more than from a car, particularly wildflowers and small architectural details. Whenever there is a choice of bus routes between two towns, the less direct one is almost invariably the better choice as it is more likely to amble through byways and country lanes free of traffic.

On the journeys described in this book the stages of bus-riding lasted between ½ and 1 hour as a rule – not so long that the ride ever became tedious, but long enough to provide a welcome rest between sightseeing in the towns and villages where I changed buses.

Friends have asked whether, with one eye on the clock and my mind on the departure time of the next bus, such sightseeing ever became a frantic dash. Dashing not being my style, the answer is no – though sometimes this meant missing a place of interest because it was on the far side of town. However, since buses nearly always go into town centres, there has invariably been plenty of interest at hand, and it is surprising how much one can see in less than half-an-hour if that is all the time available. The secret of using limited time successfully is threefold: get off at the best stop for one's purpose (ask the driver, conductor or another passenger to advise); pinpoint what's interesting on a street plan so as to waste no time hunting for it; and if you haven't already got such a plan, pop into the nearest news or estate agent and ask for one. The best idea of all, if there is a Tourist Information Centre at hand, is to ask them to pencil onto a town plan the most interesting streets that can be walked in whatever time you have and to advise you where to catch your next bus onward.

Another thing I enjoy on a bus is the contact with a variety of people. Colonel's lady and Judy O'Grady both go shopping on the same bus and exchange chat: it's a great leveller. And an extra bonus is making small discoveries unknown even to guidebook writers (all car-borne, I fancy). Several times in villages dismissed as 'commonplace' I, from my high vantage point on a bus, have spotted something of interest beyond a wall or hedge.

Gourmets read recipe books in their armchairs, gardeners while away the winter deep in seed catalogues, and I now browse through bus timetables and route maps with a connoisseur's eye – journeying in imagination to fells and waterfalls, over bridges and alongside village greens, through lanes, down valleys and beside the sea – planning in winter where next spring may take me.

It all began one autumn when I decided to journey the length of England by this means – taking days over a trip one might do in hours by express coach or train. I was warned it would be impossible. Friends painted a gloomy picture of three-day holdups for buses that run only twice a week, and of hours spent standing in the rain at a bus-stop in some industrial slum while wind blew the fish-and-chip wrappers round my ankles. But Confucius he say, 'Journey of 300 miles begins with one step'. There was only one way to find out whether these prophets of doom were right. I packed a small bag and set off.

I certainly do not want to suggest that readers should follow slavishly the routes I travelled. Much of the fun is in working out one's own journeys. I purposely do not quote bus service numbers or schedule times for this reason and because they are inevitably altered from time to time.

How that journey turned out is described later in this book. But it was just a beginning. It gave me a taste for bussing which I go on indulging whenever I can snatch a few days from the commitments of work and my family (although they sometimes come, too). The only planning involved is writing off for bus timetables – and the first chapter covers such practical matters as that.

Note: After this book had been written, a new Transport Act came into effect under which it is much easier for new operators to start running bus services. Particularly in places where it may be uneconomic for the large buses to run, it is hoped that more minibuses may start up, perhaps community buses of the kind described later in this book. As far as I have been able to find out, all the routes I travelled will still be running in 1981 – with two possible exceptions, mentioned in the text – and in at least one place – (across Romney Marsh) a service has improved since I was there. The cuts that occurred towards the end of 1980 seem mostly to have affected frequency.

1

PRACTICAL MATTERS

Selecting your route

Although this book describes a number of routes I have travelled and makes suggestions for others, remember that half the fun of bus journeying is working out routes of your own. The possible combinations are endless, and apart from avoiding big cities and industrial areas, there are no rules. The best way to start is to send for a free map called 'Principal Bus Links' which the National Bus Company will send you (see Appendix A for address). Although it does not show every single bus service, there should be quite enough for a first attempt.

Using timetables

Having made a decision about the area in which to travel, the next step is to get the relevant bus timetables (they cost only a few pence). One can obtain them on arrival at bus stations, but it is better to write off for them beforehand (see Appendix A for addresses and a map showing where each company operates). The majority of these bus companies come under the umbrella of the National Bus Company, but even if they do not their services are usually incorporated in the NBC timetables. Sending stamps to the value of 20p when ordering a timetable book will probably suffice, and the bus company can tell you if a few pence more are needed. Some bus timetables are better than others, not only for the clarity of their presentation but for the amount of extra information they give. Most will tell you when market days and early-closing days occur in each town, a few list sights worth visiting, and usually town street plans are included which show the location of important places in relation to the bus station and bus-stops. Libraries often have timetables as well as guidebooks; some county councils also issue timetables. New editions usually come out each spring.

Some people find timetables difficult to understand, so at the end of this chapter is a page on how to read them: taken slowly there's nothing difficult about them. However, it does take some time to work out a route with their help so that you can time your arrival at the town or village you want to explore and be sure of getting on another bus going where you want to go. You can always phone the bus companies for advice.

Bus stations

A bus station is the terminus of every bus route and is usually (unlike some railway stations) right in the centre of a town, which is handy. Sometimes, depending upon what you want to visit, it may be better to get off before the bus station is reached: the conductor or driver is a good source of advice on this, or look at the town street plans that are often included in bus timetable books. Some bus stations are just bare yards, others are a huge complex of buildings. Facilities vary a lot: the WCs at some involve a few minutes' walk and often no soap or towel is provided. It's worth noting on arrival just where they are, in case you are short of time on turning up for your next bus. There may be a café, a large street plan of the town and (at the biggest ones) a left-luggage office, useful only if you intend returning to the bus station and only if it will still be open then (some close early). Information offices, where they exist, have a tiresome habit of being closed or equipped only with information about their own services and not neighbouring ones – another reason for arming yourself with your own set of timetables before you set out. Bus conductors, who carry timetables, are sometimes more knowledgeable, but don't depend upon it.

Tourist information

Many towns have Tourist Information Centres now, but they are often some distance from the bus station. A list of the 550 towns in Britain which have one, giving their addresses and telephone numbers, can be obtained free from the English Tourist Board (see Appendix B). The list shows which ones will book accommodation for travellers (some charge for this service). If you want to book your own before setting out, you may like to consult a hotel guide (see 'Bookshelf'). Tourist Centres vary in their opening hours and may be closed when you arrive in the

13

evening or before you depart in the morning, so it may be worth the effort to write to them beforehand asking for their free leaflets, mini-guides to their towns, street plans and so on: with only limited time it really is worth equipping oneself with this kind of information rather than waste half-an-hour wandering in wrong directions. Some Centres confine their information to their own town, others range over a much wider area. Most have lists of places that have connections with colonial history, such as the birthplaces of George Washington and Captain Cook, which may be of particular interest to overseas visitors.

Other information sources

Guidebooks can greatly increase the interest of a bus journey. Several are mentioned in the text of this book or in 'Bookshelf' and many can be borrowed from a library. Once again, don't rely on finding what you want on arrival: get it before you start. One exception to this rule is a street plan, which is best bought or picked up from an estate agent locally.

For information about an entire region, much of it free, write to the relevant tourist board (see Appendix B) *before* you finalize your plans. This will give you interesting routes to follow.

Finally, buy local papers as you go along and listen to local radio before breakfast to get an idea of the real-life preoccupations of the people around you. There is no quicker way of picking up the genuine flavour of a community that is new to you; even the classified advertisements differ from place to place. In addition, local radio stations sometimes announce changes to bus services that you may need to know about.

Travelling light

The only advantage the car tourist can undeniably claim over the bus passenger is that the former can pack everything including the kitchen sink without much trouble. Buses have room for baggage but few of us want to carry much weight about. A nylon shoulder-bag weighs least. Forget about sponge bags and suchlike – use thin plastic bags for everything, with plentiful rubber bands to keep them secure, clothes rolled up compactly, timetables bundled together and so on. The thinnest of showercoats (with hood), pencil and paper for route-planning each day, and a 100-watt light bulb are desirable without being too heavy. Why the light bulb? Because so many hotel bedroom lights are dim, and so many timetables are poorly printed.

Timing your journey

An autumn journey is full of pleasure, and the warm bus protects one from bad weather. Spring, too, is a good time to go, particularly in the west country, when flower festivals are held – but avoid the May bank holiday weekends if you can.

Summer, yes – buses are so little used by the typical tourist, who thinks only in terms of excursions and coach tours or a car, that even in summer they are not crowded. However, the towns and 'sights' are apt to be thronged in July and August, the school holiday period. Winter is not a good time to travel because, what with condensation inside and mud splashes outside, bus windows in the country are often impossible to see through, and darkness falls very early, especially after the last Saturday in October when the clocks are changed over to winter time until late March. In spring and autumn towns are mercifully free of tourist crowds, though most of the stately homes are open (the majority close in winter). One sometimes finds more buses running during school term times, on market days, or on the days when Women's Institutes have their regular meetings.

Sunday travel may be best avoided because services are fewer then, particularly in the mornings, and information offices are closed. Do not set off early on weekdays, unless you want to be part of the rush hour to work. Market days can be fun.

What country buses are like

Country buses are different from city buses. Mostly they are much nicer though they do vary in comfort (and cleanliness). They certainly do not have the luxury of long-distance coaches, except on a few express routes: there is more noise, and some of them rattle and bump. But, with so few passengers, there is plenty of space and air, and even the single-deckers give a view over walls and fences which car passengers cannot see. Few of the buses have conductors now. You pay the driver when you get on. Fares compare well with alternative modes of transport, and in an increasing number of places pensioners travel free or for half price (children likewise). Within some regions it is possible to buy (for about £2) a pass entitling you to a day's unlimited travel on many routes, but whether this is a saving depends upon where you want to go. There is also the new Explorer ticket (see the last page).

Getting to your starting point

If you live in a big city and want to do a bus tour in another area, the starting point had better be where a train or (usually less expensive) an express coach from your city connects with the local buses. Avoid the rush hours if possible, otherwise traffic jams will prolong the agony. Londoners, of course, have by far the biggest problem, to which the fast Green Line coaches (run by London Country Buses) may provide the answer. These are the principal services, most of which run hourly.

DESTINATIONS	SOME BOARDING POINTS
Windsor (Berks)	Victoria, Kensington, Hammersmith
Cobham (Surrey)	Oxford Circus, Hammersmith
Guildford (Surrey)	Oxford Circus, Hammersmith
Leatherhead, Dorking (Surrey)	Victoria, Kensington, Hammersmith
Sevenoaks, Tunbridge Wells (Kent)	Victoria, New Cross
Hatfield, Hitchin (Herts)	Victoria, Brent Cross
Hemel Hempstead (Herts)	Victoria, Willesden
St Albans (Herts), Luton (Beds)	Victoria, Brent Cross
Ware, Hertford (Herts)	Oxford Circus, Finsbury Park
Aylesbury (Bucks)	Victoria, Brent Cross
High Wycombe (Bucks)	Victoria
Oxford	Victoria
Horsham	Victoria, Kensington, Hammersmith

Fast services from other bus companies take Londoners to Oxford (via either High Wycombe or Maidenhead and Henley), Bedford, Southend, Farnham (via Aldershot), Reading (via Maidenhead) and Tenterden or Maidstone (via Borough Green). A useful free leaflet called 'Times and Fares to 100 Destinations from London', obtainable from the National Express coach company, details express coaches from London to distant towns and cities. Write to them at the Victoria Coach Station, Buckingham Palace Road, London SW1.

Children on buses

Many of the one- or two-day tours in this book were planned with an eye to their suitability for children. Small children are more easily kept amused on buses than in cars because the children are not so confined: in the majority of journeys described in this book, there was plenty of space on the buses. Often little children chum up with other passengers; they like watching the driver, the automatic doors and the ticket machine or looking at the passing scene. A journey taken in easy stages provides plenty of halts between reasonably short periods of travelling. There is no difficulty in taking toys along for a day trip, too (or even the family dog, as a rule), and it is easy to think up innumerable spotting and scoring games – 'collecting' church spires, weather vanes in all their variety, horses, kings and queens (on inn signs), bridges or what-have-you. Several paperback books of car games are equally applicable to bus journeys. On holiday, a bus trip is the perfect solution to the problem of what to do when it rains.

Older children can get even more out of a journey – beginning with helping in the planning of it, mastering the mysteries of a timetable, studying the route map and so forth. It can become an educational experience – in an enjoyable way – if a particular theme is chosen, such as the Normans or Charles Dickens (see chapters 16 and 14), and backed up with the present of a book on the subject. The 'Discovering' series of books seems ideally suited to bus journeys. Each is pocket-sized yet deals pretty thoroughly with just one topic. Hamlyn's *Young Road Traveller's Handbook* is a good companion.

As already mentioned, buses provide a good first step into more independent travelling, when young people want to free themselves of parental control and go off on their own. Buses are very safe and more familiar to the children than most other modes of transport. If a chosen route involves changes of bus, it may be wise for a parent to check that there is no great gap (of time or distance) between the first and subsequent bus, and to write on a postcard the number of the second bus and its departure time and place to avoid possible problems (a wrist watch is desirable). Bus conductors and inspectors at bus depots are usually very helpful to young people. Obviously, more experienced young-sters can work all the details out for themselves – in fact, the challenge of getting themselves from A to B to C to D and back to A unaided can be quite a thrill, particularly if a group venture out for the day together, complete with packed lunch, cameras and perhaps binoculars.

Another 'plus' for the joy-riding habit among families with children revolves around the high cost of visiting stately homes and other tourist attractions when on holiday; the cost for, say, two adults and two children soon mounts up. To spend a day on the buses is a bargain by comparison – particularly where family tickets or cheap fares for the children are offered, but even the ordinary 'go anywhere' day-tickets provide hours of entertain-ment for very little expenditure. So does the new Day Explorer (see back page of book).

I have included in this book many bus tours which can be taken, at least in part, from typical family holiday resorts such as

Folkestone (Chapter 6), Eastbourne (Chapter 16), the Isle of Wight (Chapter 10), Torquay (Chapter 7), Bournemouth (Chapter 11) and Penzance (Chapter 13). From other resorts there are other rides, just as interesting, and some of these are more briefly described at the end of the book.

A note to overseas visitors

If you visit none but the famous (and crowded) sights you will not see the 'real' England and you may hear more foreign languages than regional English accents. However, a number of the one-, two- or three-day tours in this book can be tacked onto more conventional sightseeing – starting out from such famous tourist spots as Stratford-on-Avon, Windsor, Oxford, Salisbury, York or London itself. Others are conveniently placed in relation to the ports or airports at which overseas visitors arrive or depart. Here are some suggestions:

PORT	BUS TOUR
Newcastle	Roman Wall – London route; or Northumberland National Park
Hull	Roman Wall (from Doncaster); or Yorkshire Ale Trail
Harwich, Southend	East Anglia
Tilbury	London's Countryside
Sheerness	Dickens or Apple Blossom Trail
Dover, Folkestone	Cinque Ports route
Southampton	Isle of Wight tour, Salisbury Plain or New Forest
Plymouth	South Hams, Cornwall or Scillies
Bristol	Exmoor National Park or Cotswolds
Liverpool	Peak District National Park or Lake District

AIRPORT	
Heathrow, Luton	London's Countryside (starting at Windsor or St Albans)
Gatwick	Norman Conquest route
Birmingham	Shakespeare's England
Manchester	Peak District National Park or Yorkshire Dales

Before setting off from your own country you can obtain more information from any overseas office of the British Tourist Authority (see Appendix B for addresses). Remember that, on the whole, in the south of England spring comes earlier than in the north, and that the east tends to be less rainy than the west – an exception to both these statements is the Wirral peninsula (Cheshire).

Booking accommodation

It is possible to travel around without booking ahead, if you are not too fussy about what kind of accommodation you want. There is unlikely to be much difficulty in spring or autumn, but this method is more uncertain during summer if you go to the tourist attractions. A bus will deposit you in the centre of town, where you can either try whatever hotels are in the main streets or go to the Tourist Information Centre for help. Remember that a lot of these Centres close rather early – often at 5 pm.

Alternatively, you can make sure of your bed for the night by telephoning a hotel chosen from one of the many hotel guides – see Bookshelf – or a Tourist Information Centre in advance. Not all TICs provide a hotel reservation service (though all will give names of hotels). A free list of TICs is obtainable from the English Tourist Board (see Appendix B for address) which indicates those that do.

Hotels and inns are not, of course, the only kind of accommodation available. Some guest houses reach a very high standard of homely comfort, sometimes at less than half the price of a hotel. You may or may not get amenities like a bar, private TV, evening meal or private bathroom. In a few there may not be a sitting room. But if all you want is a comfortable, clean bedroom and a good home-cooked breakfast – often backed up by much more caring service and better cooking than some hotels give – then a modest guest house could be the best choice. (Guides to these are listed in 'Bookshelf'.) I have found a number of guest houses run by 'amateurs', often former professionals in other fields. People who prefer the hard work and independence of running their own guest house often bring to it an enthusiasm one does not always find among the staff of some chain hotels.

In addition, some private householders (including farmers) offer bed and breakfast. You may be their only guest and in some cases be treated almost as a visiting friend of the family – a chance to experience a different way of life.

Finally, there are youth hostels – for people of all ages. The accommodation can be very basic, with beds in dormitories (a few have family rooms) and washbasins in a row. Meals are eaten in refectories, and there is often a good deal of youthful noise. You can try out hostels on a guest pass before deciding whether or not to join, and a handbook will tell you which ones are on bus routes and how long it should take to get to them (see 'Bookshelf'.)

Several organizations sell books of vouchers at around £7 each which are exchangeable at bed-and-breakfast hotels on their lists. These can be very good value, and the organizers claim to have vetted the chosen hotels carefully. Before buying vouchers, however, check whether hotels in the scheme are in the places you want to visit. Examples are Woodcock, 23 High Petergate, York, and Minotel, 11 Palmeira Mansions, Church Road, Hove, Sussex. No vouchers are involved in the Guestaccom scheme – just send for their brochure of modest hotels and make your own booking (190 Church Road, Hove, Sussex). The Countrywide Holidays Association (Birch Heys, Cromwell Range, Manchester) provides good, basic accommodation at unpretentious hotels, often with outdoor activities laid on.

In praise of small hotels

When I first began writing this book I stayed mostly at old coaching inns, but gradually, as the cost of so much travelling mounted up (and so did the effects of inflation), I sought out even less expensive private hotels and guest houses which charge about £6 to £7 for bed-and-breakfast and £2 to £3 for dinner, if provided. This was new ground for me, and it came as a revelation to discover how good many of them are. In fact, my overall impression is that they are *better* than a good many expensive hotels – by my standards, that is. I do not need, for instance, porters, a huge *à la carte* menu, a dance floor or lifts. What I do value are fresh, home-cooked food; a comfortable bed; quiet; the possibility of tea or coffee at any hour; clean, well-maintained rooms with controllable heating; an informal atmosphere; and above all the presence of an owner who keeps a concerned eye on everything and cares whether his or her visitors are content. It is on this last point that small hotels often score over others charging two or three times as much, and this makes all the difference.

This also gives the small hotels their individuality: proprietors impress their own characters on their houses. It shows in everything from colour schemes (excellent to non-existent) to the style of cooking – always, in my experience, very good. In one a Cypriot was able to provide authentic Greek meals on request, at another there was home-baked bread, and at a third beautifully fresh fish was available (the owner's husband had been a fish merchant). Many proprietors of small hotels are amateurs in the sense that they have had no training in hotel management. Typical of these was an ex-salesman from British Leyland who said, 'I used to travel a lot, so when I bought this place I decided to provide everything I had myself found desirable in hotels where I stayed.' As a result, he had installed a small kitchen where visitors could help themselves to milk, tea and so forth at any hour (free), colour television in every room and advice on good, cheap restaurants pinned on a notice board. He, too, charged only £7 a night. What one gets in the way of a view, garden, bar or games room, and how big the sitting room and its TV are varies a lot; but these are variables in big hotels, too.

Small hotels often have an informal atmosphere: people do not dress up for dinner. This meal is often as early as 6.30 pm, which suits families with children. There may be a friendlier feeling (particularly towards children) than in more pretentious places. That, too, I prefer – even if, as occasionally happened, I got a bed that squeaked or a dim bedside light or very small towels (I've been given those in posh hotels, too). Small hotels are also less likely to be invaded by coach parties in summer or school groups out of season.

Eating cheaply

The traditional English breakfast, overseas visitors will soon discover, is very sustaining, so you may not need a big or expensive lunch. Inexpensive eating places include: tearooms or cafés which serve light, home-made lunches; inns with hot or cold snacks served in the bar at lunchtime; wine bars; restaurants inside department stores, stately homes, civic theatres and arts centres; fish-and-chip, hamburger, pizza and kebab take-aways; and Chinese and Indian restaurants. Restaurants that serve expensive meals in the evening often provide first-rate *table d'hôte* lunches at very modest prices. When eating at cheap restaurants, it is sometimes best to stick to those standard items such as shepherd's pie, steak and kidney pie, fried fish, omelettes and sausages.

Opening times and dates

Overseas visitors may be puzzled by English habits where these are concerned. Each district has its own rules about when its shops and bars may open. Usually all the shops in a town close during the afternoon of one particular weekday, and these early-closing days are listed in bus timetables (and a few guidebooks). However, seaside resorts and other tourist centres often dispense with early-closing days and many of their shops stay open all day every day, at least during the summer. Usual hours are 9 am to 5.30 pm, sometimes with an hour off for lunch in smaller places. Drink licensing hours are also controlled, but the precise hours vary. Bus timetables and a few guidebooks give the weekly market day of each country town that has one.

There is no generally agreed definition of the seasons. Some sights (such as stately homes) and services (certain bus routes) close down for the winter, but each picks different dates to close and reopen. The same is true of those 'off-peak' bargains in hotel accommodation offered only in the less popular seasons – each hotel determines its own dates.

Look out for . . .

. . . special savings on bus tickets. Apart from discounts in many places for children and pensioners (some areas even issue them with free tickets or sell passes entitling them to free or cheap rides), there are various economy tickets available, including family tickets for two adults and two children and cheap day-tickets. The vouchers at the back of this book can save you money on the range of Explorer tickets. Or you may pay a fixed sum for a ticket that entitles you to a whole day or a whole week on the buses, going wherever you like within the area of one or more bus companies (the former is often much cheaper). Some tickets cover combined bus-rail journeys. These special tickets may have to be bought at bus offices rather than on the buses themselves.

. . . special routes for joy riders. Several bus companies, particularly in summer, lay on extra services to travel round areas of scenic beauty such as the Surrey hills and the Peak District.

. . . special leaflets or booklets. A few bus companies produce free or inexpensive publications describing, for example, interesting walks on the Cornish coast or South Downs, with details of buses to the start and from the end of each walk. The Explorer leaflets also give information on sights, some of which may be visited at a discount, along suggested routes. The Countryside Commission's folder 'Public Transport in the National Parks' gives details of bus and rail networks in these very beautiful regions (available free from the Commission at John Dower House, Crescent Place, Cheltenham).

. . . season tickets for castles and houses. These give you free entry for a year (but check whether they are open year-round). One ticket is needed for National Trust properties, another for those in private ownership belonging to the Historic Houses Association (10 Charles Street, London SW1) and a third for Department of the Environment monuments. DoE hours are regular, but lately some monuments have been unexpectedly closed owing to staff shortages. Museums are mostly free. Note that in some houses, visitors are corralled in groups to be shown round at set intervals; this can be a nuisance if your eye is on the time of the next bus.

How to read timetables

Some people seem to go into a deep coma at the sight of a timetable – all those figures look too much like tortured hours in maths lessons. But in fact they are quite simple to follow if you set about it in the right order.

Nearly every timetable book includes a *map* showing where the bus services run. Unless you already know what's what, study this in conjunction with a guidebook (or the brochures that tourist offices hand out) in order to pinpoint which places will be interesting to visit.

Then turn to the *index* in the timetable book and look up the towns and villages that have taken your fancy. The names are at the front of the book in alphabetical order, and this index will give you the number of the bus service(s) that go to it. (Incidentally, the book will probably also tell you the market day, if any, and the early-closing day of each town, which might influence your decision about when to visit it.)

Turn to the page dealing with a particular bus service, giving its *timetable*: the services are in numerical order. Often services which do not belong to the principal bus company are listed at the back of the book on coloured paper – these may include smaller private bus companies or services run by a large company whose adjacent territory slightly overlaps. Here you will find not only the times at which the buses reach a town but also what other towns or villages they call at (and when). In the case of large towns, the list will note where its main stops are. Here is an example:

PENZANCE (Bus Station)	0905	1010	1110	1210	1410	1615	1810	2010
Penzance (Promenade)	0910	1015	1115	1215	1415	1620	1815	2015
Newlyn Bridge	0913	1018	1118	1218	1418	1623	1818	2018
Buryas Bridge	0917	1022	1122	1222	1422	1627	1822	2022
Drift Cross Roads	0921	1026	1126	1226	1426	1631	1826	2026
Tregonebris	0925	1030	1130	1230	1430	1635	1830	2030
Crows-an-Wra Cross Roads	0930	1035	1135	1235	1435	1640	1835	2035
Friend's Burial Ground	0935	1040	1140	1240	1440	1645	1840	2040
Sennen Cove	0943	1048	1148	1248	1448	1653	1848	2048
Sennen (First and Last Hotel)	0952	1057	1157	1257	1457	1702	1857	2057
LAND'S END (Hotel)	0956	1101	1201	1301	1501	1706	1901	2101

From this it is easy to see what choice of buses there is from, say, Penzance to Sennen Cove (three during the morning, five after midday) and how long the journey takes (roughly 40 minutes).

At this point, check whether the service runs every day *and* all round the year: look at the top of the page and at the footnotes, too. This is vital! Some buses run only once a week, for example. (The word weekday means Monday through to Saturday.)

Timetables are always printed in the continental manner – 1 pm is written as 1300 hours, 2 pm is 1400, 3 pm is 1500, and so on. Sometimes a name has a symbol against it to indicate that it has a rail station, a ferry, etc. These could be useful links between one bus service and another.

Alongside or below each timetable appears its twin for the return journey – it's no good arriving on a late bus hoping for an hour's stop if the only one returning leaves in a few minutes. Study this, too, before setting out.

What exactly do you want from your journey if it is not a simple there-and-back trip? If you intend to get off for a short break at, say, Sennen Cove (in the above example) and then continue on to Land's End, you may find that the next bus does not depart until two hours later, which might or might not suit your plans. Alternatively, you might want to go on to somewhere not on this bus route at all – Mousehole, let's say. A quick look again at the map and index and you will discover that if, on your return journey from Sennen Cove that afternoon, you get off at Newlyn Bridge, you can easily pick up another bus there to get to Mousehole. Turn to its timetable and you will find a choice of sixteen before nightfall and that the journey takes only eight minutes.

PENZANCE (Bus Station)	1445	1500	1515	1545	1600	1615	1645	1700
Penzance (Promenade)	....	1505	....	....	1605	....	....	1705
Alverton Estate	1452	....	1522	1552	....	1622	1652	....
Newlyn Bridge	1456	1508	1526	1556	1608	1626	1656	1708
Newlyn (Red Lion)	1500	1512	1530	1600	1612	1630	1700	1712
MOUSEHOLE	1508	1520	1538	1608	1620	1638	1708	1720
PENZANCE (Bus Station)	1715	1745	1800	1845	1900	2000	2115	2215
Penzance (Promenade)	....	....	1805	....	1905	2005	....	....
Alverton Estate	1722	1752	....	1852	....	....	2122	2222
Newlyn Bridge	1726	1756	1808	1856	1908	2008	2126	2226
Newlyn (Red Lion)	1730	1800	1812	1900	1912	2012	2130	2230
MOUSEHOLE	1738	1808	1820	1908	1920	2020	2138	2238

When doing circular tours starting and ending at the same town but not coming back exactly the same way I went out, I found I made use of three to six buses to accomplish the day's circuit – working out the routes was part of the fun, but it took quite a bit of time each evening.

It also pays to study the extra pages at the beginnings and ends of these timetable books for all the useful information they give on such things as telephone numbers and hours of ferries, train services, tourist offices and the bus stations themselves.

Distances and bus-stops

Britain is in a metric muddle at present. Though some maps are in kilometres, signposts and most other sources of information still use miles – one mile is equal to 1.6 kilometres.

Both overseas visitors and Britons new to London always underestimate its vast size. It takes at least an hour to cover the distance from the centre to one of the edges – a boring hour through mean streets and industrial areas in most cases, and often involving traffic jams. Although the quickest routes out of London are listed on page 16, it is better *not* to stay in this expensive city while making day-trips out but to move around it as described in Chapter 5.

Concerning bus-stops, usually a metal post is placed wherever buses will draw up if hailed; it may or may not state the service number of the bus concerned, and where different services run in the same place this occasionally gives rise to confusion if they stop at different posts. In the country there may be no posts because the locals are familiar with the buses' habits. The only solution to these problems is to ask someone. Incidentally, just to confuse you still further, the signs occasionally bear a number which is *not* the bus number but the number of the stop.

Bus timetables often name an inn as the stopping place. Sometimes the bus does not actually stop outside it but on the opposite side of the road, or even a few yards further along. Beware!

Incidentally, I have almost always found buses very punctual. The only exceptions are those within and near big cities where traffic and larger numbers of passengers often play havoc with schedules.

Disabled people

Buses may be the only way disabled or elderly people can explore a town or country area (the high step up into a bus can be overcome by a gadget called the 'Step-Stick', details of which are obtainable from Meadjess Ltd, 18 Appleford Drive, Abingdon, Oxon). And while on the subject of the disabled, it is worth mentioning that some bus companies provide free or cheap tickets for handicapped people. The National Bus Company has a study group considering the needs of disabled people – it is possible that the 'kneeling' bus running in some parts of Kent may be used elsewhere before long. The front of this bus can be lowered to reduce the step height when a disabled passenger wants to get on or off.

In a few places there are transport groups (voluntary associations) which take up the needs of the disabled in particular. One such exists in Nottingham, and has produced two aids which might usefully be copied elsewhere: a list in Braille of telephone numbers to dial for information on bus and train times, and a leaflet relating bus services to hospital visiting hours in the city.

2

FROM THE ROMAN WALL TO LONDON

*Hexham – Durham – Darlington – Bedale – Ripon –
Harrogate – Leeds – Doncaster – Retford – Tuxford –
Newark – Grantham – Stamford – Corby – Kettering –
Bedford – London*

This first journey was taken in late autumn, one of the driest for 200 years, from the Roman Wall to London (strictly from Hexham, the nearest bus centre to the middle of the Wall). Except after 4 pm when school children flock onto the buses, I rarely found more than half-a-dozen other travellers though they seat 40 or more, and sometimes I was the only passenger. What other form of transport offers the luxury of so much space to oneself? Yet for housewives and pensioners in isolated areas, the country buses are vital. Even if they run only once a week, they fill the essential need for travel to shopping centre, dentist, cinema or clinic – and they are a kind of social club, too, whose drivers become unofficial community officers or sometimes even social workers.

My route started in the high Pennines, passed through the great vale of York and the eastern plains and by the Chilterns to London. I wanted to explore the in-between places – not the most famous cities or beauty-spots but those towns and villages the main roads do not reach. The bus routes determined where exactly I went, which gave the journey a surprise element. I chose to go when few others would be travelling for pleasure, setting out on the last day of October. The area east of the Pennines is less prone to rain than the west.

Though there was no rain on the hills, the hunchbacked, twisted trees spoke of fierce and frequent winds, and so did the

26

thick coats of the cattle and shaggy fleeces of the sheep. The women wore knitted wool hats like tea-cosies, pulled firmly down to defeat the weather.

Hexham
(about 1 hour)

A young soldier, little more than a boy when he enlisted, was sent to keep the peace on an unruly frontier far from home. There he died – killed by one of the guerillas he was under orders to control. There is nothing unusual about this in a world accustomed to such warfare. But this soldier's tombstone commemorates the death of a Roman legionary, and it stands in a Christian church.

The Latin inscription, translated, reads:

> To the gods, the shades, Flavinus of the Cavalry Regiment of Petriana, a standard-bearer of the White Troop, aged 25, and of seven years' service, is here buried.

The stone tells more of the story than these words reveal. A carving shows vividly not only Flavinus the cavalryman on his rearing horse but, crouching in the undergrowth below, an ancient Northumbrian with his dagger thrust upwards to hamstring the horse before killing its rider.

The stone, dug up in the abbey precincts nearly a century ago, now stands in Hexham Abbey – itself built in 674 from stones brought from the nearby Roman fort at Corbridge (where Flavinus' regiment was stationed), part of the Emperor Hadrian's immense fortifications stretching across the north of England from Newcastle to Carlisle. Over a million cubic yards of stone went into the making of Hadrian's Wall and its associated forts, many of which still stand in place. The rest began to be used for the building of farms and churches when the Romans, heavily beset elsewhere, withdrew from their distant outposts in Britain, in 407 AD, after some 300 years of occupation. Some of the legionaries must have been glad to move back to warmer latitudes.

When Hexham Abbey was built (by St Wilfrid) it had no equal for size and magnificence outside Italy, and it is still impressive – starting with an exceptional Saxon crypt, though when I arrived this was occupied by archaeologists investigating discoveries made in the course of recent maintenance work. Among the arches one can find a Roman altar and other Roman relics.

The font incorporates part of a Roman pillar, and elsewhere a

Roman god passes a comfortable retirement within a Christian recess. How ecumenical can you get?

The abbey's dominant feature is the great 'night stair' descending into the south transept. Down this vast flight of steps would come, every midnight, all the clergy of the abbey for the candle-lit service of matins. Their dormitory at the top of the staircase, unheated even in the northern winter, no longer exists, but the well-worn steps are still used by choirboys who descend in a scarlet-and-white procession before services at more conventional hours. The abbey was attacked in 1296 by raiding Scots who set fire to it, and traces of molten lead from the roof still cling to some of these ancient steps.

On the landing is a small room where refugees could take sanctuary (the dispute would later be settled in an ecclesiastical court). Severe penalties were imposed for seizing anyone fleeing to sanctuary, rising in magnitude according to the spot where the interception took place: from £16 if on Hexham's outskirts to £144 if within the church itself, coupled with penances for sacrilege. But the worst penalty of all was reserved for anyone who violated the sanctuary of Bishop Wilfrid's stone seat itself, known as the Frid or Frith stool and still standing after 1200 years behind the altar. For such a one, there was no pardon. The concept of church sanctuary was not completely abolished until 1727.

The hard and violent times the abbey silently recalls are a sharp contrast to the scene just outside it on a Tuesday, market day, when the square is filled with stalls selling curly Cumberland sausages, strong boots, crabs and home-made preserves. Many of the voices have a Scots accent, and Scottish mutton pies are in most bakers' shops (a good portable lunch for bus travellers).

Nearby is the 14th-century Moot Hall, which houses changing exhibitions, and just behind it the Manor Office of the same period, now used as a Tourist Information Centre but still showing relics of the days when it was used as a gaol (until 1824). Worth a detour are Hexham's award-winning swimming pool, ingeniously created only a few years ago in a disused wool warehouse, and, near the bus station, the Midland Bank's circular building with its terracotta frieze of cherubs with early Victorian pennies, shillings and sovereigns.

From Hexham to Durham

(about 1¾ hours)

With a grinding of gears my first bus (of 20) swung out of the bus station and into roads hemmed with ancient yew and holly hedges, larch and rowan, past peat-diggings and flocks of horned and black-faced Swaledale sheep. There was a clamour of busy rooks above and a vista of serpentine rises and descents leading ahead.

'Is your mum all right? I've not seen her on the bus lately', the driver asks a girl. Everyone knows the driver, and he knows everyone. The local bus provides more than passenger transport – it's also a channel of communication and a parcel service. Shopping trailers and baby buggies are heaved on and off, old gentlemen with crutches are pushed up or handed down, news is passed on and congratulations or commiserations are exchanged. 'Can you manage, pet?' the driver enquires of a 70-year-old lady who finds the high step difficult. 'Where do you want off, pet?' (Further south 'pet' becomes 'love' and, further south still, 'love' becomes 'dearie'.)

On we go between ploughed fields and cottage gardens still cheerful with nasturtiums, Michaelmas daisies and marigolds. The prevailing sandstone, aptly called millstone grit, is dark and coarse. A pair of tethered goats nibble a grass verge. Logs are piled high ready for winter hearths. The bracken is turning brown and the birch and oak leaves gold, but a plantation of conifers spreads a patch of dark green like a baize cloth.

On the rare occasion when there is a visitor to the old people in a nearby geriatric hospital, the driver may make a strictly unofficial detour to the hospital if it is raining. But on this day the weather was as he put it, 'very canny': in fact, it was a good year altogether for the farmers.

Open-cast coal mining further along the road has made a great gash in the green hills. But the driver says only people with weekend cottages object to the sight. For the locals it means more jobs, and for the farmer who owns the land several thousand pounds a year in compensation until the fields are restored. A grass hillock which we pass, topped by a chapel and an ornate mausoleum, was once the spoil heap from open-cast mining.

The route to Durham involves changing at Consett, a steel town whose tall chimneys dominate the high horizon long before the bus gets there. One of its few claims to fame is that it produced the first Salvation Army band, in 1879. Since I was there the British

Steel Corporation have announced the closure of Consett steelworks. It is a place of gaunt, satanic shapes. The churches' blackened towers were eccentrically angular by contrast with the rounded cooling towers and the pillars of smoke. It is easy to see why Consett's mean terraces are named 'Steel Street' or 'Bessemer Street', but what faint hope inspired the naming of 'Laburnum Avenue' where not so much as a weed grows? Under the soot (which disfigures even the sheep) the stone of the wall is reddish from iron in the ground, by contrast with Hexham's grey; at Lanchester, a little further on, the stone is yellower and there are some good stone period houses built around a village green.

Durham
(about ½ hour)

Durham deserves a book to itself and at least a day of any traveller's time. But all I had was half an hour or I would miss my connection. My disappointment was tempered by knowing the cathedral already – and by making a small new discovery in the backstreets of Durham.

The city's jewels, its cathedral and castle, stand high up on what is almost an island of rock within a loop of the River Wear. You see them suddenly and spectacularly framed in an arch of the railway viaduct as the bus enters the city.

The cathedral's massive splendour dates from early Norman times and its vastness alone is impressive. It is the noblest Norman cathedral in England, perhaps in the world. Once it had red-and-black painted decorations, but now its interest lies in the variety of unusual local stones used in its construction, some (called Frosterley marble) thick with fossils, and in the elaborate carving of later centuries, particularly in the Chapel of the Nine Altars. An old account vividly describes some of the original details: 'From pillar to pillar was set up a border very artificially wrought in stone with marvellous fine colours, very curiously and excellently, finely gilt with branches and flowers.' But during the Reformation much was deliberately removed on the orders of Henry VIII, and more damage was done when Cromwell used the cathedral to hold 4000 prisoners-of-war.

Even so, it is a cathedral of exceptional beauty and so are its surroundings – the deanery, the canons' houses round a green, Prebends Bridge, the mills by the weir and the narrow streets of the old city. Next to an ancient bridge is a shopping centre that recently received an award as one of the five best new buildings in

Europe. Its shops and car parks are well concealed under a higgledy-piggledy roofscape that blends with the look of the medieval city.

My own discovery during my brief stop was a hilly cobbled road near the bus station: South Street. So steep is the climb that a handrail is provided, but the effort is worth it for the view of the cathedral's west end, seen across treetops and in a silence broken only by the shallow murmur of water slipping over the weir below. South Street itself is a gem – a backwater of Regency houses, brick and stucco, with curving sash windows or wooden bay windows projecting over the street at first floor level with decorative plasterwork, fanlights over the doors and handsome brass knockers. Jane Austen might have felt at home here. At the foot of the hill a sensitive modern development was nearing completion, which fully does justice to its setting: a terrace of small homes which, while thoroughly of today and very original in concept, uses local materials and takes up the motif of projecting windows in such a way that new is in complete harmony with old. That half hour was well spent.

Durham to Darlington
(about 1 hour)

As I ate my pie alone on the top deck I watched the flocks of gulls that had flown far inland to find *their* meal – whatever pickings a plough was turning up from the soil. They have to move fast because a diesel-drawn plough doing seven furrows at once may cover three acres in an hour – work that would once have taken more than a day. Many fields were black where farmers had burned the stubble in order to get rid of weeds and improve the fertility of the soil for next year's crop. The bridge over the River Wear at Croxdale is parallel with another (medieval?) no longer able to take today's traffic, its sharp stone cutwaters still cleaving the current. Beyond the hedges one sees from time to time the disused tracks of local railways lately closed in the interests of economic management and now vanishing under tangled weeds and waving grasses.

The bus makes a detour to scoop up passengers in Newton Aycliffe, a recently sprouted garden city with trading and industrial estates on its outskirts. Though the houses are undistinguished the corporation has at least planted road verges, filled rosebeds liberally, and put in groves of young trees that promise to hide factories from view in years to come. Then a brief ride through a landscape of rolling fields, now pale with mist creeping from hedge to hedge, and Darlington comes into view.

Darlington
(about ½ hour)

This is a town that was made famous by steam, so railway buffs immediately make for the museum at North Road Station where George Stephenson's famous engine 'Locomotion' is housed, along with other historic locomotives and a model railway. The Stockton-Darlington railway was the first public line in the world (begun in 1825), used mainly for transporting coal. Stephenson, who worked in a colliery, used whatever money he could save to buy himself an education in engineering at evening classes. The success of his Stockton-Darlington line brought him the job of designing the Manchester-Liverpool line and the famous 'Rocket' locomotive, which drew a train at an alarming 15 mph.

However, Darlington's history goes back much further than George Stephenson. The 'lady of the north', its medieval church, occupied my brief stay in the town. St Cuthbert's austere beauty makes it one of the most noble parish churches in the country, and its 200-foot tower can be seen for miles across the low-lying district around it. The Saxons had a settlement here that included a church, but the present one was built around 1180 by Bishop Puiset of Chartres, a nephew of that great patron of church builders, Henry II, England's first Plantagenet king.

Some arches in the nave lean very noticeably because of the great weight thrusting down from the huge tower – its spire alone weighs about 150 tons. The graceful spire-like cover to the font, made in the time of Charles II, is also one of the tallest of its kind. Fonts needed covers because people used to steal the sanctified water for magic or medicine.

Darlington to Bedale
(about 1½ hours)

Daylight was fading as I left. The next stretch of the journey was through a flat landscape. White-and-brown sheep grazed, ducks dabbled among reeds strangling a village pond, and a covey of partridges was busy in stubbled fields. The region had a well-to-do look, with Dutch barns crammed with hay, apples heavy on the trees and spacious Georgian houses near the fine bridge over the Tees at Croft (which also boasts a spa hotel). Lewis Carroll

(Charles Dodgson) grew up there, in the Old Rectory. By the time the bus reaches North Cowton and Brompton, villages built round greens, the architecture has changed and stone houses are outnumbered by brick ones. The day was drooping, the soaking branches dripped and the bustling rooks had put themselves to bed in disconsolate rows along the electricity cables by the time we got to Bedale.

Bedale
(about 1 hour)

What is lost in clarity is certainly made up for in atmosphere if you find yourself visiting an old church at twilight, particularly in the company of a recumbent Yorkshireman and his wife, once lord and lady of the manor, who have been lying there in stone for some four or five hundred years. One may feel more at ease in the open churchyard outside, particularly at Bedale which has a large sloping lawn with yews from which to watch darkness drop its curtain over the fields beneath. The churchyard has a number of elegant table tombs – horizontal slabs supported by six pilasters or urns – and a very ornate memorial to Nancy Day, though its red sandstone has been much weathered by three centuries of wind and rain. The church tower at Bedale, so built that it could provide a defensive post in times of trouble, has many gargoyles, which make convenient perches for the roosting pigeons whose cooing is a pleasanter sound than the rusty rasping of a brood of pheasants not far away. Through the gargoyles' throats rainwater is conveyed well away from the church walls, sometimes in a gargling rush that gives them their name.

Bedale itself, once noted for horse breeding, consists of late-Georgian houses and shops flanking a broad cobbled street where a market is held on Tuesdays. Already the shops, here as elsewhere, were beginning to put their Christmas goods on display, and their bright lights twinkled invitingly through the slight rain as twilight slipped into darkness. Wensleydale cheese, made locally, was much in evidence. As no café remained open after 5 pm, I was glad to take cover in the Old Black Swan (pubs are open round the clock on market days) until my next bus arrived. The publican collects hats which hang from every beam in the ceiling – military and naval ones, straw, felt and tweed, a fez, a beret, a Dolly-Varden, a kepi, a Tyrolean one and even a bowler – and on the walls are various bits of blacksmith's gear. Some pubs almost double as mini-museums.

Bedale to Ripon
(about 1 hour)

No moon, no stars. It was a mistake to continue travelling after darkness deepened because I saw nothing of the view except pale windows lighting up on scattered farms. I was too late in the year for October's 'hunter's moon' which, like the 'harvest moon' of September, hangs low, large and reddish as a lantern to illuminate the way.

For part of the time we were on the old Roman road known as Deor or Deer Street, now the A1, passing through Melmerby. The sole passenger, I chatted to the driver about life on the buses. The pay isn't too much but there's plenty of overtime, he said, though no one may drive for more than $7\frac{1}{2}$ hours in one day.

On his recommendation, when we reached Ripon I made for the Unicorn to find a bed for the night. This is a 400-year-old posting inn with creaking stairs, named after the Unicorn coach that used to turn in under its big arch to deposit travellers breaking their north-south journey as I was doing. The hotel is said to be haunted by an 18th-century bootboy called Crudd (his picture, in which he holds a coin between his jutting nose and chin, hangs in the hall), but no bootboy came for my shoes that dark, dank night even though it was Hallowe'en. (I returned again to Ripon, after my Dales journeys described later in this book, and had a more luxurious stay at the spacious Ripon Spa Hotel – excellent food, and a beautiful garden, surprising for a hotel virtually in a city centre.)

Ripon
(overnight stop)

'Except ye Lord keep ye cittie, ye Wakeman waketh in vain'. This cryptic message greets you in huge lettering as you enter Ripon's market square. It is carved along the top of the imposing Georgian town hall by Wyatt that faces the equally imposing obelisk in the middle of the square. What this is all about becomes apparent at 9 pm every night of the year: but first, the events which led up to the Wakeman's existence.

About 655AD a little monastery was built at the village of 'Rhypum' by Wilfrid. The crypt remains – one of the few Saxon buildings that can still be seen in England – beneath the present cathedral. The church he built was destroyed by the Danish Vikings in one of their innumerable raids two centuries later, and for a time Christianity was blotted out in Yorkshire.

It was because of the incessant Danish raids that Ripon acquired its Wakeman. Alfred the Great, who alone offered effective resistance to the invaders, gave Ripon a horn and a charter in 886AD and appointed the first Wakeman with the job of keeping a lookout all through the night ('wake' used to mean an all-night vigil before a saint's feast day, though now in the north it refers rather to traditional days off work). Every night on taking up his post he would sound his horn as an assurance to the citizens that he was on duty.

Gradually the Wakeman became an official of considerable power in the city, a kind of mayor. The night-long patrol ceased centuries ago, but the tradition of the 9 pm horn-blowing continues – one long-drawn mournful note at each of the four corners of the obelisk. The present incumbent, paid £1 a night for his services, is a young sales representative with a rubicund face, good lungs and exactly the kind of Toby-jug presence one might hope for in such a prestigious blower of horns. The current horn, dating from 1865, is from a buffalo and is resplendent with gold mounts. The horn-blower wears a buff frockcoat and a cocked hat, white gloves and a silver arm badge. It is worth going to Ripon just to see him – but a bit of an anticlimax when he drives off in his little Fiat with the horn in the boot.

By lamplight on Hallowe'en I explored some of the 'gates' of Ripon ('gate' means a way or road, in this context): High Skellgate, Water Skellgate (where a millrace once flowed), Blossomgate, Bondgate and so on, with passages leading to picturesque courtyards behind. Ripon, now a centre of the paint industry, was once a spa and the municipal baths have a grand portico as befits spa baths, with handsome spa gardens adjoining. In this direction are many of the antique dealers, craft shops and the town's old pie shop. The Wakeman's timbered house, built around 1250, is still standing and is used now as a Tourist Information Centre.

One good modern building stands among the old facades of the market square itself. It has an arcade in which are preserved ancient beams from a house that once adjoined it, premises which until the Reform Act of 1832 gave the occupant (usually the mayor) the sole right to nominate Ripon's MP. Some of the front doors of buildings in the square were deliberately set back a few inches to avoid a one-time tax of tuppence on all houses with doors opening onto the square.

The cathedral is floodlit at night, and I was there on an evening

35

when bell-ringing practice pealed out joyfully over the town. At the back of the cathedral are a house where James I stayed in 1617 (now rather spoilt by a white pebbledash finish), alms houses and the ruins of a tiny 15th-century chapel. A steep flight of steps, with flagstones and cobbles, leads up to the south door of the cathedral.

It is a most magnificent building despite eccentricities such as columns of unequal height and a round arch in the lofty nave that cuts across the pointed one beyond. After the 12th-century tower collapsed in 1450 the design was changed, for fund raising was unequal to the cost of rebuilding in the original Perpendicular style.

Among the cathedral's monuments is a painted figure of 1637, the very essence of civic pomp, which (it is no surprise to discover) is that of the last Wakeman, who became Ripon's first mayor. The big ruff fans out around self-satisfied cheeks made fat by so much puffing on that horn (and so much good living, no doubt).

There is much else to see, like the 36 fine choir stalls with oak canopies delicately carved by a Ripon craftsman, whose work became so famous that he was employed in other cathedrals, too, and his surname was changed from Bromflet to Carver (he, too, served as Wakeman, in 1511). The misericords, folding seats against which the priests could lean while standing during long services, bear on their undersides carvings of griffins, serpents, angels, a mermaid, Jonah in the whale and such homely subjects as a fox stealing a goose and pigs dancing to bagpipes. The roof of the choir is jewelled with bosses decoratively carved in stone and gilded. In the north aisle, a heraldic window tracing a family's ancestry back to Edward II incorporates the arms of the Washington family, the stars and stripes of which ultimately went into the design of 'Old Glory', America's national flag. (Washington Old Hall, the home of George Washington's ancestors, is to the north near Sunderland.)

Ripon to Harrogate
(about ½ hour)

The main road runs quickly through handsome countryside. Chestnut trees were in full autumn magnificence at the edges of rolling fields with well-kept hedges. The fields themselves were a patchwork of rich green grassland, brown earth and golden stubble. Ripley, one of Yorkshire's oldest and least spoilt villages, comes and goes too quickly, a beautiful place of pink-brown stone, pointed Gothic windows framed in white, dripstones as shapely as in the Cotswolds, and abundant flowers. There is an old market cross and stocks. Against its church walls Cromwell shot some of the Cavaliers captured after Marston Moor, the battle in which the Roundheads finally broke the Royalist hold on Yorkshire.

The women on the Yorkshire buses have a decided 'no non-sense' set to their mouths. Good sensible shoes and felt hats replace the head scarves of County Durham or the woolly caps of Northumbria. One supposes those bulging shopping bags to be full of parkins and gingerbread men, brandy snaps, fruity 'cut-and-come-again' cakes and practical woollen underwear or twin-sets.

As we neared the end of the journey, a perfect example of *homo sapiens Harrogatensis* got on – a well-matured gentleman in tweeds, deerstalker and shoes polished till they shone like horse chestnuts. He was accompanied by (what else?) a Yorkshire terrier.

Harrogate
(about 1 hour)

In 1571 a certain William Slingsby accidentally discovered a spring of health-giving water when his horse stumbled over it – and from this there grew up (but not until the 18th century, when such things became fashionable) one of Britain's most famous spas. Nearly 90 such springs are now known in the district, their origin being some ancient upheaval in the earth's crust which crumpled and split layers of rock like so much paper, impregnating the water underground with sulphur and other minerals.

So it is appropriate as well as convenient to start any walk round Harrogate at the Royal Pump Room where, in a cellar museum, one such spring still bubbles up. Taste the water and you will understand why it was nicknamed 'the Stinking Spaw'. Defoe said, 'Those who drink from it are obliged to hold their noses'. The Tourist Information Centre nearby (in the Royal Baths) has a useful leaflet for anyone with half an hour or so to spare, giving the route for a walk that takes in Farrah's (still making the toffee in blue-and-silver boxes which has brought them fame since 1840), the graceful dell known as the Valley Gardens and the Sun Colonnade, a glass-covered walk 600 feet long. Montpellier Parade is a wide boulevard that recaptures the full flavour of Harrogate in its Victorian heyday.

The town is full of Regency terraces, monumental houses clad

37

in the scarlet of Virginia creeper, and spacious streets where shops shelter behind glass canopies with white iron lacework. You may buy good tweeds, furs, jewellery or antiques – or a skipping-rope, walking-stick, flute or mint humbugs. It's a town of real leather handbags and brogues, sheepskin coats and Burberries.

Harrogate has teashops the way lesser towns have pubs, and in the Pump Room the teacups clatter discreetly to the accompaniment of a real live pianist just as they may have done when the ill-fated family of the last Russian czar stayed here. Then the streets were thronged not with buses and cars but landaus and broughams. The street names, such as Raglan and Albert, recall the heroes of the time. A statue of Victoria at her golden jubilee, looking down from a perch uncommonly like a small version of the Albert Memorial in London, seemed distinctly unamused at the temerity of a solitary skateboarder in these surroundings.

Harrogate to Leeds
(about 2¼ hours; ½ hour at Wetherby)

My intention had been to go to Tadcaster, a market town where the so-called Ark (a half-timbered house with two carvings known as Noah and his wife) houses a brewing museum that is open on midweek afternoons. But for buses out of Tadcaster neither I nor the Harrogate bus station had a timetable, and the general opinion (wrong, as it later turned out) was that I would be stuck there until the next day. So reluctantly I headed for Leeds, pausing briefly at Wetherby on the way.

Wetherby is a village of odd angles and many archways. Traffic goes round a small town hall in the middle, at the shady back of which is a stone-pillared arcade called the Shambles, where butchers tried to keep their meat cool in the days before refrigeration. Now the small shops are boutiques. Its other touch of individuality is a shop called 'The Shoe Tree', with a sprouting golden boot hanging out as a sign.

A wholefood shop provided me with excellent home-made pie to eat as the bus swung out of the town and across the River Wharfe. A memorial angel on the bridge pointed a reproving finger at the naughtily bubbling weir below. Bridges in this part of the world are often lofty because even crawling streams may suddenly run high and furious when rain falls heavily on the distant hills from which they flow.

Leeds
(about 1 hour)

There is nothing traditional about the northern outskirts of Leeds. Its suburban semis, all pebbledash and coloured paint, could be put down anywhere in England. They are succeeded by Edwardian stone mansions set on high banks with shrubberies and steep flights of steps. Then come the slum terraces, interspersed with patches of derelict land, and with these the first West Indian faces of my journey so far. Used-car lots succeed one another and are then succeeded by new-car showrooms. Old red-brick warehouses give way to new concrete skyscrapers, huge car parks, underpasses and flyovers. Nothing pleases the eye except Alf Cooke's Packaging Works, a fine piece of industrial Victoriana with Italianate red-and-white brick arches to the long row of first-floor windows and Corinthian pillars all the way along the top storey.

Leeds has a notable art gallery near its wedding-cake of a city hall (in The Headrow, not far from the Vicars Lane bus station). It is celebrated for its sculptures by Henry Moore, Jacob Epstein and Barbara Hepworth, an outstanding Rembrandt, many other fine oil paintings (mostly English) and a huge collection of watercolours. Thomas Girtin's landscapes of Yorkshire are excellent. The glass-roofed shopping arcades off Briggate are worth exploring, too. In Thornton's Arcade a pair of Jack-o'-the-clocks, mechanical figures, strike the hours below a large clock. Cast-iron curlicues, carved stone balconies and multi-coloured mosaics make a palace out of County Arcade. The mosaics spell out a Victorian morality lesson: figures of liberty, art, peace and justice are on an equal footing with commerce and labour. No miners or mill-hands would have recognized themselves in the well-scrubbed figures languidly reclining with mine lamp or spindle held in a graceful hand. But when these arcades were built no miner or mill-hand could have had the means to go shopping there.

In the shops below these fantasies, commerce is a reality. Mr Addyman, the butcher, has a window full of black puddings, brawn, 'stand' pies (more familiar to most of us as raised pies), tripe and savoury ducks – delicacies mainly unknown to the supermarket shopper. Next door to him were electronic organs. I bought a traditional 'fairing' to take home to my family, gingerbread men, and one of those solid Yorkshire cakes made with 'Old Pekulier' (*sic*) ale. Too solid for my liking, as it added

39

another 1½ lb to my bag.

Also within easy walking distance are Kirkgate Market (flanked with rows of plump cherubs) and a Jacobean church in New Briggate that still survives in the middle of 'the great town's harsh heart-wearying roar'. (That was Matthew Arnold's phrase a century ago – what would he think of today's din?) 'Briggate' means the road to the bridge – a bridge so wide that in the Middle Ages a cloth market was held on it.

Leeds to Doncaster
(about 1¼ hours)

The bus pulls out through a depressing area of housing estates set against a landscape of cooling towers, pylons, gantries and blank, windowless warehouses, sooty land and grey sky. Even in the 18th century the area round Leeds was described (by Defoe) as 'a waste of black, ill-looking, desolate moors'. The word 'slum' comes from 'slump' (which meant a marshy place), because the first factories were often sited by a river or canal with workers' houses around them – damp, ill-drained and jerry-built. About half a million homes in Britain are still officially considered slums, but many more deserve the name.

The road went through Pontefract (in the castle of which Richard II was murdered) and then at last we reached some broad sweeps of countryside again, peewits (lapwings) grazing in the sombre fields and a burst of red poppies – a reminder that Remembrance Day was near – catching the last light of the afternoon.

The rural view soon passes. Castleford has a mining college and, on the horizon, tips and pithead wheels make it plain that coal is king in the country ahead. The old miners' songs are still sung in these parts – ballads like this, once sung by a miner to his pit pony:

> I shall be glad when this shift is done.
> Then I'll be up there, out in the sun.
> Thou'll be dahn 'ere, boy, in this dark 'ole,
> Still gruntin' and groanin', pullin' this coal.

Doncaster to Retford
(1 hour at Doncaster, 1 hour to Retford)

To get from one bus station to another involves a roundabout drive on a minibus. This gives glimpses of some fine Regency buildings in South Parade and, in a shopping centre, an interesting new library looking rather like a branch of Sainsbury's (which, after all, may be more inviting to the young). A water-bus provides trips on the River Don. But for the most part, except during the racing season, Doncaster has a very workaday face, as befits a town which owes its living to coal and the building of locomotives.

A pearly-pink sunset provided the backdrop to the trees of the Bawtry Forest as we passed into Nottinghamshire. The bus started off full of schoolchildren but many had alighted by the time Bawtry was reached. There several wide-arched coaching inns surround the market place. Soon afterwards we left the A1 – the Great North Road of coaching days – to get to Retford and the well-named River Idle just before nightfall, and I booked into the last room left at the White Hart.

Retford
(overnight stop)

A large cannon in front of the church points directly at the White Hart, but it is a long time since it fired a shot in anger. Retford has had other troubles, though. In 1528 it had its own great fire when the whole town was burnt, including the church. In 1651 a storm blew down the church tower. Later, plague repeatedly hit Retford, and the parish register contains a recipe (early 18th-century) for its cure: a pennyworth of dragon water, a pennyworth of olive oil, some methrodate and treacle. The patient is then to scrape out the middle of an onion and fill it with pepper, roast it, add it to the previous mixture and drink it. The recipe further advises sweating and putting soap and bay salt on one's feet at night. 'With God's Blessing', it concludes, 'you shall recover' (though whether from the plague or from the remedy, who shall say).

The fine Perpendicular church is dedicated to St Swithin, of whom a quaint little Portuguese statue stands above the south door. I was lucky to find the church floodlit after nightfall, and the bell-ringers were hard at practice on the ten very melodious bells. This change-ringing (the peals being rung in varied permutations, quite different from playing tunes) is something peculiar to England.

Though Norfolk is the county whose churches are famed for their carved oak angels in the roofs, I found them in Retford, too, and in other churches from here to Bedford – plain, painted, gilded, soaring, kneeling or playing music. The superstitious

41

believed real angels hovered invisible in the roof of every church. When the Cromwellians destroyed other images lower down in the churches, the angels escaped because they were too high to reach.

Early morning saw stall-holders already setting out their goods under colourful striped awnings in the market square. The sun was bright and the air breezy. Once, all goods sold in markets were subject to taxes that went to king or lord and later to the township. Now stall-holders pay rents instead. The cross which some markets have in the centre was often called a butter cross, because it was there that farm women sat to sell their butter and eggs. In the 16th century, market halls were sometimes built to shelter them in a pillared area, and the room above was used for meetings of the town council and similar purposes.

One of Retford's more attractive parts is Grove Street, off the square, which has attractive 18th-century doorways with fluted pilasters, bow windows and good ironwork. The local council has dealt kindly with this road, planting laburnums and well-designed wood seats. Instead of a kerb, a wide new gutter of purplish-red bricks seems to give the little street greater width.

Retford to Tuxford
(about ½ hour)

In this part of the world sugar beet is one of the important crops. Harvesting it that year was heavy work, for the rust-red soil was dry and hard to break – so hard, said the bus driver, that the annual ploughing contest had had to be abandoned. The fine weather meant prolonged summer in the cottage gardens, still full of flowers, and Askham, a village on the brow of a slight hill in this otherwise flat region, was looking particularly pretty. The bus follows lanes that wind among the villages and crosses the old Chesterfield canal, where a traditionally painted narrow-boat was moored (70 feet long but only 7 feet wide, so as to pass through the narrowest canals). In 1830 William Cobbett described quite well-to-do Yorkshire families, of farmers or skilled artisans, crossing England by canal to Liverpool in one of the first waves of emigration to America, as 'fugitives from the fangs of taxation'. Many of the cottages have red pantiles in place of the slate roofs which are universal further north.

Tuxford
(about ½ hour)

How did such a small place as this come to have such a fine grammar school? No longer a school, alas, but the handsome Jacobean building houses a library (in marked contrast to that supermarket library at Doncaster). One of the windows is now a fake. Long ago bricked in to avoid the window tax that was imposed between 1695 and 1851, a *trompe l'oeil* window has been painted in its place. (Householders paid double if they had more than ten windows and double again for over 20, so it could sometimes save a lot to brick up just one.)

Across the way is the medieval parish church. Never was any church more damp and chilly, but it is worth a visit all the same for the sake of its fine Perpendicular woodwork – the screen in particular. Though the church is dedicated to St Nicholas, it has two memorials to St Lawrence (martyred by being grilled on a kind of toasting-rack): a 15th-century stained glass window and a carved stone of the same period showing the saint and his gridiron. There are some alabaster tombs from the time of James I and a fine roof with carved bosses and painted angels. Alabaster, mined in the Midlands, was popular for effigies because it was easy to carve.

This is hunting and shooting country (the hunting season began that day), and Tuxford houses both a gunsmith and a maker of pigeon traps. There are few other tradespeople in the village, yet between them the shops can sell you anything from pigs' trotters to coal tongs, catapult elastic to shoehorns, things hard to find in city shops. Facing the big coaching inn, the Newcastle Arms (named for one of the greatest dukes in the Dukeries), is a signpost that could claim to be the prettiest in Britain. All curly iron with a lamp on top, it was erected in 1886 and restored about ten years ago. The village was once known disparagingly as Tuxford-in-the-Clays, but that is at least a little better than another unambiguously called Foul Mire. 'Good land, bad travelling' says an old country proverb of these clays, spread over the East Midlands when the glaciers of the Ice Age melted.

Tuxford to Newark
(about ¾ hour)

Flat though most of this route is, it goes through some especially pretty villages – Normanton and Sutton in particular – with half-timbered houses, black and white like the local magpies. All that is left of a windmill is the brick stump, looking sadly amputated. Such brick windmills came in during the 18th century (the earlier ones being made entirely of wood) when building in brick first became popular. There were blackberries in the hedgerows still, at least where the mechanical hedge-rippers had not yet been busy, tearing and mutilating as they go. Dozens of brown-and-yellow buntings take wing as we pass.

The stone houses of the north have petered out. Walls here are mostly whitewashed or bricks are used in a chequered pattern. The grass seems particularly green and lush, the broom yellow as butter. The small roads used by the local buses give one a distinctly superior feeling whenever they spring over the tops of motorways beneath – there are all those poor folk pounding along at 70 mph and seeing so little of England as they go.

Newark's lofty church spire comes in sight above the trees and then its castle ruins on the banks of the River Trent, that long river which, rising in the west, used once to bring 4,000 tons of Cheshire cheese a year right across England for consumption here in the east.

Newark
(about 2 hours)

Newark's 12th-century castle, where King John died after his flight across the Wash, was largely destroyed by the Royalist armies in 1646. The town, held by the Cromwellians, had been under siege for three years. Even in Saxon times it had been regarded as the key to the north because of its commanding position where main roads and river meet. Some relics of that siege remain in the town museum, including square coins specially minted inside the beleaguered town and a hoard of nearly 500 silver coins buried in a panic and never dug up again by their unknown owner, who may have died in battle.

The museum (in Appleton Gate, only a few minutes from the bus station) has an extraordinary collection of bygones which bring alive the details of daily life the way it used to be: tinder boxes and sulphur matches needing a flintlock to ignite them; a man-trap to catch poachers; a spiked collar put on dogs used in bear-baiting (legal until 1835); sharp cock-fighting spurs; clumsy, rusty dentistry tools. From an old chemist's shop came a large wooden panel listing sixpenny 'cures' on sale: 'Nerve and digestive tablets', 'Back drops' and 'Pink pills', described as being 'for pale people'. The formulae are given, too – a cure-all simply called 'Family Doctor' consisted of nitric acid and mint in water.

Not many yards away is Chain Lane, leading to the Market Square and the old shop of a modern chemist – but, thank goodness, not so modern as to have thrown out the great glass flagons of coloured water and the rows of old pharmacy jars, still half full, with labels like 'Ol. origami' and 'Tinc. camphor'. The excellent Mr Cherrington still sells some of the things that have vanished from the shelves of the chain chemists, such as real sponges from the seabed, those spouted china cups for feeding invalids with beef tea, and 'Dr Nelson's improved inhaler'.

Newark's vast Market Square is undoubtedly the richest I encountered on my journey. Its town hall is everything that a town hall should be – portico above steps, arches above portico, balcony above arches, columns above balcony, and pediment over all – with Justice teetering on top, scales crooked, sword bent, but still loyally supported by a mangy lion and unicorn. Down the next side of the square are a stone colonnade and two former posting inns from the time of Edward III. The courtyard of one now houses a betting shop and the other is sadly neglected, the rows of carved angels on its facade gradually mouldering away. The little pasties at the Olde Pie Shop are to be recommended for a bus lunch (or to picnic by the town weir below the church). Beyond the shop an arcade leads to Stodman Street and the house where Prince Rupert, the Royalist leader, stayed in 1645 after his defeat at Marston Moor.

The shops were selling seasonable muffins, chestnuts and cobs, and fireworks (only three days to Guy Fawkes Day). I was sorry I had not turned up on a Wednesday, when there is not only a food market but a cattle market, too, and an auction on Beast Market Hill. However, the quaint backstreets of the town are entertainment enough for so brief a visit.

And, of course, I took a quick walk round the magnificent church, started in 1160. More roof angels (recently restored with paint and their wide-spread wings gilded), medieval stained glass, a huge brass to a 14th-century merchant, and throughout a feeling of loftiness and light. There is a colourful and poetic monument to John Johnson, twice mayor of the 'loyal and unanimous' corporation of Newark, who died in 1659. It begins:

> Noe gawdy tryumph nor a flattring verse
> Can gild his fame or add unto his herse . . .

and then goes on with a considerable length of 'flattring verse' surrounded by much gilding. Where medieval epitaphs pray for the soul of the departed in the next world, later ones vaunt his or her achievements in this one.

The church has a chantry chapel endowed by a wealthy parishioner in order that masses might be said for his soul in perpetuity. Thomas Mering bequeathed for this purpose 'all my clipped wole and all my floke of shepe'. Another memorial, to Anne Markham (1661), shows the lady with all her seven children in miniature. Like many churches in the area, this one suffered from Cromwell's campaigns. Newark's spire, 240 feet of it, is said to have been built high in an attempt to outdo Grantham's, but in this it fails, for the Grantham spire is taller by over 30 feet.

Newark to Grantham
(about 1 hour)

The countryside continues to be rather flat with heavy clay soil. Warm red brick predominates in the villages, well set off by white-framed windows with leaded panes and porches of white trellis, like a red dress with snowy collar and cuffs. The names of some houses, recently refurbished, show how village communities are shifting and the old order changing – names like 'The Old Vicarage', 'The Old Smithy', 'The Old Schoolhouse' and even 'The Old Post Office'. One fine manorial-looking house has decorative gables in the Dutch style, a reminder of the many links between the Netherlands and Lincolnshire, the southern part of which was once called 'Holland'.

This part of England has always been celebrated for its geese (the first fowl ever to be domesticated), a flock of which grazed oblivious of the fact that this is the time of year when roast goose appears on the table and goose fairs used to be held – the Nottingham and Stamford ones were famous. The weather around Martinmas (11 November) is often fine, and this year was no exception. Called in Germany 'old wives' summer' and in England 'goose summer', this is the time when one may some-times see gossamer (from 'goose summer') in the fields. It comes from a species of small spider which spins threads that may fly through the air and then fall to ground, where dew can condense on them.

Innumerable old sayings foretell that a fine autumn like this one, with many berries and leaves still on most trees, will bring a hard winter. (And it did!)

Grantham

(about 2 hours)

The bus rides in along a road lined with Georgian houses raised up on a bank, as so many are in Bath. It passes 'the oldest hostelry in Britain' (the limestone 13th-century Angel, with a weatherbeaten angel carved in a doorpost). Originally a hostel of the Knights Templar, it was visited by Edward III, housed King John's court for a while, and was the place where Richard III first learned that his friend the Duke of Buckingham was leading a revolt against him and then signed an order for the execution of 'him that had most cause to be true, the most untrue creature living'.

Grantham may pre-date the Romans, but little is known of its far past. It was the scene of Cromwell's first notable victory in the Civil Wars when in 1643, although outnumbered, he defeated 24 troops of the king's force, doing much damage to the town and the church. Sir Isaac Newton attended the grammar school which still stands beside the church. With the coming of the railway age Grantham lost its previous importance as a coaching centre, and now even the motorway bypasses it, which makes it a pleasant town to visit.

Close by the bus station and hidden away above the public library is the town's museum – small but excellent, for it has been well designed and lighted. Its exhibits are mainly of local life from the earliest time onwards. The night watchman's rattle and the town crier's bell share a case with one of the splendidly decorated truncheons issued during the General Strike of 1926 to special constables enrolled to help the police keep order. There is an interesting set of bronze weights (trons) with the town arms on them, used by the tronator – an official who checked the weight of wool brought to market. Cutters for making quill pens, candle snuffers, silk winders, goffering mangles for ruffs, pocket pistols and irons heated by the insertion of a glowing coal – these 'unconsidered trifles' together build up a picture of home life long ago. The case devoted to Newton starts with a sundial which he cut in stone at the age of nine, and ends with a model of an Apollo Saturn V rocket and a commentary relating the conquest of space to Newton's theories.

Before going further, call on the excellent Mrs Gibbons, receptionist at the Guildhall. No tourist office or library is a better fund of information, maps, free booklets and enthusiasm than she, covering both Grantham and Stamford. Quite near the Guildhall is one of Grantham's famous pubs. Not a spacious coaching inn, but a modest little place called the Beehive, its sole claim to fame is its sign, an actual beehive in a tree outside. A verse reads:

Stop, traveller, this wond'rous sign explore.
And say, when thou hast viewed it o'er and o'er,
Grantham, now two rarities are thine.
A lofty steeple and a living sign.

The road leads on to 14th-century Grantham House, now a well-furnished National Trust property only occasionally open to the public (but the garden deserves a glimpse at any time), and to the church. If the verger can be found to open it, its ancient library of chained books is worth exploring. It dates back to Tudor times when books were too valuable to be left accessible to thieves. Building of the church began in the reign of Henry II, and probably its magnificence is due to the fact that the masons who built Salisbury Cathedral worked here too. It was not completed for nearly 300 years, and St Wulfram's is now a mixture of Norman, Perpendicular and Decorated styles of architecture. It is one of the most richly ornate churches in this area.

This is a church of angels: up in the roof of the choir (blue and gold), on the reredos behind the altar, on the organ, and on the cusps of tomb arches – but these last have had their heads hacked off by Cromwell's men. There is some fine modern stained glass in this church and a marvellous font cover with a carved spire that reaches almost to the roof of the church. By the font lies an unusual register of baptisms – every page has a country flower hand-painted on the vellum, with old-fashioned names like fumitory, enchanter's nightshade or codlins-and-cream. Curious and sometimes grotesque little stone heads peer at you from every corbel.

There is much more to Grantham – the George Inn where Dickens had Nicholas Nickleby stay on his way to Dotheboys Hall, the ancient market cross, the town conduit built in Elizabeth I's reign and still providing fresh spring water, and many quaint backstreets. A pleasant spot to end a visit is Catlins – a grocery that smells as few do now of freshly roasted coffee, cheese and ham, with a panelled tearoom above in which hot buttered toast or a featherlight cream cake and a pot of tea will still leave you change from 50p. A Cromwellian sword was found under a floor there during recent renovations.

Grantham to Stamford
(1½ hours)

'Coming with me, luv?' enquired the driver as he saw me hovering uncertainly at the bus station. The bus on this stretch of the journey was an express, luxuriously comfortable by comparison with the local buses, and dearer.

The trees were almost bare on this windswept road, silhouetted against a mother-of-pearl sunset. There were only four of us in the warm cocoon of the bus, and chat sped the journey along until I left the bus to head for nearby Red Lion Square and the 17th-century Crown Hotel in search of a bed for my third and last night on the road.

Stamford
(overnight stop)

'Here you die young if you die before 80, it's so sleepy', said Miss Mason as she served my dinner at the White Heather café later that evening. She was a fount of enthusiastic information about this unique town. Sleepy it may be, but its attractions were lively enough to keep me walking until well after dark, and I was up early next day to explore it further. Stamford really needs a whole day to itself.

It is an ancient town of stone on the River Welland (Stamford derives its name from 'stone ford'), a town of alleyways, arches, steep steps and many spires, crypts and cellars. Much of its creamy limestone came from the nearby Ketton quarry. Like so many other towns in the east of England, it has seen war after war. Boadicea pursued the fleeing Ninth Legion of the Romans across the ford in 61 AD, the marauding Scots attacked it in Saxon times, and the Vikings from Denmark ravaged it in the 9th century as they did so many towns on that side of England. In 1460 the Lancastrians stormed it during the Wars of the Roses, and it knew the upheavals of the Civil Wars. But later it was spared an even more disruptive effect than war – a proposed railway junction – and so one can still see this town very much as it must have been in medieval and Tudor times, particularly now that the A1 bypasses it.

The stone town owes its character to the fact that it is surrounded by quarries in the belt of limestone that stretches diagonally across England from south Yorkshire to the Cotswolds. Once its square mile was enclosed by defensive walls (one bastion still remains, in West Street), within which flourished a dozen monasteries or friaries and 14 churches, six of which are still there (but mostly kept locked up). Over 600 houses, ranging from one to four hundred years old, are officially listed as being of historic importance. Stamford has always been a prosperous town and was famous for its cloth (prominent at Henry VIII's meeting with Francis I on the Field of the Cloth of Gold in 1520). Even after the blow of Henry's dissolution of the wealthy monasteries, the town recovered and grew rich again on the wool trade. Much of this money went to pay the Tudor masons and wood carvers whose work still makes Stamford so beautiful.

The houses tucked away on Barn Hill (off Red Lion Square) are mainly of a later period, however, fine examples of Queen Anne and Georgian architecture. I walked up it at dusk and by lamplight read a plaque describing how in 1646 Charles I spent one of his last free nights in hiding there, fleeing next morning disguised as a servant. Two days later he was betrayed and taken into the captivity that was to end with his beheading. The lane winds round to Scotgate, on the opposite side of which alms-houses are hidden away around a peaceful courtyard. Further along is a disused brewery in which an interesting museum has been set up (morning tours around it end with a beer tasting).

At the other corner of Red Lion Square the High Street, now a pedestrian way, is full of buildings with character and side passages over which upper storeys almost touch, virtually shutting out any glimpse of the sky. A left turn leads to Broad Street, wide as its name suggests, and lined with houses that have the handsome porches and fine bay windows typical of Georgian times. Behind their dignified fronts are now conducted the mysteries of Chinese take-aways and hairdressers, surveyors and solicitors.

Browne's Hospital, comprising 15th-century almshouses and a chapel with exceptional stained glass, carried on its door a 'Visitors welcome – please ring' notice, but as no one answered my ring I wandered in the gloaming through cloisters where the scent of roses drifted heavily on the humid evening air.

Next morning, in bright sunshine, the shops in St Mary's Street were opening up: Kelham's, a bow-fronted grocery selling green gunpowder tea, ham on the bone and Spring's Lincolnshire mincemeat; Battels, for pottery and dolls made from the disused wooden bobbins of an old woollen mill; Lamb the ironmonger, whose shop front is adorned by five gold cherubs with garlands sadly in need of a lick of the paint he sells. Many of the women with empty shopping baskets were heading further along, however, to join the queue at the early Georgian Assembly Rooms (now an arts centre with a chandeliered ballroom) where the Women's Institute opens its doors at 9 am for its weekly market of home-made cakes and jam, home-grown herbs and fruit.

Next door, carpenters were at work in the old theatre, which was about to throw off a century of silence and dust. This little gem is one of England's oldest provincial theatres, built for £800 in 1768 so that touring actors should no longer have to perform in inns or stables. Macready, Kean, Kemble and Mrs Siddons all played there – and so did acrobats and can-can dancers. Some-times charity performances were staged: one was to benefit sol-diers disabled at the battle of Waterloo, another was for cotton-mill workers made unemployed when the American Civil War cut off supplies of cotton in 1863. After 1871 the theatre fell on hard times, its fittings were stripped and it was eventually reduced to taking in dog shows, bazaars and a disco. By the time the Duchess of Gloucester reopened the 170-seat theatre, much of its original elegance had been restored – and perhaps its reputed ghost will tread the boards once more.

South of the river, in the district of St Martins, stands the famous George coaching inn with its gallows sign – a beam stretching right across the Georgian High Street (at one time this was a common device, but few are left). The George is a place of inglenooks and underground passages. At the back is a cobbled garden, bright with hanging baskets of geraniums and fuchsias, that is lamp-lit at night. Once pilgrims walked there, for it is on the site of the 'House of the Holy Sepulchre', a Norman hostel for those on their way to the Holy Land. The sunken lawn was once a carp pool providing Friday fish. The present building goes back to Tudor times. In its heyday as a posting inn, 40 coaches would daily come and go through its courtyard on their way to York or London. Highwaymen, kings, Sir Walter Scott and the Duke of Cumberland, fresh from his victory at Culloden in 1746, were among its visitors.

A portrait of another famous customer, Daniel Lambert, hangs in the hall: he weighed 52 stone when he died in 1809. You can still eat well at the George.

St Johns Lane is a mere crack between houses. It leads down to the riverside, pretty paved gardens behind the Olde Barn rest-aurant, and the little Gothick Bath House (now someone's home). Further along stands what was once a watermill owned by the Crown, now imaginatively restored as a day school for mentally handicapped children. Sacks of flour can still be seen in Kings

Mill Lane and, through an open door, I saw a baker hard at work.

Stamford to Corby
(about 1¼ hours)

The two-decker bus climbs up High Street St Martins, turns a corner and suddenly one is in the countryside and the next county without any suburban or industrial sprawl. Gentle hills, stone farms, ancient oaks and a crocketted church tower – the view must be the same as in coaching days. Then, as we passed through pretty limestone villages such as Easton, Duddington, Kings Cliffe and Bulwick, the 20th century showed itself again in a mobile shop, from which a woman was choosing her weekend joint, and a plane landing at the RAF base at Wittering.

The branches of oak trees lashed the roof with a quick, sharp crack and the road switchbacked up and down all the way. The winter sun, low in the sky, emphasized the textures of hay, thatch and stone walls. Thatched roofs become more common as one nears the reedy Fen country, some having decorative scallops along the ridge of the roof and all wearing wire hairnets these days to keep out birds (or beasts: rats, too, appreciate a cosy bit of thatch). Reeds are also sometimes brought from Scotland, or the straw from wheat is used. Thatch over 15 inches thick not only keeps homes warm but should last nearly a century (it needs to, since re-thatching can cost £5,000 or more). Thatching was a dying craft until newcomers who could afford to pay for it began buying up derelict country cottages.

In these parts, hay is now mechanically gathered up in the shape of a giant toilet roll rather than in brick-like bales. Sheep, cows and pigs lay dozing in the fields, and swans idled amongst the reeds.

The soil in this region is chocolate brown, sometimes almost black. Right across a newly-sown field a farmer had stretched wires between trees and strung up multi-coloured plastic sacks as a latter-day 'scarecrow' that gave the field a circus gaiety. Outside one village near Corby a real circus was setting up. Travelling entertainers were once part of the great fairs held on certain saints' days, when goods were brought from far afield and, even in fairly recent times, labourers would line up hoping to be chosen for hire by local farmers.

Many of the cottages have decoratively fretted bargeboards under the eaves or at their porches. Their demure lattice windows and the neat rows of leeks and cabbages in their gardens give them a storybook air – this could be Hansel-and-Gretel country (even the bricks are marzipan colour, and the white paint is like icing).

But before long a view of factory chimneys announce the presence of Weldon. Its main street has a terrace of mean Edwardian houses, whose builder's sole effort to give them individuality was the casting in concrete of such hopelessly inappropriate names as 'Myrtle Cottage', 'Woodbine Cottage', 'Hawthorn Cottage' and the like (memorial slabs to the wildflowers which once were there, perhaps).

But, Weldon apart, the longish ride from Stamford was one of the prettiest on my route, and I shared the feeling of the stout woman who heaved herself off at Corby saying to the driver, 'Thank you for a beautiful ride! I enjoyed that – it were *luvly*.'

Corby to Kettering
(about ½ hour)

'The manufactures I take to be as well worth a traveller's notice,' said Defoe, 'as the most curious thing he can meet.' No traveller can fail to notice Corby's main manufacture, for the steelworks outside it stretch for miles and the air smells of sulphur. (Since I was there, the Corby steelworkers have been threatened with unemployment if the British Steel Corporation goes ahead with plans to cut production drastically.) But Corby itself is a shiny new town of concrete, Snowcem and Marley tiles. Its shopping centre has escalators, and its houses are like those ideal homes you see in television commercials. It is bright and breezy with lots of open space and municipal lawns mown smooth as billiard cloth.

North has now imperceptibly changed to south, or nearly so – along the main street comes a London-type taxi with its 'for hire' light on. It's only a short way to Kettering, past the interesting new children's centre at Rockingham Dene. Roca's *ing* (family) had their *ham* (village) here in Saxon times. Next to this is the boot trade's research association, for this is Northamptonshire, the shoe industry's prosperous stronghold. You won't see many down-at-heel feet getting on and off the buses here.

Kettering
(about ¾ hour)

On this visit Kettering let me down. The art gallery was closed for repairs. The Tourist Centre was closed for the season. The library had no information to hand out about the town. The ancient church had an impressive exterior, but was stark inside. Its high tower houses an outstanding peal of bells (a full ten of them, which is rare, the earliest dating from Charles I's reign), but they were silent on the day I turned up. One of the bells has recently cracked, and until over £5,000 has been raised for recasting it the full peal will stay silent.

I looked among the market stalls for some local produce to take as a picnic among the pansies in the art gallery gardens, but found only Leicestershire cheese and prawns from Thailand. Feather cornice-brushes, mugs with the Muppets on them, plastic ones with names of football clubs: these are the kind of trivia which have replaced the cheap ribbons and laces that first gave us the word 'tawdry' from 'St Audrey', on whose feast days were held fairs with cheap trifles for sale.

Kettering to Bedford
(about 2 hours, including ½ hour at Rushden)

A rattlebones of a bus trundled me through an area of marshes and trickling brooks. Gipsies (or more likely, just ordinary 'totters' and not the true Romanies of Indian origin) were camping in deluxe motor caravans by the wayside – all white paint and chromium without, frilly curtains and plastic knick-knacks within. Higham Ferrers has a pleasant square and a long street of stone houses, but there is little else of interest until Rushden.

There I broke my journey to look at the unique strainer arch in the church that stands high above the rooftops. The lacy carving of this unusual arch across the nave looks too delicate to be anything but ornamental, yet on its strength depends the entire structure. Without it, the 600-year-old spire and all the church would crash in ruins. It was inserted in 1370 when the pillars in the nave started to give way.

The church has much else of interest, too: an angel roof, a rare Wyclif pulpit, a newly restored and repainted Elizabethan monument, medieval glass and ancient heads carved in stone both inside and outside the church. The most elegant lettering I have seen was on two 18th-century memorial tablets outside the eastern wall of the church, the words and decorations delicately incised in the slate by a mason who was as much artist as craftsman. They are so obscurely placed that few but the chirruping sparrows are likely to see them.

Though the land from here on is so flat that any small mound seems like a hill, the bus twists and turns along lanes where trees meet overhead in a mingling of green, gold and russet. Sharnbrook is a village of whitewash and thatch but there is little else to see until, gathering speed on the main road and with the wind whistling by us, we approach Bedford.

Bedford
(about 2 hours)

This is John Bunyan's town – remember Kipling's poem 'A tinker out of Bedford . . .'? Plaques mark where he was baptized (in a stream), tried, imprisoned for 12 years and where 300 years ago he wrote *Pilgrim's Progress*. Sculptures of scenes from that book are on the walls of the library and the base of his statue. But most interesting of all are the Bunyan church and museum. The latter contains, among much else, editions of *Pilgrim's Progress* in 200 languages, the portable anvil he carried everywhere, a violin he made in metal and a flute made from the leg of a stool in his prison. The church doors are particularly fine with scenes from the book cast in bronze. Usually nonconformist chapels are plain, even ugly, but not this one.

Having visited the Bunyan museum and church earlier in the year, I decided to concentrate on other things this time. Behind shops near the bus station is the new Harpur Centre, built on the site of an old school. The splendid 1804 Gothick facade has been carefully retained on one of its sides. The core of this new shopping centre (designed by Frederick Gibberd) is a brick walk spiralling gently down from one level to another – not only an imaginative architectural feature, but kinder to toddlers and the elderly than a staircase would have been. Leaving by the Harpur Street exit (still flanked by splendid scarlet, gold and black Victorian lamp posts) one soon comes to the church and, on Wednesdays, a ploughman's lunch in the vestry if you are so inclined. Here is another magnificent angel roof, carved screen and misericords dating from the time of Agincourt; an unusual brass showing a knight wearing both armour and mayoral robes; and a very early stone pulpit from which Wesley once preached. Brasses came in between the 13th and 15th centuries to replace the great tombs with stone effigies that took up so much space. Britain has some 4,000 brasses, ten times more than the rest of Europe. Inconspicuously lodged in the south porch is a sad little gravestone of someone of no importance: Patience, the wife of a publican, who died aged only 37 when George I was king. During her brief life she bore 25 children, and the last childbirth killed her.

The church and path lead towards the river, its embankment

gracefully balustraded with stone pillars where once there were wharves for the shipping of corn to Holland. The River Ouse is always busy with swans and in the distance a white iron footbridge springs in a delicate arch across the water. Along the embankment is the local museum (a hotchpotch of toys, horse-drawn fire engine, pots, an Egyptian mummy and old prams), but it is best to keep as much time as possible for Bedford's least publicized treasure-house – the Cecil Higgins Art Gallery, a few yards further along, near the fountain and scented garden for the blind.

Mr Higgins, a local brewer, was a man of taste as well as wealth. At his death in 1949 he bequeathed to Bedford his exceptional collections – of watercolours and prints, glass, porcelain, lace and *art nouveau* furniture. Not only are the contents superb but so is their setting, a purpose-built gallery, which is itself a delight to the eye and with perfect lighting. Downstairs are pictures by Constable, Blake, Fuseli, Turner, Rouault, Cézanne, Dégas and Renoir – how many other provincial towns can muster such an artistic role as this? Upstairs are the glass and china with, at the far end, the surprise of a lily pool over which a life-sized Chelsea swan seemingly floats, together with Meissen ducks, on a rosewood raft. Mr Higgins used to serve his guests soup from this virtually priceless swan tureen, and it must have reminded him of the herd of swans on the Ouse which are such an inseparable part of the Bedford scene. Swans, once valued for their meat, used to be under royal control, and special swan courts dealt with anybody who kept or killed one without a licence. Beaks were marked to indicate ownership. (The Crown still exercises such rights on the River Thames.)

And so to London
(about 1¼ hours)

The sky was like clotting cream as I boarded my last bus. We were soon through Bedford's industrial outskirts where the tall chimneys of the brickfields loom over claypits drowned in stagnant grey. The few trees were already bare of leaves.

This part of the world was one of the earliest brick-making areas in England, partly because the technique was learnt from Holland and partly because clay for brick-making was here in abundance. In Tudor times bricks were used only for important buildings, but the demand for fire-resistant homes grew after the Great Fire of London (1666) and accelerated as supplies of timber began to run out in the 18th century. When the railways came, bricks began to be distributed even to the parts of Britain that had formerly used stone. Their widespread use in lieu of timber and stone was deplored then just as we now deplore the ousting of bricks by concrete.

I had been impressed by the skill of the drivers in Bedford's big bus station on a Friday at rush hour, each slotting his big craft into the right bay at exactly the right angle while a dozen others were coming or going at the same time. The company liveries varied - green, white or red – and some of the buses were double-deckers, some singles. There are clean buses and dirty buses, smooth ones and boneshakers, some with well-upholstered seats and others with utilitarian plastic-and-metal. Drivers come silent or chatty, spruce or grubby, young or old, but I had not encountered a single sour one (unlike some in London, where traffic conditions make bus driving an ulcer-ridden occupation).

Despite the hour, even this bus to London had only a handful of passengers – as always, mostly women shoppers. The darker the haze outside, the cosier the bus seemed. A long string of tiny streetlights defined a distant horizon as passengers got on at Houghton, well-muffled up against an English November night.

At Ampthill we were held up by the only traffic jam of my entire journey (and we were late arriving, also for the first time). The bus had to mount a kerb in a narrow street in order to get through what was once a tranquil centre of lace-making and millinery. The engine panted and hummed. Vast lorries laden with bricks strained their way through. How Ampthill's little Georgian houses must be shaken (and their occupants' nerves, too).

Night blanked out the rest of the journey until London, when it was at last time to alight: four days (17 hours on the road), 300 miles covered, 17 towns visited and 11 counties and 13 rivers crossed since I left the lonely spaces of Hadrian's Roman Wall.

Looking back

A journey like this – cutting one lean slice down the length of England – brings home the tremendous variety the English scene can offer within a single trip, even though my journey was down one side of the country only and through the less spectacular lowlands. But it is a part of England particularly rich in villages, old spires, markets, coaching inns, limestone buildings and traces of historic events from the Romans to the Industrial Revolution.

In the north there is stone everywhere, for bridges as well as houses. In the south, where rocky moorlands give way to woodlands, timber is more in evidence for both, until black-and-white timbered houses begin to predominate.

The roads themselves are full of diversity. The coach routes, often going over lengths of Roman roads, contrast with those twisting lanes which – apart from the Celtic ridgeways across the hills, going from one Iron Age hill fort to another – are probably among the oldest roads, made by the Saxons. Zigzags often indicate that once the lane turned and turned again in order to go round the edge of an old bog or outsize oak long departed, or round some field that was hedged in a thousand years ago. Exceptionally narrow lanes usually pre-date wagons or coaches and so may go back before Tudor times when goods were normally carried by packhorse (low parapets on small bridges also date from those days, to accommodate the packs that bulged over on either side of the horse). Straighter, wider roads between village and village, with broad grass verges, are likely to have been laid out in the 18th century as part of the general reorganization when the common lands were enclosed. Now some of the scenery has changed yet again as farming, building and road-making methods have changed. There are many losses, but they are few when measured against the whole beauty of England, still to be found not far off the beaten track, where the little buses go.

Note: As mentioned, I deliberately avoid most big cities. However, it is possible to do this journey slightly differently in order to take in famous historic centres. There is a leaflet called 'East of England Heritage Route' which details a six-cathedral trail (Durham – York – Lincoln – Peterborough – Ely – Norwich), available from the East Midlands Tourist Board (see Appendix B).

3

SHAKESPEARE'S ENGLAND

*Oxford – Woodstock – Stratford-on-Avon – Banbury -
Oxford*

In summer all the world pounds through Stratford-on-Avon, and
the multi-storey *coach* park is full. But there is nowhere better for a
quiet winter or spring break (though even then the accents of
America, Japan and Australia can be heard in inglenooks and
alleys, and it is wise to book well in advance if you want a seat at the
Royal Shakespeare Theatre). In this part of the world they really
do know about log fires and hot punch before a roast beef dinner,
with deep armchairs to follow.

I stayed at inexpensive bed-and-breakfast houses, finding
two which had that vital necessity – a really welcoming landlady
or landlord who offers you hot milk at bedtime or books restaurant
tables for you. The Earlmont Guest House in Oxford is a short bus
ride from the centre; the Salamander Guest House in Stratford is
within walking distance of most places of interest.

Oxford

Of my starting point, Oxford, whole books have been written and
it is impossible to compress here an account of all that can be seen.
If time is limited it is best to make for Carfax in the centre and the
nearby Tourist Information Centre to get their free map, which
has a two-hour walk marked on it. This includes over a dozen colleges and also one of my favourite places (even in winter), the
17th-century Botanic Gardens by the river.

Shakespeare must have known Oxford and its inns well. The
13th-century tower in Carfax is a relic of the church where he
stood godfather to the child of an innkeeper (the inn is now hidden
behind an 18th-century frontage at 3 Cornmarket).

The bus to Woodstock goes out past the Ashmolean Museum,

classically elegant with urns and wreaths, cornices and Ionic columns, in a combination of cream and white stones; along wide St Giles; past the Radcliffe Infirmary, sedate Victorian houses and immaculate cricket fields; and so out into the countryside.

Woodstock

Woodstock is often overlooked by motorists, for its interesting buildings and cobbled ways lie off the main road. It is a small town of very old houses that were 'modernized' with new facades in early Georgian times. Bay windows, shops, porches with lanterns, white shutters and iron-studded front doors are characteristic of the place. So are the roof tiles of local stone, their sizes skilfully graduated down each roof from small to large. Once off that main road, the quiet is very noticeable. Woodstock is memorable, too, for its stocks with *five* (!) leg holes; and for glovemaking. I sought out the glove-maker's premises off Chaucers Lane (Chaucer's son lived in the house on the corner), down which there are glimpses of a walled garden and a flight of old stone steps. I chose a pair of hand-made kid gloves at 'half the price of London shops, my love', as I was credibly assured.

The Bear is an old coaching inn where bear-baiting used to take place. There has been an inn on the site since at least 1232, but 'inn' is now a misnomer for a hotel that is world famous. Stone, tapestries and pewter give the restaurant its special character; such traditional food as roast sucking-pig and jugged hare are served. Woodstock is full of historic buildings offering good food (and the local beer of Hook Norton): the Dorchester, the Marlborough Arms, Vickers (where there is a barbecue in a walled garden during summer) and the Terrace Restaurant of Blenheim Palace itself, close to the famous fountains. Woodstock has a particularly good museum of rural life in a house which is itself a museum-piece (and which has a coffee lounge). Sometimes there are craft demonstrations.

Woodstock is overshadowed by its most famous home, Blenheim Palace, a showy masterpiece designed by Vanbrugh and enriched with painted ceilings, carved woodwork and other embellishments that took 70 years to complete. It was started as a gift from the nation to the Duke of Marlborough after his victory over Louis XIV at Blenheim in 1704. Winston Churchill was born in one of its rooms (and is buried in the nearby village of Bladon). The palace is surrounded by a park designed by Capability Brown – he dammed a river to create its lake (everything about Blenheim is on a grandiose scale).

I prefer the grounds to the palace, with all its pomp and glory. One first sees the swirling shape of the lake in its valley, blue as the sky above, with a view over the trees of the 120-foot column bearing a statue of Marlborough. On the other side of the palace is a formal French garden smelling of box hedges, with a fountain splashing. There is a traditional knot garden, huge gilded dolphins in a pool (the sunlight reflected onto them by the water was dazzling), topiary birds and beasts, sweeping lawns, and shrubberies where the only sound is the plop of a fir cone or the scuffle of a pheasant in the undergrowth. The park was deserted when I was there, with not a duke in sight.

The same bus service continues to Stratford-on-Avon (1½ hours away), passing through autumn scenery that glows with the metallic colours of copper beeches and oak leaves turning gold, on the edge of the Cotswolds. Chipping Norton, where tweeds are still woven, has an old guildhall, 18th-century houses and earlier almshouses. 'Chipping' means market, and the market place is in the heart of the town (now full of antique shops, too). The road is dotted with charming villages built from local stone, many on the banks of the winding River Stour. Along the ridge between Shipston ('sheep's town') and Chipping Norton are flocks of grazing sheep which make it obvious why this is rich wool country. Gradually they give way to cattle and mixed farming.

Stratford-on-Avon

Out of season, Stratford-on-Avon can really be appreciated. It shows itself to be beautiful and spacious – a market town that is the essence of what the whole world regards as 'typically English'. That so many superb timbered houses have survived for four centuries is due in part to a timely decline in Stratford's fortunes when other places were busy tearing down and rebuilding themselves. Stratford had to make do with what it already had, and thus many buildings are still as Shakespeare knew them. They have survived not merely the passing of time but, in many cases, the tramp of a quarter of a million pairs of feet a year (and the vibration of traffic to match). At Shakespeare's birthplace a section of wall has been exposed to show its simple wattle-and-daub construction between the great timbers. Will modern materials last as long?

Shakespeare's father was a merchant and alderman, and the house where he was born was naturally a fine one. So were his own house, New Place (which he bought in 1597, dying there in 1616), and his daughter's home, Hall Croft (she married a Dr

Hall). This last is one of the most interesting yet least visited of the Shakespeare properties. All are open to the public in winter (not all of them on Sundays), though little is left of New Place. Their gardens are beautiful, even in winter. The birthplace has been planted with flowers and trees mentioned in Shakespeare's works, and quinces hung like yellow lanterns on the wintry branches (see *Romeo and Juliet*!).

Even if Shakespeare had never lived there, Stratford would attract visitors to its lovely streets, the banks of the Avon, Clopton Bridge (with its 14 arches built in the 15th century), the lanes of little shops and its ancient inns full of dark beams, inlaid or carved panelling and log fires. In the comfortable lounge of the Black Swan a big wall painting has been uncovered telling the story of Tobias and the Angel. Good eating places are almost too numerous to mention, but the Marianne (in Greenhill Street) provides particularly good French cooking for the very modest *table d'hôte* price.

Traditionally painted with castles and roses, the canal boats waited for next season in the waters by the Shakespeare memorial garden, where ducks and swans gather; further along the river, past the famous theatre, is Holy Trinity Church with Shakespeare's grave. At that time of year, with the sun low in the sky, long shadows were cast by the leaning tombstones and the tall yews.

It is impossible to describe all that makes one day in Stratford far too brief a visit. And when the town has been explored, there are still the nearby villages to which buses go – particularly Shottery, with the picturesque thatched farmhouse where Shakespeare's wife, Anne Hathaway, grew up, and other lovely houses further along the road.

Banbury

The return to Oxford can be by a different route, taking the bus to Banbury (1¼ hours). This was an especially lovely ride, wandering this way and that to serve little villages off the beaten track, some still flowery. There are noble churches, houses of tawny stone with a suntanned look, old inns, sparkling streams, here a small market square and there a row of almshouses. The bus passes the site of the Battle of Edgehill (1642), the first of many in the Civil War. It might have been the last, for Charles I was almost defeated.

Banbury cakes (for eating) and Banbury Cross (for the nursery rhyme) please the child in everyone. The cakes, which are in fact pastries filled with spicy dried fruit, were made even before Shakespeare's time, while the original cross was one of a chain erected by the grieving Edward I to mark each place where his wife's coffin rested on its journey to London for burial. Into the present cross, put up in 1859, were later incorporated statues of Victoria, Edward VII (improbably clad as a Goth) and George V. Banbury has an unusual Palladian church dating from 1791 with 'pepperpot' towers and, amongst all the bustle of a busy town, quite a few interesting old buildings, including the comfortable Whately Hall Hotel. Some are of ironstone, some brick and some timbered. The 16th-century Reindeer Inn is worth a visit for its Hook Norton beer as well as its interior. After the ancient houses of Market Place and the High Street, the waterfront near the bus station is worth exploring. There is a tip-up bridge over the canal (originally built to bring coal from the Midlands), a boatyard beyond the lock where canal boats are repaired, and a mill converted into an art centre (the bridge over the millstream was built in the 13th century). But to discover all of Banbury that one can within an hour or so, it is best to get the leaflet 'A Walk Round Banbury', sold by Banbury Museum just off the High Street. With any luck you may find that the museum is showing one of its lively special exhibitions with themes like 'Hats and Thatch' or 'Drink and Sobriety in Victorian Banbury'.

Finally, I rode back to Oxford (in 1¼ hours), with plenty to look at on the way. Adderbury's fine church has gargoyles and a 150-foot spire, there are thatched cottages and two village greens. Deddington, between two tributaries of the Cherwell, is a decayed town with large houses left around a big square. Steeple Aston's name tells its story – 'steeple' was originally 'staple', which means a wool market. The bus crossed the Oxford canal, which more or less follows the road after Banbury, to finish the journey along a road lined with turreted Victorian houses, sprouting crockets like broccoli – typical north Oxford architecture. And so I was back again in the 'towery city, branchy between the towers' from which my journey started.

4

BUSES FOR BOOKWORMS
THE COTSWOLDS

*Cheltenham – Painswick – Stroud – Cirencester –
Chedworth – Burford*

Some people's idea of a good day out is to spend it browsing in one bookshop after another – the kind of place where bookish dust has not been too vigorously brushed away and there is a faint aroma of old paper and even older leather. The books are usually crammed from ceiling to floor or even stacked on the ground, and the owner may live like a mole in the dim rear of the shop, half-hidden behind precarious piles of volumes. No one seems to mind too much if after an hour's gently grazing in literary pastures you spend a pound or less – possibly getting, for a fraction of its original cost, a well-illustrated and well-bound book printed on good paper with wide margins.

This harmless activity can be pursued in many parts of England and, as pleasant bookshops and pleasant surroundings often go together, it is an easy matter to combine book-hunting with bus riding for pleasure – particularly in winter. Planning a route is helped by leaflets obtainable from the antiquarian section of the Booksellers Association (154 Buckingham Palace Road, SW1) and the Provincial Booksellers Association (c/o Francis Books, 3 Crescent Road, Worthing, Sussex). Say which county interests you and they will send a leaflet listing a few dozen bookshops within it giving their addresses, opening hours and what kind of books they stock. The latter also issues a calendar of book fairs.

After that it is a fairly simple matter to look on the map of bus routes to see which ones you can reach in a day's ride. One warning, however. I have found that booksellers are wayward and don't always open at the hours printed in these leaflets.

I chose the Cotswolds for a bus tour covering six towns with very pleasant rides in between. I started by staying on a Thursday night at Cheltenham, then moving on to Cirencester with a 'budget' weekend in Burford. The rolling hills, houses of honey-coloured stone, sparkling rivers and churches of immense grandeur make the whole region a place of outstanding beauty no matter what the season.

Cheltenham

Cheltenham was built for pleasure in the 18th century. A spa where Handel and Dr Samuel Johnson once 'took the waters', its climate is mild and it is a centre for festivals and racing. Above all else its parks and parades provide a marvellous temptation to while away the time doing nothing in particular. Among the many shops of quality are several booksellers conveniently near one another: Alan Hancox at 101 Montpellier Street, Barrie's at 4 Montpellier Walk and Robert Wilson (who specializes in illustrated books) at 115 The Promenade. At the other end (49 Clarence Street) is Mr Heynes' shop where there are bargains to be had for as little as one penny, and in between lie shops with new books such as the Promenade Bookshop and Preedies at numbers 22 and 88 The Promenade. If any time is left after this bookish orgy, one can visit the art gallery for its Dutch paintings or (further out, near lovely Pittsville Park) the Gustav Holst museum in the house where the composer was born.

Cheltenham's spine is its great Promenade, running from north to south. I arrived at the coach station near the north end and made my way first to the nearby church and Clarence Street (with museum, art gallery and Heyne's bookshop) before strolling slowly to the south end (with the fascinating Montpellier quarter, more bookshops and Suffolk Square, where I would spend the night). A whole day in Cheltenham is little enough, there is so much to enjoy.

The church, tucked away, has a spectacular rose window 700 years old and interesting memorials, including one to Captain Skillicorne, whose discovery of a mineral spring in 1738 was the beginning of Cheltenham's fame as a spa. The Skillicorne family was still supplying the town with mayors into this century. The peaceful churchyard is famous for its elegant tombstones and quaint epitaphs – especially this one, of 1825:

Here lies John Higgs
A famous man for killing pigs.
For killing pigs was his delight
Both morning, afternoon and night,
Both heats and cold he could endure,
Which no physician could e'er cure;
His knife is laid, his work is done,
I hope to heaven his soul is gone.

The local museum is a good one, with everything attractively displayed and well explained. For instance, a glass case exhibits pots dating from the 15th to 17th century on one side and others by modern craftsmen on the other, showing how the latter are continuing old traditions of shape, decoration or glaze. Upstairs, the ways in which local rocks were formed is clearly demonstrated, with jars of different local soils to compare and an explanation of how these determine the variations in vegetation.

One room is devoted to pieces made by Gimson, a Gloucestershire furniture-maker of renown in the 'thirties. His style was a return to earlier simplicity but with decorative detailing of legs, drawer handles and the like. Another room is full of mementos of Dr Wilson, who died tragically with Scott in the Antarctic. Cheltenham was his home town and his statue (by Scott's widow) stands in the Promenade. It seems to me badly sited – Wilson stares right into a chestnut tree and only the birds can stare back at him.

One could spend a day in Cheltenham simply looking at all the different capitals on its innumerable columns or at the endlessly varied patterns of the wrought iron balconies. Even the Post Office and the local newspaper's premises look like Greek temples. There are plenty of seats on the wide pavements from which to watch the world go by, and plenty of cafés; the *boulevardiers* give the town a rather continental air. In summer the flowerbeds are bright with begonias and Canterbury bells; around Christmas the great chestnut trees sparkle with lights (their switching on in November is the occasion for a festive procession of choirs, dancers and bands). And the shops! All the temptations of Vanity Fair are displayed there. Cheltenham is the place for antiques and hand-made shoes, oriental rugs and china dolls with straw bonnets, and in the tea-rooms you may order jasmine tea or a cup of hot chocolate with marshmallows.

Yet this is no longer primarily a town of colonels and

memsahibs retired from running the empire (the empire is long dead, and most of its colonels, too). In fact there are lots of young people around, for Cheltenham has more than the ordinary quota of colleges.

Nevertheless, change comes slowly and the town still has a distinctive character. Even though such retailers as Habitat, Wallis and Jaeger have forced their own house styles into the Regency Promenade, plenty of mahogany and gilt survives. Such idiosyncratic characters as Mr Sales, who runs the Spa Pharmacy, have not allowed modern packages to take over their windows completely. Among the spouted beef-tea cups and old pharmacy jars he displays some 1880 advertisements for quack remedies, and two staring pairs of glass eyes. Down a backstreet (every Cheltenham backstreet has its surprises) a grocer claiming to specialize in bacon has his wall decorated with a realistic mural of a flitch of bacon: the old chap himself was still busy at the great slicer when I passed by late in the evening ('. . . for slicing pigs was his delight; both morning, afternoon and night').

Just off the Promenade is the grand town hall, inside which are great blue pottery urns from which you can help yourself to spa water. It is not chalybeate, as in other English spas, but very alkaline, and it tastes salty.

On the other side of the Promenade Neptune presides over a fountain that draws its water from a river flowing under the road, surrounded by willows grown from cuttings of those that shaded Napoleon's tomb in St Helena.

At the far end of the Promenade I came to Montpellier Walk, famous for its dozens of caryatids – larger than life-size, scantily draped ladies supporting the shops' upper storeys on their heads. This and the surrounding streets are full of curio shops. After exploring them I sat under a cedar in the gardens opposite to enjoy the scene. The mansard roofs of grey slate slope down to balustrades of creamy stone above facades with large sash windows. This upper storey is hemmed, as it were, with a white band of decorative moulding to separate it from the shop fronts and caryatids at ground level.

The shops were closing. I walked on to find my guest house, passing on the way the Rotunda, now a bank (with dome and anxious-looking lion) and an unusual statue of Edward VII, 'the Peacemaker' – as a plaque at the back calls him – in plus-fours and holding the hand of a barefoot child. Although the Willoughby modestly calls itself a guest house, its facade – with 30-foot Corinthian columns and a great portico – would not disgrace a 'grand hotel' in lesser towns than Cheltenham.

Next day the bus out of Cheltenham took me through other fine streets such as Bayshill Road (flanked by Cheltenham Ladies College), Montpellier Terrace (pretty little villas) and Bath Road (the impressive buildings of Cheltenham College). Once into the country, the route lay through fields with the Cotswold hills in the distance. Gradually the road wound its way upward, swishing this way and that, the countryside growing lovelier as we went and the views stretching ever further into the distance. We looked down into treetops through which stone chimneys and rooftops occasionally peeped.

The Benedictine abbey of Prinknash lies along this route to Stroud. The monks make pottery for sale, the medieval fishponds have been restocked with trout, and there is a bird park with pheasants, swans and geese.

Painswick

I stopped at Painswick, one of England's loveliest stone villages (its bookshop is in a former inn, the Golden Fleece), with a celebrated churchyard containing 99 skilfully clipped yews standing in ranks, some twinned to form great green arches and all at least 200 years old. Though it is for the yews that this church is most famous, it has a very lovely interior. If one is lucky, the Ancient Society of Painswick Youths may be heard in action. 'Youths' may be a misnomer, but 'Ancient' is true enough: they are the bellringers and their team dates back to 1686 (so do some of the twelve bells, gifts of local cloth merchants whom Cotswold wool made rich). Their record-breaking peal was of 13,001 changes in under nine hours (1920). I imagine that afterwards they headed for the nearby Falcon Inn.

So did I, and I wandered with a glass of local ale to look at their bowling green (laid down in Tudor times), a pretty place with flower beds, thatched arbour and old stone walls around it. A coaching inn and one-time centre for cock-fighting, the Falcon also once served as a courthouse.

Painswick is a cobweb of little lanes – Tibbiwell, the Cross, Friday Street – lined with picturesque stone cottages. Its main street has houses of great dignity in the same stone but smoothly dressed, punctuated with well-spaced sash windows and topped with colonnaded parapets. Down by the stream are three mill houses (one still in use for making hairpins).

The best way to explore Painswick is with the little leaflet with an annotated walk produced by the local Women's Institute. One can get a bird's eye view from the top floor of Fiery Beacon, an art gallery whose owner welcomes sightseers.

Stroud

The bus to nearby Stroud continues through the hills to where five valleys meet. The town's narrow streets climb steeply up and down, crowded and bustling. Wool made the town in the beginning, and woollens are still woven there. Alan and Joan Tucker have two shops for new books by the station and five rooms of secondhand ones (in particular they stock modern literature, the arts and wildlife). There is little else of interest in the town: the church is Victorian, the museum very poor, and the old buildings few. But from there it does not take long to get to Cirencester, a busy market town and once the second greatest city of Roman Britain.

The bus passes through the so-called Golden Valley where the old woollen mills still stand, though some are used now for very different purposes from electronics to making corn dollies (the latter, at Chalford, can be visited). In amongst the hills that follow are pretty Cotswold villages such as Sapperton and Daglingworth – the former with a lattice-windowed village school and (unusually) a Queen Anne church, where Stafford Cripps is buried, and the latter with an old circular dovecote of which one gets a glimpse (on the right). This was a journey of great variety and memorable beauty.

Cirencester

The streets of Cirencester have some wool-merchants' tall houses of the 15th century, a weavers' hall and a magnificent church built with the proceeds of the wool trade. It is near this church that Paul Wellar has his shop in Dollar Street, with 70,000 books, new and old.

The bus enters the town through some of the most interesting of the old streets and draws up by the church – almost like a cathedral in its grandeur. To the original church the great tower was added in 1415 (it houses the oldest peal of bells in the world). A lifetime later the enormous porch went up, and it did duty as a town hall with meeting room above and a cellar below; its lovely fan-vaulting is well lit, and the multitude of odd creatures carved on the exterior are easy to see. Soon after, the nave was rebuilt with Perpendicular arches soaring high on slender pillars, a breath-taking achievement. The colourful windows, the carvings in the roof, the 'wine glass' pulpit (named for its shape) and the wall paintings are just some of the enrichments within. And without is a peaceful old graveyard, reached through a slit of an alleyway with some plant troughs and copper wall lamps.

Before exploring the town it is a good idea to visit the museum (which has won a number of awards for excellence), because it explains Cirencester's past so vividly in a series of spacious and lively displays. For instance, there are not only superbly restored Roman mosaics but recreations of a Roman sitting room and a kitchen, neither wildly dissimilar from home comforts of today. Models of Iron Age barrows make plain what archaeological remains often do not. The techniques of processing wool in the Middle Ages are shown, and so on.

Many streets in Cirencester were interesting, but some I remember in particular. Cicely Hill, for instance, is a serene and beautiful street of stone houses leading up to a splendid tree-flanked vista through the great Park. The wide curve of the Market Place, in which honey-coloured stone alternates with stucco in blue, soft pink or cream, was made even more gay on market day by the striped awnings of stalls. The Old Brewery is now converted to provide workshops for craftsmen ranging from a painter of clock faces to a traditional baker (there was also a basketmaker who had even turned his skill to the making of a double bed in wicker).

In the market a farmer from Dymock was selling his own cheeses. After buying from him some real Gloucester cheese, but with a variation (it had nettles in it), I awaited my next bus outside the church, with time to take in all the detail of the Market Place buildings. At sky level there was an infinite variety of cornices, dormers, pediments, gables, mouldings and cupolas with chimneys round or square, made of stone, terracotta or brick.

The bus left town through where a Roman gate had once stood in the city wall, and ahead the Roman road stretched up and down, straight as far as the eye could see. But after a bit the bus left it for winding lanes to little villages.

A signpost pointed to Chedworth Roman villa but we pressed on to the picturesque Chedworth villages (upper and lower). Not only are the old cottages very pretty, but so is the new village hall, where a couple of other passengers helped to heave an old lady off the bus. She stood to wave goodbye as we rattled off once more. Another, white-haired, was short of change for her fare: 'I'm not going to worry about it', said the driver, 'so don't *you* go grey about it!'

This was one of the best bus routes I'd found, through unspoilt countryside and with views for miles, the road winding down and up all the way and at each turn bringing a new rural scene into view. There were Jersey cows standing in a stream to drink, white geese grazing, a waterside farmhouse with old millstones leaning against the wall, and worn steps up through a little garden to a cottage door. At Yarnworth there is a very tiny church actually in a farmyard. The bus goes to Northleach, a small country town with a 'wool' church almost as fine as Cirencester's (and with outstanding brasses). This was a busy place in coaching days. Alas, its only bookshop had closed down, I discovered.

Burford

We went on through rolling country, typically Cotswold landscape, to Burford. This is inevitably my favourite place in the Cotswolds, having spent my honeymoon at the Bay Tree Hotel, a great place for complete comfort, good food, graceful antique furniture and, in winter, four log fires in its various sitting rooms. The original owner, a Tudor magnate, has his resplendent tomb in the lovely church on the banks of the river Windrush. Burford has plenty of other good hotels (the Lamb in Sheep Street, for instance) and almost as many bookshops, of which my favourite is Jubilee Books – well-stocked, carpeted and spacious. But there are many other distractions, too, such as craft and antique shops, cobbled courtyards and old inns.

On this visit the Windrush had flooded the meadows for miles around and the water had turned into one vast ice rink. Light snow sugared the tussocks of moss topping old stone walls until they looked like so many meringues. Sunday was spent (with plenty to read!) in a deep chair by one of those crackling log fires.

Note: This area is served partly by small private bus companies and many services run only once or twice a week (often only on market days). The timetables of all of them are combined in one booklet obtainable from the Public Transport Department, Shire Hall, Gloucester.

5

LONDON'S BORDER COUNTRY

*Gravesend – Wrotham – Ightham – Sevenoaks –
Westerham – Reigate – Dorking – Leatherhead (or
Guildford) – Windsor – Amersham – Hemel Hempstead
– St Albans – Epping – Waltham – Tilbury*

Every year millions of Londoners go streaking off far away for a
holiday – racing through (or flying over) interesting places
without a second glance. One year I decided to take a few days'
holiday touring through seven counties yet never finding myself
much more than an hour away from Piccadilly Circus. My route
formed a circle round London through the Downs to the south
and the Chilterns to the north. I crossed the Thames upriver
where it is the boundary between Surrey and Berkshire and
downriver where it separates Essex from Kent. The journey
through hills and valleys was full of contrast, and as the scenery
changed with the geology, so did the architecture – weatherboarding, stone, brick or whitewash-and-thatch came and went as
county succeeded county.

One could start from any of the towns listed; some are even on
the Underground. Others can be reached by train, fast coaches or
express buses (see Chapter 1). 'See London's Town and
Countryside' is a useful guide and map; it is free from London
Country Buses, Lesbourne Road, Reigate.

Gravesend
Most guidebooks do not even mention Gravesend, yet once it was
a fashionable resort for Londoners who flocked onto steamers for

day-trips to its pleasure gardens. And, although its heart has now been ripped out, it still has a lot going for it. Right in the middle is stranded a pretty little Georgian church and beside it a lively statue (presented by Americans) of the American Indian princess, Pocahontas. She married John Rolfe, pioneer of the Virginian tobacco plantations, after saving the life of another Englishman from hostile Indians. Her husband brought her to the court of James I but, as they began the voyage home again, she fell ill and died on board ship as it was passing Gravesend; here therefore she was laid to rest. A memorial window inside the church shows her in Jacobean high fashion, but her statue is as Rolfe might have first seen her in Virginia.

Gravesend has a covered market (it was chartered – licensed – in the Middle Ages) in a vast, classically pillared hall; and a weatherboarded smugglers' inn, the Three Daws (jackdaws), with a verandah over the waterfront from which to watch the ships go by – including, with any luck, one of the old sailing-barges with huge red sails set. Better still, one can have a good meal in the restaurant on the end of the town pier next to the Three Daws, eating right out on the river while looking across to Tilbury, where there is an old fort and very often a Russian liner moored outside its port. A few yards downriver is a tiny church, once a mission to seamen but now an arts centre: and near the Clarendon Hotel some archaeological excavations are in progress.

The Gordon Promenade (with an old fort, now a museum) is named for General Gordon, who was responsible for planning fortifications here to repel any French invaders who might have come up the Thames during one of many invasion scares. Further on, yachts are moored in the old canal basin. Once this canal joined the Thames to the Medway, passing through a long tunnel in the chalk hills, but as delays caused by tides made it less than a short cut, much of it was filled in and a railway now runs through its tunnel.

If there is time, take a bus to reach Windmill Hill, not only for the fine view of the Thames and its multitude of craft – from great tankers and container-ships to the small boats carrying the river pilots who navigate the big ships through the tricky estuary – but also because the twisting lanes on the hill still have many of the villas and rustic cottages dating from Gravesend's heyday.

Two buses are needed to get to Sevenoaks, the first going through Meopham and Wrotham to Borough Green. Once out of Gravesend, the bus soon passed suburban gardens colourful with forsythia and flowering currants and drew up by Meopham's huge, triangular cricket green, overlooked by the beautiful smock windmill that has stood there since 1801.

Walls made of flints dug out of the chalk are a characteristic feature along this ride; so is decorative brickwork: grey and red bricks make chequered or diapered patterns on house walls. There are huge timber barns, weatherboarded houses (both very Kentish, deriving from the times when wood was plentiful in the Wealden forests) and lovely stretches of road from here onwards. The trees bear a great weight of ivy and there are tremendous views from the top of the hilly road. The road goes over a new motorway in the course of construction; it is like a lunar landscape of chalk, gouged ruthlessly out of the gentle hills.

Wrotham

Wrotham is a dozy place now, yet once it was busy with comings and goings at the archbishop's palace next to the old Bull Inn (what is left of the palace is now a private house, the rest of the stones having been removed in 1349 to build a new palace in Maidstone). On a wall nearby, a stone commemorates the assassination in 1799 of an officer who was shot by a deserter here. Roughly opposite is a handsome medieval house, Wrotham Place, from which it is said (but of other places too!) Henry VIII watched for the signal that Anne Boleyn's head had fallen at the executioner's block in the Tower of London.

St George's church has a number of unusual features such as an arcade cut through its tower to allow religious processions to pass under it. This was necessary because the tower abuts on the road, leaving no room for processions to go round it without leaving holy ground. The attractive statue of St George above the door is by a modern sculptor, Willi Soukop, and replaces an older one that was stolen. There are a lot of medieval brasses inside, and, if one peers high up, tiny windows can be seen in a gallery concealed in the stonework dividing nave from chancel. Here nuns could watch the services while remaining hidden from the public eye. The higgledy-piggledy old houses in the High Street are popular with sparrows, which noisily build nests under their generous eaves.

We went on to Borough Green (a characterless place) to change buses for Ightham, which is soon reached after a drive between leafy hedges and buildings of Kentish ragstone (a name well describing its rough appearance).

Ightham

Ightham deserves an hour's break in one's journey. It is a village of half-timbered houses, an old inn (the Green Dragon, with flavoursome real Kent ale called Tusker, from Fremlin's Faversham brewery) and a tiny stream chattering its way among the houses.

The church, a little uphill from the village, is full of interest, beginning with the steps up to a mounting-block by the lychgate, from the days when worshippers arrived on horseback. It was at its best when I was there – the yellow and white flower arrangements from Easter Day still decorated every sill, the pulpit and the font. There are carved Jacobean box pews, a life-size effigy of a knight of 1374 in chain and plate armour (very similar to that of the Black Prince in Canterbury Cathedral) and a memorial of 1641 to Dame Dorothy Selby, a redoubtable dame to judge by her portrait bust sculpted by Charles I's master mason.

The leaflet about the church is well worth reading before looking around, otherwise one might miss details like the carved heads up among the 15th-century roof timbers; the elegant brass (under a mat) of a lady in the sugarloaf hat and ruff that were fashionable in 1626; and the simple memorial of 1921 to a local grocer who became an archaeologist of international renown.

Much of the church's interest lies outside, in the tombstones. Typically Kentish are the ones shaped like head and shoulders (double ones, for husband and wife, look uncommonly similar to bedheads) with a skull incised crudely in the 'head'. Others have cherubs, and one (behind the church) is covered in coats of arms – the work of a famous Victorian architect, William Burgess. An anvil decorates a blacksmith's tombstone, an anchor a sailor's. The most moving of all was small, simple and hard to find among the weeds and ivy: that of General and Mrs Luard, 1908. A few weeks previously my husband had bought for 50p an old volume entitled *Great Stories of Real Life*, from Rasputin to the Marie Celeste, among which the Luard mystery was related. Mrs Luard, a wholly respectable lady and much liked, was shot while walking not far from Ightham, and neither the murderer nor any motive was ever determined. Her stricken husband received a number of anonymous letters accusing him, and he later committed suicide by throwing himself under a train. What the book does not reveal is an earlier Luard tragedy, which a neighbouring tombstone chronicles – the death in action of their son only a few years before. The onward journey goes past the estate (Frankfield) where the murder took place.

The hawthorns in bloom spread their white lace in the hedges, and the banks below were bright with starry yellow celandines. The conical roofs of oast-houses are a conspicuous feature on the

75

way. There are woods of beech, birch and pine along here that are ideal for picnicking, beyond banks of golden, prickly gorse. Beside the sunlit road winding down to Seal, striped with the shadows of slender tree trunks, were tile-hung, half-timbered and weather-boarded houses.

Sevenoaks

Sevenoaks was built strategically in a gap in the North Downs. Its greatest jewel is one of the largest private houses in the country – Knole, built in the 15th and 16th centuries. Filled with valuable paintings and furniture and surrounded by a great deer park, Knole is a small palace – the stone buildings alone occupy four acres – with a mass of turrets, gables, ornate chimneys, battlements and towers outside; inside are galleries, carved panelling, elaborately plastered ceilings and state apartments still with their original furnishings. It is worth staying overnight in Sevenoaks in order to have plenty of time for Knole.

As to Sevenoaks itself, the most interesting part of the High Street is at the far end from the bus depot (and in the lanes which run between it and London Road to the west). After a pleasant lunch at the Chantecler (not only the proprietor but even the bay tree on the patio came over from France 25 years ago), I strolled among the little shops and old houses, and down Six Bells Lane (a quaint byway of cottages, cobblestones and small courts) to the church. Next to this stands old Chantry House, its name indicating its connection with the chantry chapel inside the church. The medieval well-to-do would pay for prayers to be chanted for their souls, in perpetuity, in a chapel (chantry) endowed for that purpose. To provide the money, land would be given to the church, and Chantry House stands on such land. At the end of the street is Sevenoaks School, an impressive yet simple building with a few marble statues in niches contrasting rather oddly with the homespun look of the ragstone walls.

Sevenoaks is a good spot from which to go bussing about into the countryside (a digression from my 'round London' circuit), so I stayed overnight at the Moorings, a comfortable private hotel on the London side of the town, and dined at an above-average Indian restaurant, the Mumtaz. Buses go to such beauty spots as Ide Hill and the Darenth Valley, and on Sundays in summer the local bus company runs special 'Rambler' buses.

The next bus on my 'round-London' circuit moved out to Westerham with views, as it went up and down, of the chalk cliffs quarried in the hills. Much of the beautiful woodland along this route is preserved by the National Trust. The road is fairly busy (though not as bad as it used to be before the new motorway siphoned off traffic), but with plenty of interest. There is a great variety of house-building styles, old inns, dignified houses surrounding the green that gives Bessells Green its name, and willows, bright of bud, beside a stream at Sundridge. Near Brasted sheep grazed in a noble park. Brasted itself is a picturesque village with a green, old stone walls and a lot of tile-hung houses with fine doorways and fanlights; some have grotesque figures carved in their timbers. As in many places on this route, antique shops are numerous.

The road winds on, the tops of the surrounding downs vanishing into mist. Bare boughs were hung with rain like chandelier drops and the wet moss on the beach trunks shone bright green. A smell of wood smoke drifted in when the door of the bus opened.

Westerham

Westerham church came into sight, squatting low on a hilltop, and then the bus drew up beside this little town's steeply sloping green. Here sits Winston Churchill, slumped in an armchair, looking as settled as the church itself. The statue is on a great rugged plinth of Yugoslav stone presented by Marshal Tito and could hardly differ more in style from the other statue on Westerham Green – General Wolfe, elegantly poised, almost as graceful as a dancer, on an urn-shaped plinth. These are Westerham's two famous sons, whose houses can both be visited. Wolfe was born there and Churchill spent many of his later years there.

The National Trust owns Quebec House, the childhood home of General Wolfe, a Tudor mansion of mellowed red brick. Not far off is Squerryes Court with more Wolfe mementos. Churchill's home, Chartwell, and its lovely gardens are a magnet for sight-seers. Though Victorian, the house is a place of space and light, with marvellous views. Its rooms are filled with his things, as if he were just about to play a game of bèzique, finish a painting at his easel or continue writing at the desk in his study. (Getting to Chartwell involves a two-mile detour on another bus.) Jane Austen's novel *Pride and Prejudice*, incidentally, is set near Westerham.

The church is worth visiting not just for its interesting interior but because the hillside churchyard with its old tombstones, adorned by well-weathered cherubs and skulls, looks down over

77

the town's old roofs and the valley below.

Westerham has many restaurants among its antique shops: I ate well at the Henry Wilkinson wine bar, all pine furniture with brick walls painted a mossy green. It is named after a local artist whose engravings hang on the walls and can be bought. After lunch I wandered down Water Lane, which leads off the green and goes by streams and stiles to green fields and a pleasant walk below the town, ending up at the far end of the main street.

The bus onward into Surrey was a double-decker with good views from the top. There are rustic bridges over a stream meandering through the outskirts of Westerham, followed by groves of silver birches, pastures, old barns, roadside gorse in golden bloom and attractive houses – some modest, some of consequence. The stretch of road is high and gives long-distance views. The bus detoured through Limpsfield with its terraces of picturesque cottages (the composer Frederick Delius is buried there) and then to Oxted where more substantial homes lie behind high hedges of copper beech. We climbed the steep street of Old Oxted, its ancient houses and inns crammed together as if fighting one another for a grip on the precipitous hill. The almost empty bus swooped and swayed up and down the hilly road through this prosperous part of Surrey.

Downhill the bus goes into Godstone, where the reddish buds on a tree tapped the bus window as we drew up by the huge green with its round pond and its fringe of well-mannered houses. The cricket field, sodden with rain, waited forlornly for better days. If you should stop at Godstone for lunch, the White Hart provides not only old-world atmosphere but the agreeable old-world custom of carving the roast beef at your table or serving steak-and-kidney pudding from the basin.

Beyond Bletchingley, a village of white- and pink-painted houses in a wide street, the road descends and there were views of the Downs' crests before we whisked over the top of the motorway that snaked through the landscape below us. At Nutfield children played in the yard of a traditional old village school. There is a castellated priory looking as if it might be haunted by something grisly out of a Hammer film. Finally we went through Redhill's unlovely suburban sprawl and down into Reigate.

Reigate

Reigate is an attractive town at the foot of the North Downs. Under the remains of the castle on the hill is a tunnel built to save the Prince Regent the bother of going round the hill. The tomb of

Lord Howard of Effingham (hero of the Armada defeat) is in the old church, which lies a little away from the town centre. There are a number of interesting old buildings in the streets, including the Market House in the middle of the main road. Just by this and alongside Lloyds Bank a narrow cobbled slit leads upwards to the gardens that are where the castle used to stand. It is a pretty spot above the hum of the traffic and with views of the roofscape below – a medley of cupolas, chimneys, clocks and weathercocks. Reigate also has attractions of a different kind down below. At the Peer Gynt restaurant, among genuine Norwegian furniture and decorations, a smorgasbørd luncheon is served; and the lovely Priory Gardens have a lake, limes, mansion and garden with clipped yews.

The next bus moved out through a street of sedate houses and past more village greens, a classical bridge over the River Mole and flashes of bright scarlet from pyracanthus berries still thick against cottage walls.

Dorking

Dorking's origins are Saxon and its main street was first laid down by the Romans. Dickens stayed at the White Horse coaching inn (in Tudor times it was the vicarage, and before that a pilgrims' hostel), which is where the bus stops. With such a history behind it Dorking is a fascinating place, and down every alley is something interesting. One, for instance, leads to 'Equations of Time', a workshop where two young cabinet-makers create grandfather and wall clocks to the highest standards of traditional design – future heirlooms – or restore old ones. The smell of pine from an old coachyard (where a crafts market is sometimes held) leads to another workshop where pine furniture is made. Part of the pavement is on a bank raised above the level of the road, presumably to protect pedestrians from mud and other hazards of coaching days. Some of the shops have bow-fronted windows, an ironmonger's front is elegant with Corinthian pillars and what was once a small inn is now an aromatic Culpepper herb shop. There are gunsmiths in Dorking, leather goods, and – particularly in West Street – craft and antique shops galore, with more along North Street (which leads to the bus station and has many good restaurants to choose from).

North Street also has, facing a group of *cottages ornées* with rustic or Chinese-looking porches, a little printing company of so unusual an appearance that I knocked on the door to ask its origins. They told me that the ecclesiastical look of the place, with three stained-glass windows and inscriptions carved in the stonework, was conceived by the founder of the firm over a century ago. A one-time architect, he acquired stained glass and other fittings from churches being busily 'improved' with Victorian zeal and re-used them here.

At this point I had to make a decision about which of several routes to follow in order to get to Windsor. The quickest also had the advantage of remaining within the territory of the London Country Bus Company, so that I could keep using their cheap day-ticket.

A more appealing alternative, however, was to go via Guildford, an attractive town, and Bracknell. The road from Dorking to Guildford is very lovely indeed, passing through some of the most picturesque villages of the North Downs, with marvellous scenery. Between Bracknell and Windsor, too, are attractive views – one can go through Windsor Great Park or take the Sunningdale-Egham road, which runs by woods, the lovely lake of Virginia Water and Wentworth golf course. However, I took the most convenient route and rather regretted it – though the first and last parts were enjoyable.

The bus turned north, passing white houses set well back behind tall pine trees and cedars and almost vertical chalk hills with trees clinging to them by the merest toe-hold. This was once the main coach route to London. On the right is the Burford Bridge Hotel, a traditional hotel set, long and low, in particularly fine gardens at the foot of steep Box Hill. Nelson, Keats and Robert Louis Stevenson all stayed there for a while. There are no box trees left on the hill because they were all cut down in the 18th century, when their fine-grained wood was in demand for making the blocks used by picture-engravers. The river flowing under the bridge is the Mole again.

There the bus left the main road to clamber up Juniper Hill, a lane that winds and climbs between black-and-white houses and flint walls characteristic of chalk regions, and by a flint church with old stone heads. The red brick houses have decorative red tiling and lozenge-paned windows.

Leatherhead

Leatherhead has several bridges over its rushing river; beyond it Bookham Common is a place of tangled woodland followed by a narrow lane and little bridges across which the bus squeezes with difficulty. After the prosperous suburban comforts of Stoke d'Abernon come the village green of Cobham and flooded fields.

Road and river (the Mole still) run together for a while, weirs frothing white. Much of this part of the journey is suburban. However, occasional stretches of larch trees, rhododendron groves, old farm buildings and a pool glimpsed over a wall (hiding it from the sight of motorists) made for some relief. The sky was then a pearly salmon colour as daylight began to fade, reflected in the river where pleasure craft waited by a pretty iron bridge. Outside the Georgian houses round Chertsey's cricket green the pyracanthus berries were still thick and red.

Recently the acres of gravel-pit pools beside the road from Chertsey to Staines have been landscaped and turned into Thorpe Park. This now has a hundred acres of lakes and land with displays illustrating maritime history, a Celtic farm, a Roman port, a Viking longship and much else including water sports.

Buses from Staines to Windsor run beside the Thames for most of the way, crossing Runnymede (where King John put his seal on Magna Carta) and past the memorial to President Kennedy, with views of locks, weirs, islands and boat-houses along the way. Finally Windsor Castle rose into sight above its Home Park.

Windsor

Berkshire's royal town provides plenty of good reasons to stay the night, not only because there is so much to see but because the old House Hotel (once Wren's home, beside the Thames) is irresistible. The food is excellent and all the handsome rooms are furnished with antiques, several lined with carved panelling.

Many books have been written about Windsor, but for the purpose of a flying visit the free Green Line leaflet provides a good guide to the main sights, beginning (of course) with the great castle begun by William the Conqueror and improved by almost every monarch since. At 13 acres, it is the biggest inhabited castle in the world.

Windsor's most interesting shopping street curves downhill in the shadow of the castle walls until reaching the old bridge (now reserved for pedestrians only), with Eton on the other side. There is a promenade by the river, usually gay with pleasure boats and swans. Church Street and nearby Market Street are places to linger in for their Tudor houses and little speciality shops; and Wren's columned Guildhall is nearby. Elegant Park Street, lined with Georgian houses, leads to Windsor Park and its magnificent vistas of the castle to the left and the Long Walk to the right, stretching in a straight line to George III's statue three miles away. One of Windsor's best-kept secrets is that the royal mausoleum in the park, normally closed to the public, can in fact be viewed on a few dates each May. It is incredibly beautiful: a little jewel in early Italian style, housing the great tombs of Victoria and Albert side by side, and surrounded by a stream and garden. Behind it lie the very simple graves of members of the royal family who have died in recent times, the latest burial being that of the Duke of Windsor.

Eton, immediately across the bridge, also deserves unhurried exploration. The 15th-century part of the college can be visited together with its superb Gothic chapel, containing carvings and wall paintings. In the High Street leading to the college, every second building seems to be an antique shop at which you may buy anything from a clay pipe to a chandelier; most of the rest are old inns or restaurants such as the bistro-like Eton Wine Bar. Yards built for coaches now hold large tubs of flowers. I stayed at the Christopher Inn, behind which the coachyard has been lined with elegantly furnished bedrooms each like a mini-cottage, equipped not only with bathroom, TV and so on but also with fridge, kettle and toaster for self-sufficiency.

This made an early start next day easy, but first I walked along the river. Canada geese grazed on the banks undisturbed at that quiet hour except when a group of ducks flew in. I walked past a bowling green, dormant at that season, and by beds of daffodils braving the unseasonable chill, until I came to a backstreet leading to a narrow stairway which, rising this way then that and around a Tudor house, emerged into Curfew Yard and the High Street. It was still only 8.30 am and the town was almost deserted. I could see and enjoy as never before the fine Georgian sash windows, the skyline of gables and pediments, shop fronts pillared or arcaded, old red brick contrasting with the smooth stucco of upper storeys in blue, yellow, apricot or dove-grey and the swinging shop signs.

And so to the bus. One is, fortunately, in and out of Slough in a matter of minutes. Beyond, flanked by flat meadows, the Thames is particularly beautiful. Blue and white pleasure craft, freshly painted, were moored in a creek ready for summer to bring tourists, and gulls rested in ploughed fields that were waiting for the spring sowing.

The journey onwards to Berkhamsted in Hertfordshire is a long one. It can be broken at, say, Amersham (Bucks) or to visit Stoke Poges, just off the bus route. The road goes up and down as pussy willows, holly (still bright with berries) and oaks give way to pleasant suburban houses set well back in gardens. In the leafless trees last year's nests were exposed to view, and already noisy rooks were beginning to make repairs for the new season, flying in with new twigs to add to old nests. Pines and rhododendrons were succeeded by silver birch and gorse on the commons at Gerrards Cross and Chalfont St Peter, suburbs by fields where cows grazed at the verge of a stream. At Chalfont St Giles a flying glimpse was possible of the pond beyond which John Milton's cottage lies. On through low hills and pastures, past one old inn after another, and soon we reached Amersham.

Amersham

Here I stopped, because it is a very pleasing old town with quaint almshouses and 17th-century market hall in its spacious main street, sheltered by the surrounding hills. Of its many fascinating old inns the Mill Stream (passed on the way in) is the most unusual, for the stream actually flows through it. Wandering among cobbled courts and alleys, I found thatched cottages tucked out of sight.

But the first thing I noticed, opposite the bus depot, was a warning on a cottage wall (dated 1811): 'The Magistrates Acting for this Hundred have given peremptory orders to constables to apprehend all common beggars, ballad-singers and other vagrants so that they may be dealt with according to law.'

Suppressing any urge to burst into song, I wandered along the main street and into the church – like its churchyard, beautifully maintained, a place of light and spaciousness. Amersham and the whole of this area have a history of religious dissent, with Puritan martyrs and Cromwellian associations. There is something Quakerish in the simplicity of even the parish church with its whitewashed walls, a polished pale floor and simple oak chairs. But against these the baroque monuments, carved pulpit (with the four evangelists coloured and gilded) and the royal coat-of-arms stand out even more splendidly. The 'heavenly' chancel ceiling is blue with gold stars.

Behind the pillared market house and its old lead pump lies Market Walk, where ten small speciality shops have tucked themselves into one building. Brief Encounter nearby is a good spot for a light, home-made lunch, and bar snacks are served at the 15th-century King's Arms further along. The whole length of the street is worth a lingering walk: brick-and-flint, or timbered houses, wisteria and other creepers, Dutch gables and rippling roofs, print galleries and antique shops – everything is a pleasure to see.

The most direct route to Chesham and Berkhamsted is

semi-suburban. Although there are some attractive views of the pretty River Chess and of beech woods as the bus climbs up and down, the roundabout way via Great Missenden is more picturesque. Throughout this route the Chiltern Hills provide marvellous views, particularly in autumn when the great old beech trees blaze with colour and the ground glows with a carpet of their crisp, fallen leaves. In summer, when the trees are green, they create a pattern of dense shade and flickering sunlight on mossy banks or bluebells. Bricks combined with flints make a characteristic style of architecture for this region.

Berkhamsted is still largely unspoilt despite the busy traffic through it, and it has an old beamed inn (the King's Arms) at which the buffet table provides the best value in hot meals that I encountered on this journey. A little way down Lower King's Road – beyond antique and book shops – lie the Grand Union Canal and the ruins of a Norman castle. The canal, built in the 18th century to bring goods from Northamptonshire to London, today has more pleasure boats and ducks than working barges.

Hemel Hempstead

A short run alongside the canal (and its locks, gaily painted narrow-boats and a former watermill) leads to Hemel Hempstead, its new town bright and busy but its 18th-century High Street still surviving in the old part.

It has something of the quality of Amersham but is less self-consciously picturesque. One can have a very inexpensive but appetizing lunch in the town hall's gallery, where art students' work hangs and dining tables overlook the yews of the old churchyard (but there are plenty of other eating places, from the Spinning Wheel to the Lautrec or White Hart, in ascending order of sophistication and price). At the far end of the High Street is an old pump of 1848, now done up in attractive colours, and on the corner of a tiny street called Cherry Bounce is a shop selling every article that can conceivably be made of basketwork – even a pram. As the sun was then shining and the view of the river, lacy white iron bridges and cottages was so attractive, I continued to walk to the village of Piccotts End.

No one ever paused at Piccotts End, except for petrol, until about twenty years ago first one and then another sensational discovery was made. There are two adjoining 14th-century cottages, whose previous sole claim to fame was that once they were employed as a cottage hospital – in fact, the first ever set up, by the surgeon to George IV. Later they reverted to humble dwellings until, on the death of their solitary 78-year-old occupant, some refurbishing was put in hand by the new owner. What started as a simple job of stripping wallpaper suddenly became a great revelation – no less than six layers of paper on one of linen collapsed off the wall in one great mass, uncovering on the plaster beneath a fantastic wall painting that had been preserved in perfect, vivid condition for four centuries. As if that were not enough, a further mural almost as old was revealed in the adjacent cottage some ten years later.

The earlier mural is an enigma. Many of the symbols entwining the conventional representation of the crucifixion and of the Virgin Mary are not just unusual but have associations with heretical beliefs. Was there once in this neighbourhood a group of Cathars, a forbidden sect from the Pyrenees, and is this why their wall painting was kept so carefully hidden from view under a cloth? Both cottages have been lovingly restored and filled with medieval and Tudor furnishings, and they were well worth my stroll from Hemel.

The next part of my ride was suburban at first, until along came fields and farmhouses, and suddenly the great abbey of St Albans appeared on the horizon.

St Albans

I got off before the bus entered the town in order to look at the Roman theatre – unique in Britain. Its small stage and larger central space suggest that it was probably used for religious ceremonials rather than for acting plays. It stood to one side of the Roman city of Verulamium, which extended downhill towards where today's town stands. That town grew up *outside* the Roman walls, possibly where the Romans had their cemetery, and as I walked down Fishpool Street to reach the town I was passing the ghost of the Roman city.

On the way I visited the Roman museum, whose finds range from delightful mosaics to the nail-cleaners and ear picks of 2,000 years ago. A few yards further on, ducks were crossing the road in one direction and swans in the other. Beside their home, the River Ver which gave Verulamium its name, stands a 16th-century watermill restored to order and open to the public. In one of its store rooms a group of enterprising local women had set up the Calico Tree, a shop selling pretty things in gingham and patchwork designed by one of them (an artist) and made at home by the others.

Fishpool Street winds on and on downhill, lined with Queen

Anne, Georgian and Regency houses – some gracious, some quaint, most with individualistic porches and doorknockers. The 16th-century Manor House is now an elegant hotel with five acres of lawns beside the River Ver. The road turned and abruptly I found myself at the foot of the abbey.

The Saxons built the first cathedral (in honour of Alban, a Christian martyred by the Romans), but the present great abbey is largely Norman and 13th-century work. A lot of fine medieval wall paintings have been uncovered inside during the last century or so as the Puritans' whitewash has gradually been cleaned off; once all the walls must have glowed with colourful painted scenes, and its great interior would have been thronged with people. But when I was there, in the twilit gloom there was stillness until a little procession of two priests and a dozen small choristers (red-robed and white-ruffed) entered to sing evensong for a congregation of two. In the cathedral I bought an excellent paperback, *Cathedral and City*, with first-rate essays on the history of St Albans by various contributors including Robert Runcie, its former bishop who, that very week, was to be enthroned as Archbishop of Canterbury.

I stayed the night at the White Hart, a half-timbered coaching inn right by the abbey, wondering whether my beamed bedroom may have been the one where Lord Lovat stayed in 1746 on his way to the Tower and execution for treason.

The town of St Albans is rich in old inns, historic buildings, byways and (like many other towns on this circuit of London's countryside) antique shops. If you do not want to buy a guidebook to the city, use the free Green Line leaflet which illustrates a walking tour round the most interesting parts starting from St Peter's Street (where, ever since Saxon times, a Saturday market has been held), going along French Row (where French prisoners were housed in the Middle Ages) to the medieval curfew belltower and the gate of the Waxhouse where candles were made.

To get to Waltham I went via Potters Bar and Enfield – a dull route, though there are a few interesting buildings surviving among Enfield's bustle. The town of Waltham Cross is notable only for an unusual inn sign of swans on a beam stretching right over the top of a busy road.

Waltham

Waltham Abbey, however, is breathtaking and well worth the journey. Its richness, size, antiquity and its stormy and emotional history are all exceptional, and it is also enhanced by the fact that one comes upon it in surroundings that are very undistinguished.

To start with: the legends about it. In 1030 a Somerset carpenter was instructed in a dream to dig in a certain hilltop. Seventy feet down, a black stone crucifix was found. This was taken (again, by mystical direction) to Waltham, on the edge of the then vast Epping Forest. There it was housed in a wooden church until – six years before the Battle of Hastings – King Harold built a monastery to house it, to which later monarchs added. The remnant of this Norman church is all one can see, but *what* a remnant! The total structure must have been one of the wonders of the Norman world, for although the Conquest was still to come, the masons (and the stone) were imported from Normandy. When Harold prayed before the black cross before he went to do battle, it is said that the head of Christ bowed down (an ill omen). Harold's corpse was brought back for burial after the Battle of Hastings, and his grave can be seen.

Though the present nave seems colossal, the original was three times as long until Henry VIII tore most of it down. But what remains is impressively strong, simple and grand, now enriched by Sir Edward Burne-Jones's stained glass and an elaborately painted ceiling.

In the narrow streets of the town that grew up round the abbey one can still see many ancient timber-framed houses, some leaning at tipsy angles. The walled gardens of the abbey deserve a lingering visit, too.

The onward road climbed among white, weatherboarded cottages through woods of birch and beech (vestiges of Epping Forest) and along an open ridge with far views of distant hills. As the bus splashed through puddles and the driving rain outside lashed the windows, I was dozily lulled by the warmth inside and the rhythmic squeak of the windscreen wipers until Epping and lunchtime arrived conveniently at the same moment.

Epping

Epping has some pleasant Georgian houses at each end of its wide High Street but, fighting with the wind for possession of my umbrella, I was more interested in steak-and-kidney pie at the Thatched House (not, in fact, thatched, but a low-beamed inn).

It is possible to complete the circle around London by going via Ongar, Brentwood and North Ockendon to Tilbury, where there is a passenger ferry to Gravesend. But there is also a tube station at Epping from which one can get back into central London again (unfortunately, the very pretty stretch of Underground line from

Ongar is threatened with closure); and the rest of the journey is one of the less interesting stretches. However, I pressed on.

Ongar must once have been picturesque, but it has been badly neglected, and Brentwood seemed to have little to commend it. I was glad to move on to North Ockendon to pick up my last bus. This part of Essex is fairly pretty, though one never goes for long without pylons or distant factory chimneys springing into view. However, there are lots of tree-lined lanes and half-timbered houses. The nearer we got to Kent, the more Kentish did the scene become – a church tower on which flints and ragstone alternated and some weatherboarding, for instance. The scenery is varied by streams and lovely mansions, one near where a new motorway was being hewn across our route. The bus drew up outside the local museum – easily worth half an hour for its well-designed displays telling the region's history from the Stone Age flint industry to the great docks of the present day. Then, after passing more flat fields with grazing cows against a factory background and yards stacked with timber newly arrived from Sweden, we suddenly arrived at the railway terminus of Tilbury.

Tilbury

The Thames itself is out of sight, hidden behind a high sea-wall and iron floodgates that are ready to slam shut if, one day, the Thames rises to flood levels (a perennial fear). A grey tide was rolling in when I arrived, frothing impatiently. The wiry-necked cranes crowded along the dock sides a little way upstream. I walked downstream along the sea-wall – not just for the fine views of shipping in Gravesend Reach but to visit Tilbury Fort, a 17th-century defence against the Dutch and French with a lavish triumphal gateway. Where the military were once quartered private citizens now have their homes, but the ramparts and guardrooms can still be visited. The World's End, a weatherboarded old inn nearby, has a cosy and interesting interior.

As I waited on the jetty for the ferry to come, I could see Gravesend church spire on the opposite bank (white with a blue-and-gold clock) and the Town Pier. A container-ship laboured slowly past, its twelve great containers looking like children's bricks – green, red, yellow and brown. The ferry soon took us across and I stepped ashore to the cry of gulls and the splash-and-clang sound so characteristic of the Thames, made by waves on the iron hulls of moored barges called *Dutch Courage* and *Dutch Treat*. My journey had come full circle and once more I was back in Kent.

6

THE CINQUE PORTS

*Sandwich – Dover – Hythe – New Romney – Rye –
Winchelsea – Hastings*

Because the ancient Cinque Ports (now seven, despite their
name) are close together along the Kent-Sussex shore, one can
reach them all within a few hours, but they are so interesting that a
few days' holiday, stopping overnight at two or three, would be a
far better way to do them justice. That would also give time to go a
little way into the surrounding countryside. The local buses are
convenient and frequent. I went early in spring – a spring that
seemed reluctant to let winter go. Despite the nip in the air, it was
an enjoyable trip – not least because there were few other
travellers.

This stretch of coast faces Europe and has always been the part
most vulnerable to invasion. Caesar landed here, and later the
Romans had to build forts to defend it from the Saxon tribes of
Germany. William the Conqueror landed a little further west and
in his turn built defensive castles along these shores. Many of
Henry VIII's defences against the French can still be viewed, and
so can some of the 70 dumpy Martello towers put up when an
invasion by Napoleon was feared. Today's invaders, tourists from
Europe, are more welcome than their predecessors.

The Cinque Ports gained their unique status in national
defence in 1278 when Edward I gave them a charter under which,
in return for providing ships and sailors to defend the shore, they
were granted valuable privileges of self-government, trading
rights and exemption from military service. They thus grew not
only powerful but rich, as the remaining medieval houses and
noble churches show.

However, the ports' fortunes later declined. When Charles II
built up England's navy their services were no longer so vital and,

worse still, nature had taken a hand: their harbours were by now silted up (Dover excepted) by the great masses of sand and shingle that are swept in by the Atlantic and deposited along these shores. Because of this Sandwich, New Romney, Rye and Winchelsea are in fact far inland now. Virtually all privileges were eventually withdrawn from the ports.

This journey is therefore one of great historical interest, through country studded with the massive relics of invasions or invasion scares (from the Romans right up to the Second World War). It runs along a coastline that is still in the making – or unmaking – with scenery as varied as the white cliffs of Dover and the wild, windy marshes around Romney.

Sandwich

My journey started at Sandwich, most senior of the Cinque Ports, but if you prefer to start at the beginning – chronologically speaking – you could make nearby Richborough the first visit, for here stand the massive ruins of the Romans' greatest fortress, built to keep the Saxons out. It is not only the earliest relic of Roman Britain but arguably the most spectacular. From here started the great Roman road, Watling Street, which ran all the way up to Shropshire.

Sandwich is a delightful town of narrow streets and high-gabled houses jumbled together – medieval, Tudor or later. As well as its riverfront it has a strange artificial stream, the Delf, wandering amongst and under the houses – an early means of water supply. There is a barbican of chequerboard stone, an old guildhall, and ramparts that are grassy mounds providing a very pleasant stroll around the old town. There are plenty of places to stay: I enjoyed the food at the Weavers and, in one of its low, beamed bedrooms, Thomas Becket (Canterbury's martyred archbishop) once stayed, so it scores on ambience, too.

One can go direct to Dover, but it adds little to the ¾-hour bus journey to take the route via Deal – not a Cinque Port but interesting for having the best of the Henry VIII castles. It is also where Julius Caesar landed, despite fierce opposition from the Britons, who drove their chariots into the sea against the armoured legionaries as they tried to disembark. A small seaside resort favoured by artists, it is on an attractive bus route that skirts Kent's only coalfield, which in no way spoils the scenery.

The view out to sea is of the notorious Goodwin Sands, their lightships and wrecks, and of the minor shipping busily passing between them and the shore. Here a familiar landmark is the time ball, twin of the one at Greenwich to which it was electrically linked until recently. Its function was to signal the hour by the dropping of the big ball on its spire, so that ships at sea could check their chronometers. (The Tourist Information Centre is here.) The promenade by the long shingle beach leads to Deal Castle, but it is worth visiting first the Georgian backstreets which have great charm, relics of the days when Deal was a prosperous and bustling port.

The castle was built to defend the ships that moored at low tide between the Goodwins and the shore. Though treacherous when high tide barely covers them, the sandbanks at other times form a protection from rough weather in the Channel. Henry VIII's small castles are built in the shape of a rose, not for any aesthetic reason but because the rounded, petal-like bastions provided for tiers of cannon, each able to fire over a very wide arc. The interior is a maze of passageways.

Walmer, too, has its Henry VIII castle (within walking distance, and on the bus route to Dover) as well as a famous lifeboat, usually to be seen drawn up on the shingle. The castle, altered a lot since it was built, contains exhibits about past Lord Wardens of the Cinque Ports such as the Duke of Wellington (including his boots) and Winston Churchill, and it is surrounded by lovely gardens.

Dover

In ¼ hour the bus reaches Dover and its castle – a very different fortification, overwhelming in size and site, high up and with spectacular sea views. For thousands of years there has been a fortress here, and still standing within its walls is the 50-foot stump of a Roman lighthouse. When the Normans burned Dover they rebuilt the castle so well that the beseiging French found it impregnable in 1216. It is still an important defence and was used in both world wars, and its great central keep is one of the largest in Britain.

The bus down into the town stops in the centre, conveniently near most of Dover's historic sights such as the recently discovered Roman house which accidentally came to light when a car park was being levelled (it is in a down-at-heel lane that gives no hint of the treasure it holds). It was possibly the house of the admiral in charge of the port. Its painted walls survived because, in erecting a new fort, the Roman army built a great wall right through it, and this was banked up with a mound of clay that preserved the colourful house walls buried inside it. The underfloor heating system also survived intact.

As Dover is not only a port but a garrison town, it is big and bustling. But there are pleasant promenades, cliff-top walks, riverside gardens, a 4,000-foot pier (the view from the end of the castle and the famous white cliffs shows them in all their grandeur), and a honeycomb of underground passages. Dover is also a great place for statues and other memorials.

Tiny St Edmund's chapel is worth seeking out, built by one English saint (St Richard of Chichester) in honour of another, in 1253. Bulldozers were whining and lorries changing gear outside, but inside were sanctified peace and simplicity – whitewashed walls, a floor of cobbles and ancient oak roof-beams fastened to one another with wood pegs. The chapel is near the Town Hall ('Maison Dieu'), which has great coloured windows telling of royal comings and goings through the port: Edward III off to the Hundred Years' War, Henry VIII embarking for the Field of the Cloth of Gold, Charles II's restoration. The floor vibrated to a crescendo from the organ in the great hall, and all the pomp and circumstance were in complete contrast to St Edmund's.

Next door is a typical town museum, a hotch-potch of local bric-à-brac alongside souvenirs donated by intrepid Victorian travellers. On television that night David Attenborough was showing trees in Arizona's petrified forest and that morning I stroked the polished, stony remains of one – in Dover's museum. There are plenty of restaurants in this area – home-made food on cane tables at the Dovorian, for instance, or more sophisticated cooking at Flicks Diner.

Flints from among the chalk go into the building of walls hereabouts, and they were much in evidence on the short bus ride to Folkestone. Beyond lie the high hummocks of the North Downs.

Folkestone

There are two Folkestones – low and high, one old and workaday and one leisured and more recent. Decimus Burton laid out the latter in the grand manner early in Victoria's reign. I got off the bus in Castle Street and walked back a little along The Stade beside the old harbour. I could smell fish before I saw it displayed on stone slabs in the fish market. Out of the Channel mists a ghost ship suddenly loomed – the Sealink ferry from Boulogne.

The long climb up Remembrance Road to the other Folkestone is worth the effort. Along this road thousands of soldiers marched (many to their deaths) to embark for France during the First

World War. As well as a conventional memorial at the top, the city fathers planted this road with rosemary ('for remembrance'), bay and pines. These scents now mingle with the tang of the sea below to give an almost Mediterranean aroma to the air.

Folkestone, once described as 'a miserable little fishing town', got a new lease of life when the railway came in 1853. And at the top of Remembrance Road one is suddenly transported into this new world of stately Victorian hotels with names redolent of nobility, saints or statesmen of a century ago. The buildings stand at attention along a wide promenade of neat box hedges and still neater lawns, deserted when I was there except for a worker repainting the curlicues and ships on the wrought-iron street lamps. At the centre of the Leas, as the promenade is called, William Harvey (who discovered the circulation of the blood and was born in Folkestone in 1578) clutches his still, cold heart with fingers of bronze.

Opposite Trinity Church in Sandgate Street I waited by a Victorian pillarbox (hexagonal, with a pie-crust top) for the bus to Hythe. It makes its way between Sandgate's timbered buildings, some with wood balconies or shutters, and beside a shore where surf thrashes the shingle ceaselessly.

Hythe

Not only the Martello towers in this area recall how lively was the fear that Napoleon would invade: the road into Hythe sees the beginning of the Royal Military Canal, built as a defence against the emperor and still found useful in the two world wars. The canal was in effect a 60-foot-wide moat, its inland bank built high, which deliberately followed a zigzag route so that cannon could be strategically placed at each angle. Now people fish and boat on it, it is flanked by gardens, and a glorious 'Venetian' water carnival is held every other summer.

The little streets of Georgian houses around the church are attractive and the church itself is one of the finest in Kent, built with the once-rich proceeds of herring fishing. Children are fascinated by its more macabre side – a crypt stacked with thousands of skulls and bones, believed to be Roman, but more probably medieval. They also enjoy (and so do adults!) the miniature railway that steams its way for 14 miles across the marshes to Romney as an alternative to getting there by bus. The ten steam locomotives are mostly replicas (one-third size) of main-line expresses of the 1920s. There is a railway exhibition at New Romney station, and near Dungeness are an old lighthouse and lifeboat station to be visited.

A worthwhile detour, 10 minutes by bus, is to Saltwood Castle, where the knights plotted Thomas Becket's assassination. It is a romantic semi-ruin draped in creepers, but its gatehouse is still occupied by the family of Lord Clark.

Hythe is soon going to be separated from its peaceful canal by a multi-lane roadway to accommodate the juggernaut lorries from the Continent which at present pound through the narrow High Street. The best way to escape them is through the colonnade below the town hall (an incised stone says 'All Persons are requefted to unite their Endeavours to keep this Place clean and to prevent BOYS or others from dirting the fame') and thence up a narrow hill leading to the church and to the backwaters of Bartholomew Road, Malthouse Hill and other lanes lined with ancient houses.

At the hill's foot is the old malt house, now an antiques market, within sight of the Red Lion bus-stop. A few yards away, I gave in to the temptation of a generous cream tea at Betty's in what was, from 1892 until 1921, a tram shed (the tramlines can be seen in the cobbles of the forecourt). The trams, nicknamed 'toast-racks' – photographs make the reason plain – were horse-drawn. An alternative for a quick snack is Flapjax (where they flip a pretty pancake); there are also several good but pricey restaurants in or off the High Street.

The bus shelter stands right by one of those strategic zigzags in the canal, and from there the bus reaches Dymchurch in a few minutes (unless one breaks off to visit Lympne Castle first).

From Hythe onwards the ground is utterly level – onetime marshes (now drained), flat as a billiard table, stretch out into a misty, never-ending distance. There is little to see, a total contrast to the Downs at the start of the journey. The high sea-wall blots out the view on the other side of the bus.

Dymchurch, once pretty, is very sleazy now. Its vast sandy beaches are an attraction to children, but its only other claim to attention is a Martello tower housing a museum of anti-Napoleon defences. The tower was sited here to defend the sluices which control the drainage of the marshes: the land lies many feet below sea-level and if the sluices were destroyed the sea would flood it. This was smuggling country, and Dymchurch is where Russell Thorndike set his series of novels about Dr Syn, the smuggler-parson, whose deeds are now celebrated in a biennial Dr Syn carnival.

The marshes here and beyond New Romney have not always existed. Once the sea covered the area, exposing only muddy saltings at low tide. The Romans built not only the sea-wall but another (the Rhee Wall) alongside the River Rother which, at that time, flowed through the saltings where the Appledore-New Romney road now runs. Thus the Romans turned the saltings into drainable land they could use as pasture. Later Thomas Becket, among other landowners, drained more saltings on the other side of the Rhee Wall and created Walland Marsh between New Romney and Rye, now some of the richest soil in the world. Its grass is so excellent that the hardy Romney Marsh sheep need no extra feeding (nor any shelter) in winter. Their shepherds, known as 'lookers', lead isolated lives on these windswept marshes. Ask the bus driver where to get off for New Romney: some buses only pause outside it and then whisk off elsewhere.

New Romney

New Romney was new in Saxon times (old Romney having been superseded when its harbour silted up). It used to be an important port before the River Rother left it, suddenly changing its course after the great storm of 1287. The Georgian houses in its wide street were in many cases the homes of 'owlers' (smugglers) who, even during war with France, carried on illicit bartering of wool for contraband silk, brandy and tobacco. The extent to which the land in these parts changed its level is made vivid at the church, a particularly splendid Norman one, where the ground is now more than halfway up some of the older pillars. The church is often locked against vandals, and I had to content myself with wandering among the tombstones where lichen -- gold, green, grey and even crimson -- obliterates the inscriptions with its patterns. Down West Street are old priory walls. another reminder of the town's vanished status. A good place for a rest after exploring all the quiet lanes is the New Inn, a rabbit-warren of nooks.

New Romney is a sleepy place and, except for antique shops, does not go out of its way to attract tourists. Nevertheless I chose to sleep there at the Ship Inn. Exterior and prices are modest, but the food is home-cooked and generous, and the inn itself dates back to the 12th century. Ancient beams stick out oddly through the plaster here and there, like bony limbs through old clothes.

The bus journey is about 12 miles across the Wall and Marsh with its drainage ditches, isolated farms, very few trees and an occasional old inn. It is a place of vastness and solitude.

Rye

Beautiful Rye seethes with tourists during summer, but in spring only the locals were out and about, and not many of them. I could see the cobbled streets and medieval buildings as never before. It is worth picking up a street plan from the Tourist Information Centre before venturing into the warren of little streets perched on Rye's hill, which was once almost an island surrounded by sea on three sides.

Conduit Hill (up which water was once pumped to a great cistern in the churchyard) leads to the High Street where above the shop fronts are upper storeys of scalloped tiles (known as beavertails) and timbered overhangs leaning at precarious angles. Some shops hang out signs, such as an iron kettle at the iron-monger's and a brass pestle-and-mortar at the chemist. For over three hundred years the grammar school has dominated the cen-tre, its red brick slowly mellowing. Now one can rent a holiday flat in it. Down sidestreets one can glimpse cobbled yards and ancient cottages, wreathed in forsythia and clematis, or brave Bessie, a ship's figurehead of 1820 standing guard outside a crafts shop.

The road continues down the winding slope of the Mint, a street of old houses that have oak doors with carved linenfold panels and worn stone steps. A few have pargeted walls (decorative plasterwork). Past the many potteries (one makes the decorative house-name plaques which are a feature of Rye) lies the Strand, with wooden warehouses converted to restaurants and antique shops along the waterfront.

Ascending back again to the centre, I strolled up one of England's famous streets, now almost deserted – Mermaid Street. It is worth pausing to look back every few yards at changing perspectives of cobbles and window boxes. At the end, to the right, lies the Tudor house where Henry James once lived – its lovely garden alone is worth an unhurried visit – and the marvellously preserved square surrounding the ivied church-yard. Every other house seems to be of outstanding interest architecturally or historically, with evocative names like St Anthony of Padua, Friars of the Sack, or the Old Stone House. Off it is another fascinating byway, Watchbell Street, with glimpses of gardens and courts at each side. At the end is a lookout over the boats and marshes lying far below the town and a view of the distant ruins of Camber Castle, wreathed in mist.

The great church has windows of the most vivid blue and a very unusual, very ancient clock – its enormous pendulum hangs right down into the nave, the steady tick-tock louder than the murmured prayers of worshippers. Rye's old bells sound a splendid peal over the marshes.

Ypres Tower, nearby, is another lookout point. It is a forbidding grey bastion (now a really interesting museum) which in its time repulsed the French and housed prisoners. The curious oval Water House, on the way back to the town centre, was built in 1732 to provide a supply of water to the top of this hill town; people brought their buckets to the pump outside it. Now the great gauge outside shows it is empty, its function taken over by progress and plumbing.

The log fire, Tudor beams and home-made food of Fletchers (in Lion Street) provided a welcome break. The house is named after the Fletcher of Beaumont and Fletcher, 17th-century dramatists, who lived there. Then I went down East Cliff, through the great stone Land Gate and thus, reluctantly, back to the bus station. Rye is so full of good places at which to stay, eat, shop or just look that one could happily linger for days.

The bus onward circles round the bottom of Rye's hillock and, looking backward, one can see how the town is heaped up above what was formerly sea – the ridge far to the right of the bus route was once a sea cliff. Now the only water is in the narrow river running alongside the road and the drainage ditches, the haunt of moorhens.

Winchelsea

Winchelsea is another town on a hillock that was once a sea-girt island. The bus climbs into it by a steep road with hairpin bends, passing one of the ancient stone gates that date from the time when this was a defensively walled town.

What a contrast with busy Rye. This sleepy 'town' of 500 people is unique – an example of town planning 13th-century style. There was another Winchelsea once, but the great storm of 1287 swept over it and buried it under sand. Those who survived built a new Winchelsea, laid out in 39 squares and with a magnificent church of Normandy stone and Sussex marble. It is fortunate that this was built just when the Decorated style was in its early days, an outstanding period in English architecture. What stands now is only a fragment of the whole, the 70-foot choir, for the French destroyed the rest. Its stone effigies of knights and other worthies are dappled with the light from exceptional modern stained glass (the blues are particularly rich) with intricate designs that deserve unhurried study. It is said that some of the great marble figures were retrieved from the old, inundated Winchelsea.

Many of Sir John Everett Millais's paintings were done at Winchelsea, some in the church. The town flourished when it was a port for wines from Bordeaux (the later houses built on old foundations have enormous ancient wine cellars), but, as the sea receded, it became a quiet retreat and is mercifully free of traffic still.

The New Inn is a good spot for cheap, piping hot food by a flaming fire. The church bookstall provided me with a particularly well-produced 'Town Walk' booklet which took me through one fascinating street after another. At Manna Plat is a former 13th-century wine cellar, now a coffee shop and art gallery.

Perhaps because of its history – apocalyptic storms, four invasions, the Black Death, and finally the catastrophic departure of the sea which ruined its life as a port – there can be few places as calm as Winchelsea now. One can stay inexpensively at the New Inn or in a romantic 600-year-old house, the Armoury, which has beautiful gardens.

A half-hour bus ride runs through fields and orchards with views of rolling hills and the villages of Icklesham and Guestling. Here and there are converted oasthouses and an old wooden windmill.

Hastings

The bus makes the long descent into the middle of Hastings, right through the middle of the old town. This road is called the Bourne because once it was a river, and the streets flanking it were on its banks. This is a good place to get off in order to wander in the old town. But first I strolled round the nearby fishmarket and among the teetering black wooden sheds on the beach in which, for some two hundred years, fishing nets have been hung to dry. The pebbly beach is covered with fishing odds and ends between the colourful boats drawn up above the tide (for there is no harbour: it silted up centuries ago). Behind rise many-coloured sandstone cliffs hewn into odd shapes by centuries of weather. There is a fisheries museum in a disused chapel.

At the start of All Saints Street, once the east bank of the Bourne, is a gigantic winkle (symbol of Hastings' Winkle Club, a fishermen's charity, one of whose members is the Queen Mother). The street itself has pretty houses with low oak doors, windows of leaded panes or bottle-glass, and half-timbered overhangs. There are beamy inns such as the Stag, which has a collection of mummified cats, and curiosities like the wedge-shaped cottage called the Piece of Cheese, sometimes open to the public. One of the pavements is raised high on a bank, presumably once a necessary precaution against flood and mud.

All Saints Church, at the end, is majestically enthroned uphill. Its main claim to fame is a medieval 'doom' painting high on the wall dividing nave from choir, with a lively devil casting souls into hell, but the much later Catholic church across the Bourne is arguably more beautiful inside though it has a plain exterior. Next to it stables have been converted into a theatre on the other side of which runs the old High Street. Of the many tiny cottages, number 118 is the quaintest – sheer Hansel-and-Gretel, with a chimney almost as big as the cottage.

St Clement's 14th-century church is oddly designed to fit the shape of the land (it was perched here because an earlier church on level ground was destroyed by the sea). It is a place of space and light, dedicated to the saint of fishermen. From here I went puffing and blowing up Coburg Place – narrow twisting stairs that run behind, between and even under houses to get to the top of West Hill, where William the Conqueror built his first castle.

A vast network of tunnels in the hill was originally gouged out by underground streams, but humans have had a hand since – most recently with figures of Churchill and others carved in the soft sandstone. No one knows how long ago the caves were first put to use, but they have often been used for refuge – from Vikings and from bombers in the Second World War, for example. Smugglers found them extremely useful hideaways, as did Wellington's soldiers when garrisoned in Hastings. Eventually the entrance was walled up. (Was one soldier inadvertently walled in? Some years ago a skeleton was found, said to be nearly 200 years old.) The caves were then more or less forgotten until a gardener digging a hole fell into them, and after that they became his life's work. He carved many of the figures and miles of pillared 'cloisters' with niches for candles. Occasionally candle-lit processions are staged there. Young people have a weekly disco, and the TV play 'King's Dragon' was filmed down there. All events are presided over by Nina the cat, who never loses her way in the labyrinth that is her home.

Hastings was the most important of the Cinque Ports until Dover overtook it a century ago. This was in spite of the fact that it had to be recreated three times after the sea swept over it. Now the picturesque old town, with its antique shops and restaurants, is a very small part of the whole. Modern Hastings (go down West Hill to it by means of the lift) is a bustling holiday resort, full of entertainment. On the other side of the old town is East Hill and a country park with picturesque glens and nature trails.

Hastings cannot be appreciated in only an hour or two, so I stayed overnight at the Chimes, Silverhill, a few minutes by bus from the centre. This small and ordinary-looking hotel has an out-of-the-ordinary host in Clifford Pugh, a scientist turned hotelier, whose attention to detail is exceptional. For instance, he keeps a huge range of guidebooks (even a bus timetable – how rare!) to help visitors. A specialization of the hotel is excellent wine from Kentish vineyards, with cooking by Mrs Pugh to match – and all this at very ordinary prices. The hotel is, incidentally, close to express coaches to London and elsewhere.

Should you want at the end of the journey to return to your starting point, the coach that goes from Hastings to Dover in two hours during the summer will speed you back most of the way, or there is a through bus that takes three hours. There are also coaches and trains to London and elsewhere (but you may need to book a seat on coaches).

7

THE SOUTH HAMS

Totnes – Dartmouth – Kingsbridge – Plymouth

'Ham' means 'sheltered', and the South Hams area of Devon is so sheltered that it has the mildest climate in Britain, which makes it a good choice for a few days' break even when other places are still wintry. It is entirely a farming area with no industrial ugliness to spoil the idyll, and because no fewer than five rivers run hither and yon, indenting the coastline where they reach the sea, any bus ride is full of interest as it goes up hills and down into valleys. Farming and trading have always prospered here, so towns contain handsome houses and the thatched cottages of the villages have been kept up well.

Totnes

I chose Totnes (on the River Dart) as a good base from which to explore the area by bus, and right by the bus park found the Royal Seven Stars Hotel, a coaching inn which dates from Charles II's day. The coachyard is roofed over to make a stone-flagged entrance hall with an imposing staircase descending from a gallery, and a long row of old room bells, now silent, hangs on one wall.

The inn stands at the foot of steep Fore Street, which is spanned halfway up by an immense blue-and-white gateway beside which are steps leading up to the ramparts of this ancient borough. Founded in Saxon times, it was once an important town, and at its quay merchandise has been loaded for nearly a thousand years.

Fore Street is lined with houses in pastel pinks and yellows, some with bay windows, some with little courts that can be glimpsed between them. A characteristic of Totnes is the use of slates decoratively hung like fish scales on the upper storeys. In the street are the kind of small, old-fashioned shops which still have evocative smells – of toffees in a sweet shop or leather in a shoe shop, for instance – almost vanished from memory in this packaging-and-plastic age.

The rampart walk leads past the old stone Guildhall (now a museum) in its picturesque, colonnaded corner and to the 15th-century church with a really spectacular rood screen, its delicate tracery of carved stone amazingly intact after all these centuries and with some of the old gilding still surviving. On the elaborate monument to Christopher Blackhall, who died in 1633, are his four wives (successive not simultaneous), each in the fashion of her day, whether ruffed or lace-collared.

Beyond lies the castellated castle on a mound, neat and round as a child's sandcastle. It remained undamaged, I was told, because the burghers of Totnes were always quick to change sides in any war when the going became really rough. From here there is a good view over the tumble of rooftops below. The High Street beyond is where the most interesting shops and small restaurants are, many in columned arcades, some decorated with black-and-white fancywork and some with carved grotesques. In Totnes a great variety of building stones have been used, including red sandstone, granite, limestone and tuff (a stone formed from volcanic ash).

Plenty of bus trips are possible from Totnes – out onto the moors, for instance, or to lovely Dartington Hall nearby (a school and arts centre combined and set in exceptionally lovely gardens – the great lawn, flanked by grassy terraces, was once a tiltyard for jousting). I lunched from the hot buffet served at the Cott Inn near there, ducking my head at each low doorway. This is one of the oldest inns in the country, its thick white walls made of cobb (a mud-like mixture), its roof of dense thatch. Torquay, Buckfast Abbey and Paignton are all within an easy bus ride, too.

The bus route to Dartmouth runs between high hedges, pines and oaks, with views of fields where brown Devon cattle graze or ploughed earth shows up red among the green. It is a winding road, punctuated with streams and picturesque inns, rising and falling, often with trees meeting overhead. Descending steeply into Dartmouth, there is a lovely view across the water with its swans and bobbing boats to Kingswear: colour-washed houses are piled up on the steep bank, and a steam train puffs slowly along the shore.

Dartmouth

Dartmouth is one of my favourite places by the sea, perched precariously on steep cliffs beside the estuary, a little harbour at its heart. Picturesque and historical, it is a place of coves and cobbles, old houses and sub-tropical gardens, a waterfront castle and trips on the river through spectacular scenery. From there one can take a further bus along the sandy coast to Kingsbridge, or Kingsbridge can be reached direct via Totnes by an inland bus ride that offers distant views of Dartmoor's smokey-blue hills and close-ups of the steep banks so characteristic of Devon lanes, with primroses, moss, hart's tongue ferns, celandines, holly, ivy and occasionally violets.

The Dartmouth-Kingsbridge bus route is particularly attractive, going close by the Slapton Leye nature reserve with a good view of waterfowl on the lagoons, and the sea on the other side of the road. The Start Bay Inn is a good place to stop for a seafood lunch.

Kingsbridge

Kingsbridge is a little town on another estuary. Like Totnes it is on a steep hill by the river, and like Totnes it has an arcaded Butterwalk or Shambles that goes back to Tudor times. On Wednesdays, market days, it hums with activity, and the old King's Arms inn does a busy trade. Where the buses stop there is a good place for lunch: Wooster's wine bar.

Plymouth

From there it does not take long to get by bus through more pretty villages to Plymouth, which has just celebrated the 400th anniversary of Drake's voyage round the world on which he set out from Plymouth, his home town. There is the famous Hoe (where bowls are still played) overlooking one of the most beautiful natural harbours in the world; beaches of sand and rock; brilliant gardens; the cobbled streets and fishmarkets near the steps from which the Pilgrim Fathers embarked on the Mayflower; and old lanes and little shops (big ones, too – Plymouth has a vast shopping centre). Although much-bombed Plymouth does not have many old buildings, it has so much else going for it that it is a big holiday resort now, with sights, excursions and restaurants enough to occupy one for a fortnight. Open-top bus tours and a viewing platform at the top of its Municipal Offices skyscraper make the most of one of its greatest assets: the views. Whether inland or out to sea, every prospect pleases.

8

ENGLAND'S ONLY PRAIRIE
SALISBURY PLAIN

Salisbury – Amesbury – Marlborough – Devizes – Wilton – Salisbury

Wiltshire is a county often underestimated by tourists, who hurry in to 'do' Salisbury Cathedral, Longleat or Stonehenge and then dash on elsewhere. It is worth spending longer and, using Salisbury as a base for a couple of nights, one can make very varied bus trips in each direction (see end of this chapter). This is an account of just one, crossing Salisbury Plain from south to north, climbing up into the Marlborough Downs for contrast, and then returning across the Plain again by another route.

The Plain is a vast expanse, still holding many ancient secrets. People have lived there for at least 4,000 years, and the traces of far-off occupation are numerous yet often mysterious even to archaeologists. The great circles of which Stonehenge is the most famous remain the subject of argument (were they temples? sundial-calendars for farmers? No one knows for sure, and it is even uncertain how such colossal stones were raised into position). There are literally hundreds of prehistoric burial mounds and traces of Iron Age forts and earthworks on hilltops – each adding to the landscape's distinctive contours. Some ancient tracks may well have been trodden by the feet of Stone Age people, and the famous white horses of Wiltshire's hills, cut through the turf to reveal the white chalk below, were in some cases created over a thousand years ago (others date from the 18th, 19th or even 20th centuries). Horse-spotting is a good way to keep small children occupied on bus rides to the north of the Plain.

Salisbury

But first there is the starting point, Salisbury itself. The cathedral's 400-foot spire is known world-wide through reproductions of Constable's famous painting of it, and this is unquestionably its most beautiful feature. The soaring and lengthy interior is impressive, yet rather bleak. The spire was added a century after the cathedral was built early in the 13th century, and its 6,000 tons added such an extra strain to the foundations that there have been problems ever since.

Within the cathedral is the oldest clock in the world, and its clacking iron mechanism attracts a bigger group of sightseers than any of the monuments. Having been working for 600 years it is quite possibly the oldest bit of 'living' machinery in the world. The cathedral has the largest cloisters in England, an octagonal chapter house with biblical scenes carved in stone, and a tiny chapel with exquisite fan-vaulting. Children may enjoy spotting one of its special though not very conspicuous features (binoculars are a help): some 60 stone faces very high up in the nave and elsewhere. Each is a portrait of somebody once notable, but very few have been identified. Some may also enjoy picking out (with the help of a booklet sold in the cathedral) the hundred or so saints and kings in their niches on the west front. With the largest cloisters, oldest clock and highest spire Salisbury cannot but be one of the most impressive of cathedrals.

Around the spacious green that is the Cathedral Close are old houses such as the medieval bishop's palace, canonry and deanery (some open to visitors), and to the north of it lies a network of historic streets, churches and inns. The most interesting shops and eating places are in the High Street.

Five winding rivers meet in a tangle at Salisbury. The banks of several are gardens or meadows, so the countryside seems to penetrate right into the heart of the city. It is worth taking a bus to Harnham and walking down to the old mill, the spot from which Constable got his famous view of Salisbury's spire (one can then return to the city by a short walk across meadows and bridges over two of the rivers). The mill is now a small hotel, and one can lunch on open sandwiches, Danish-style, at the adjoining tearooms.

The bus ride to Amesbury was brief but attractive, through unspoilt countryside, and the wintry sun burnished every stream and puddle so that the watery landscape was illuminated here and there. New calves were sparkling white. Looking backwards before entering Amesbury, one can still see the lynchets on the hillside – strips that were ploughed, seeded and harvested by generations of medieval villagers – and two old tollhouses, now cottages. Then come the lovely cedar trees that mark the approach to the town.

Amesbury

Amesbury recently celebrated its millennium, to mark which Prince Charles planted the whitebeam now growing up among the ancient yews in the churchyard. One day it may be a noble tree some 60 feet high, the undersides of its leaves pure white. I wandered across the nearby footbridge over the Avon as it hurries on its long journey to Salisbury and the sea. This metal bridge spans the river alongside a stone one bearing the date 1775, waterweed clinging to its cutwaters. The only sounds were the rush of water over a little weir known as Tumbling Bay, the raucous rooks and mellow chimes from the church.

Amesbury's history goes back to the Stone and Iron Ages, with legends to match (Arthur's Queen, Guinevere, was reputedly buried here, and the Vikings raided it). It later prospered, being on the junction of main coaching roads – hence the many inns that line the High Street – but it is a quiet town now.

The bus route to Marlborough follows the Avon upstream through the valley it has carved out of Salisbury Plain. On the way out of the town the bus passes, on the left, two curious buildings of dressed flint – a skilled technique almost forgotten now – with octagonal towers (one is named 'Diana her hous' and dated 1600). They were once gatehouses to the park of the long-vanished abbey. At the crossroads, Countess Farm has a fine collection of great 18th-century barns, evidence of the agricultural riches of the area.

Along the twists of the valley road were cottages of thatch and half-timbering or of brick alternating with flint bands, views of hills bare except for clumps of trees, swans on the river, and in the air two parachutists floating down and a glider. At Pewsey, King Alfred's statue stands in the street – a reminder of battles long ago when he repelled the invading Danish Vikings. Opposite one of the inns is a narrow hill called Brunkards Lane, and I wondered at whose genteel behest that 'B' had replaced what was once no doubt a 'D'!

The road to Marlborough crosses the Kennet and Avon Canal where pleasure boats idled below. Many of the thatched roofs are topped with a straw pheasant (some thatcher's personal trademark). The road climbs high, rounds a bend and suddenly the towers, spires and roofs of Marlborough were at our feet. The bus swooped down, crossed a lovely river, ran alongside a very lengthy copper beech hedge, passed Marlborough College and drew up in the vast main street – exceptionally wide and long, with a church at each end.

Marlborough

The town was devastated by a great fire in 1653, which is why so many of its houses show an 18th-century front to the world – but Tudor or medieval remains can still be found behind the many alleyways that are threaded between the buildings. Some shops are sheltered behind arcades. There are lovely lamplit courtyards, old coaching inns and the tranquil lawn and spring flowers of the old priory gardens tucked behind a modern cloister-like building in the middle of the street, which slope down to the River Kennet.

It is a short distance, through the Marlborough Downs, to Avebury – a village surrounded by a circle of prehistoric stones and earthworks in many ways far more impressive and mysterious than the more celebrated Stonehenge. The whole area abounds in such remains: Silbury, a man-made hill 130 feet high; Windmill Hill, made 5,000 years ago; the colossal long barrow tomb of West Kennet – and much more. Avebury deserves a lengthy visit for there is so much to see: Avebury Manor, a Tudor mansion and gardens; a very interesting church (part Saxon); and, in a great barn, the Wiltshire Museum of Rural Life.

Devizes

Devizes, a traditional market town, is not far away. At its heart is the big market square, decorated with an elaborate fountain in memory of some long-forgotten worthy and a market cross of 1814 carrying a discursive tablet which begins 'The Mayor and Corporation avail themselves of this monument to transmit the record of an awful event in 1753 as a salutary warning . . .' It then goes on to relate in great detail how Ruth Pierce, who had defrauded two other market women over a purchase, 'protested that she had paid her share and said she wished she might drop dead if she had not. To the consternation and terror of all, she instantly fell down and expired, having the money concealed in her hand.'

The buildings around the square are columned, garlanded, domed, pedimented and porched. They are bedecked with clocks, cherubs, medallions and statues. The Corn Exchange of

1856 is particularly splendid, with sheaves of wheat and a huge if rather crumbly sandstone Ceres on top. On the day I called there Ceres was presiding over a dog show in the Exchange, and it felt as if all of those one-hundred-and-one dalmatians were present, along with assorted spaniels, greyhounds and a snow-white poodle so fluffed up (and so somnolent despite the chorus of barking) that I at first mistook it for a heap of angora knitting. Brushing was brisk and busy, rosettes shone silky and satisfied, and the din was indescribable.

Off the square, St John Street leads to the church (passing a mock castle to the right and an alley of medieval houses hidden on the left). This has a Norman chancel of exceptional intricacy and beauty, its complex arches intersecting, each one with elaborate geometrical decoration – uniquely beautiful. As in Salisbury cathedral, there are a lot of carved portrait heads: they seem to be a Wiltshire speciality.

And so I travelled back again via Salisbury Plain once more, this time not through a river valley but across wide open spaces beyond the ivy banks and overhanging trees of the outskirts of the town. The first village, Potterne, has an impressive 14th-century church tower (square, battlemented and pinnacled) and a 15th-century timbered house with a huge porch overhanging the pavement. The landscape beyond is intersected with rivulets and the thatched roofs are often mossy. As the bus went further the Plain opened up. The fields are vast – between road and sky is nothing but ploughed earth without hedges or trees, and only the occasional tank track (the Plain is much used by the army for training exercises). Houses are few, villages even fewer. In great contrast to the leafy roads earlier in the day and the stone archways or gateposts with urns leading to mansions, this was a landscape – or skyscape – in which the elements dominated, and it was constantly changing.

Half way is the isolated, attractive village of Tilshead, its cottages typically banded and its church chequered (flints from the chalky local soil alternating with stone). Next came Shrewton, where the River Till (little more than a stream) trickled by the road, with a quaint little domed lock-up for wrongdoers and more thatched cottages. The Till runs into the larger River Wylye at pretty Stapleford, from which it is only a few minutes to Wilton. Pollarded willows mark the route of the frothing river; a barn perches on rickstones (precaution against rats) and an old hay wain added another Constable-like touch to the scene.

Wilton

At Wilton, England was born: that is to say, it was here that, in the year 838, the two kingdoms of Kent and Wessex were united into one. 'Wiltshire' in fact means Wilton-shire, for Wilton was once the capital of the Kingdom of Wessex. Under Georgian Kingsbury Square and pretty streets nearby are buried the remains of a Saxon king's palace.

Magnificence is still to be found, though, in 17th-century Wilton House, designed by Inigo Jones. Its collection of paintings, furniture and gardens are all on a palatial scale. So is its collection of toy soldiers, all 7,000 of them. Other sights to be seen in the town include medieval stained glass in the church, the famous carpet factory (three hundred years old) and, if you happen to be there at the right time, the Sheep Fair. Within minutes the bus had whisked me back to Salisbury again.

Other good bus trips out of Salisbury

These include, for example, Stonehenge; Tidworth (reached through the valley of the River Bourne); Shaftesbury (a hilltop town with abbey, ruins and cobbled streets, with fine scenery along the way); and, for a longer trip, the seaside resort of Bournemouth (pleasant countryside, and the interesting villages of Breamore and Downton with half-timbered and thatched cottages are along the route). And there are lots of others. The Hants and Dorset Bus Company, which covers much of Wiltshire, too, has published a useful leaflet called 'Around Salisbury by Bus' (see Appendix A for address).

9

AN EAST ANGLIAN JOURNEY

*Colchester – Ipswich – Orford – Woodbridge –
Felixstowe*

I arrived at Colchester by bus through water meadows where
cows grazed near a winding stream and hawthorns blossomed in
the hedges. The bus strained up into the town via North Hill
(where antique shops, bookshops and restaurants are located) and
along the arcaded High Street with its resplendent Edwardian
town hall and coaching inns.

Colchester

The bus station is at the end of the High Street and conveniently
near the main places of interest – castle, museums, and so forth.
But I did not head for them immediately, preferring to seek out
Colchester's oldest remains first: the massive encircling wall the
Romans started (down Priory Street, to the east). It is both
impressive in scale and, with yellow ragwort and wallflowers
springing from its crevices, beautiful too – but scarcely a pleasant
walk, because there is a car park along its entire length. I was glad
to turn aside to the ruins of the Norman priory (itself built from
stones and tiles taken from Roman buildings). There is a
spectacular doorway, its huge arch outlined with row upon row
(twelve in all) of axe-hewn decorations. A pigeon had rather
lowered the tone by building a nest in a crevice, loosely
incorporating a large plastic bag that flapped in the breeze, but
pigeons are always untidy builders, with little appreciation for
ancient monuments.

Threading my way through Vineyard Street and another car
park flanking the southern stretch of the Roman wall (exit of
Roman sewer as clearly labelled as any nobler relic), I came via the
quaint houses and little shops of Trinity Street to the rural crafts

museum (housed in a disused church, partly Saxon) where lifesize exhibits show how thatching is done, how a windmill works and so forth. The recreation of an old laundry was fascinating – it had everything from wooden pattens (footgear to keep one's feet clear of puddles on the stone floor) to a box mangle, a huge box filled with stones that was rolled to and fro over the wet linen. 'Operating the mangle was tiring work' said the caption – the understatement of the age.

It was a short walk to Balkerne Gate (in the west wall of the city), the greatest Roman gateway still surviving in Britain; the modern Mercury Theatre (where I had a good, inexpensive lunch); and Jumbo – an extraordinary water-tower which has dominated the city for the last century or so. By the time I'd had a good look at the town hall and the old byways tucked behind it, I was glad to reach the gardens surrounding the castle and sit on the grass in its shadow.

The very early Norman castle is, in every sense, Colchester's high spot. It covers a vast area and was once immensely tall, too. The huge stump of it that is left houses an extremely clear and well-devised museum, with models that vividly interpret all one has seen while walking about. The 1648 siege of Colchester by the Cromwellians is clearly explained in a vast panorama of fortifications and troops. There are models of how the city was in Roman times (where the castle now stands was once a temple to the Roman emperor, Claudius). Even the plethora of statues from the town hall facade are reproduced in plaster and explained. There are, of course, a lot of archaeological exhibits, the oddest of all being a horse's coffin from the Iron Age.

Nearby are two other good museums in interesting buildings. In an old church, children clustered round the ichthyosaurs and iguanodon that are among the dioramas and other displays of local wildlife, and in an early Georgian mansion surrounded by beds of violas and wallflowers is housed a collection of old furniture, costume, toys and so forth. A child's lesson book called *Reading Disentangled* was full of precepts like 'My dear children, I hope that you will never swear like some poor boys in the street'. Another social comment could be read into the caption to a portrait of Mary Wates who, by the time she died in 1620 at the age of 93, had 367 grandchildren and great-grandchildren (having herself given birth to 16 children). I suppose if you were tough enough to survive all that child-bearing (and the Tudor doctors), it was a simple matter to go on surviving into your nineties.

Before returning to the nearby bus station I walked past the handsome Jacobean plasterwork of Alderman Winstanley's home and into the light and elegant 15th-century church where his ornate tomb stands. The church has a dark oak roof adorned with bright angels, painted and gilded, a typical East Anglian touch. (Incidentally, in summer an open-top bus does a 1¼-hour tour of Colchester and its environs.)

My bus swung out and down steep East Hill – lined with Georgian or half-timbered houses, walls leaning and roofs at odd angles – over a bridge of blue-and-white ironwork, with a weir to the left, and past Siege House, pocked with bullet-holes from the Civil War and masked in dust raised by the passing traffic. Once clear of the suburbs, the route passes through 'Constable country', though East Anglian fields are often prairie-like in size now. It goes by pool and stream where upended ducks were plunging to find food, rises and falls as pink and thatched cottages are succeeded by orchards and then skirts the gold-and-silver of gorse and hawthorn hedges, until the busy county town of Ipswich is reached.

Ipswich

I stayed overnight at a comfortable (if overheated) small hotel, the Gables, though to reach it involved a half-hour walk uphill through the beautiful park which is one of Ipswich's outstanding features. Next morning another guest gave me a lift to the opposite edge of the town – the quayside of the River Orwell. Among the working ships from all over the world are moored others in honourable retirement, such as the great old sailing barge *Phoenician*, now being converted for disabled people to sail in, an ex-Navy steam tug being restored by enthusiasts, and a scarlet lightship with seemingly top-heavy lantern.

Heavy lorries belt by old houses that were once the homes of sea captains and merchants, the handsome Custom House and Wolsey's Gate – sole relic of a college founded by the cardinal, an Ipswich man.

There are interesting old shops, wine bars, craftsmen, mullioned windows and courtyards to be found up St Peters Street and Silent Street. ('Silent'? Even at 8 am Ipswich has motor cyclists buzzing about as if a wasps' nest had been disturbed.)

Then I found a total surprise. Whereas some business houses have tried to blend their new premises into old Ipswich by designing in a traditional style (Barclays Bank, for instance, has built itself an imitation of a riverside warehouse), an international insurance company has gone to the other extreme – and with great success. Ipswich's most exciting building (in Friar Street) is the biggest glasshouse in the world, accommodating over a thousand workers. It is low (only three floors); it has a flowing, curved shape; and it is of a tinted glass that reflects the church spires and other old buildings around. Its roof is made of grass – an acre or so of lawn which (along with swimming pool, gymnasium, restaurants and suchlike) helps to make this a very agreeable workplace. Curiosity, as always, overcoming discretion, I walked in and was given a handsome brochure about this incredible building.

Though there is more to see in Ipswich there was only time, before catching my next bus, to walk along the Buttermarket to Hatchard's big bookshop, a riot of carved wood outside and in. The facade is covered with pilasters, swags of fruit, lions' heads, oriel windows, pelicans in plaster and representations of the four continents (Australia was the as yet undiscovered fifth when the house was built, in Tudor times). From the bus station, in the curiously named street of Dog's Head, there is a view of three church towers – all beautiful in the morning sun, but in completely contrasted styles. One is simple, flinty and rectangular, beyond it is a slender spire, and finally the third is a chequerboard tower topped with lacy stonework of great delicacy.

The bus threaded its way out through narrow streets, past a new Sainsbury's with a wall textured in cobbles, bricks and mosaic; pleasant little early Victorian cottages; suburbs; and then a heath of gorse and birch with the morning haze still lingering on it. Further on, householders have planted the road's verges with spring flowers. Then came an imposing group of almshouses in hot red brick, a narrow street packed with ancient homes, and abruptly we found ourselves in the great, quiet square at the heart of Woodbridge, dominated by the Tudor Shire Hall and courthouse in the middle and a century-old pump in a pumphouse, and ringed with old houses painted buff, terracotta, dark or pale green. As I intended to call here later, I stayed on the bus – enjoying the Suffolk voices of the women who exchanged local news with the bus driver as we went steeply down, only just missing the overhead sign of the 15th-century Bell and Steelyard Inn – an astonishing weighing-arm that stretches out across the road (for the inn was once a steelyard).

The journey then became really rural – heath alternating with big ploughed fields, across the wide river at Melton (the tide right out), running by woodland and pools, past an air force base and through a pine forest where signs warned that deer sometimes wander out of the shadows and onto the road. Great barns and walls of knapped flint are characteristic of this area. A tractor hauling bales of hay slowed us to a crawl behind it in the narrow lane that approaches Orford and then, just as suddenly as at Woodbridge, a turn released us like a cork from a bottle into a great open square.

Orford

Everything of interest is close to this square or down towards the now distant quayside (as on much of this coast, the coastline has shifted its position over the centuries, so Orford is no longer a port). There is the partly Norman church, impressive in its own right and also used to house various local relics. The wooden roof has carved bosses and, like many East Anglian churches, there are poppyheads at the ends of the choir stalls. Under floormats are a number of brasses – one shows a mother and the 12 children she bore who all died before they grew up. Stone coffins, the village stocks and old bells from the tower are dumped in one corner, near an ancient board detailing the terms of Brett's Benevolence, a fund for 'deserving poor Widow Women of the Parish'. The church's greatest treasure is a painting by one of Raphael's pupils. The church was cold, and I returned gladly to the sunny churchyard and the ruined arcade behind it, lingering over ancient epitaphs, telling of ancient griefs.

Small though Orford is, it has a huge castle, many attractive houses, a choice of old inns and good eating places, picturesque corners and many stories to tell – of ghosts, floods, mermen and shipwrecks (it's worth buying the local guidebook, sold in the church). In fact, the village deserves an overnight stop, for from it one can visit the bird reserve on the island of Minsmere and watch oyster-catchers and other waders close up (from a hide). To do this it is necessary to write in advance to the bird warden - appropriately named John Partridge – at 30 Mundays Lane, Orford.

If you have breath to climb 90 feet to the top of the castle (built for Henry II about 1170 as a defence against invaders from Europe) there are spectacular views of sea and countryside.

All the inns are interesting. I sampled the local brew at the Kings Head, a coaching inn which was also a smugglers' base, then walked across to the Buttery for a fish lunch (oyster soup followed by eel-and-salmon mousse) eaten at a marble-topped table. Orford's Buttery is famous for its smoked fish and local oysters.

My next bus took me back to Woodbridge again but by a different route, colourful with the faded reds of last year's bracken and oak leaves, and with pheasants' copper breasts iridescent in the sun. The pheasants strutted boldly at this season when shooting is over, scarlet and green heads showing up bright above their white clerical collars. There were partridges about, too. A row of dead moles hung along a fence – destined perhaps to make a velvety moleskin waistcoat?

As usual, there were few people on the bus and all but me were well known to the driver. His remarks floated up to me on the top deck: '. . . if I see Jack, I'll tell him you asked after him . . .' and, to a child getting off, '. . . and wait there till Mummy comes; don't you go running across the road.'

At Melton the tide was in and the moored pleasure boats bobbed happily. We passed a disused rail station, squeezed tightly through Woodbridge's narrow streets again, and ground to a halt.

Woodbridge

Woodbridge is famous for its 200-year-old tide mill down beside the River Deben, its wheel worked by the ebb and flow of the tide. All round here are cobbled lanes leading to quays and a scene of boats and boat-building. This is a town of great charm. Up its steep streets are many old houses (all porticos, fanlights and iron balconies), and it has some interesting shops. The Music Shop sells antique instruments, there is an art gallery, furniture, book, rod and gun shops abound, and so do inns.

The next bus chugged along, gently rattling and squeaking, on a straight road between fields of sheep (now a far less common sight than a century ago, when Suffolk was one of the great wool counties). There are picturesque inns along this route as well as cottages with immaculate thatch capping their dormers and shaped into eyebrows over bedroom windows. A pheasant strolled casually in front of the bus.

Primroses on a river bank, periwinkles tumbling down a wall, pink cottages, a field of chestnut mares with newborn foals – such pictures seen through the big bus windows came and went in swift succession. The earth thereabouts is reddish, some fields deep-furrowed and others ploughed to a fine tilth. At Hollesley, where there is a colony for delinquents (a constructive alternative to prison), we passed a boy leading a great carthorse, others loading cabbages and some busy in a blacksmith's shop. There are many huge water-towers in this region, because of the chronic lack of rain on the eastern side of England.

Another aspect of east-coast life, however, has less pastoral charm. As in every century, England is on the defensive here. Much of the land belongs to the Ministry of Defence. Rotating scanners came into view, and suddenly we passed near a row of great missiles, lined up and pointing their sharp warheads out seawards and to Europe.

After another sharp turn red sails and then hundreds of little boats at anchor sprang into sight. We drew up by a small sandy beach at Bawdsey where children were playing. I, by that time the only passenger, got out to await the ferry which would take me from Bawdsey to the Felixstowe side of the Deben estuary.

Felixstowe

Mr Brinkley, the ferryman, comes from generations of local fishermen (I had noticed the name in accounts of Orford's history), some of whom still brave the North Sea in their eighties. Listening to his anecdotes of people he had encountered on the ferry, I lost track of the time, missed my bus and so had a long walk into Felixstowe – along the sea wall, past bathing huts and Martello towers and across a golf course. A lark was singing high out of sight and a peacock butterfly alighted at my feet. Golfers were out in force and a salt breeze flicked the wiry grass as it passed. The only other sound was the sea on the shingle until I reached the outskirts of Felixstowe.

That was the end of my two-day tour, in a town very different from the others I had explored – a sedate seaside resort with magnificent, manicured gardens in which every lobelia and every bachelor's button knows its place, the palm trees grow straight as lamp-posts, and no one ever moves faster than wheelchair pace. Within two hours I was at home in London.

Note: As this book went to press, I learned that the Orford and Bawdsey buses may cease to run, unless local people start an alternative service.

10

THERE'S SOMETHING ABOUT ISLANDS
THE ISLE OF WIGHT

Ryde – Bembridge – Sandown – Shanklin – Ventnor –
Yarmouth – Freshwater Bay – Newport – Cowes

Any island is bound to have a character all of its own, no matter how narrow the strip of sea that separates it from the mainland, and islanders are known for being stubbornly independent. The Isle of Wight is no exception: even the usual 'Keep Britain Tidy' posters are missing, and in their place hangs 'Keep the Island Tidy'.

For a bussing-about holiday on Wight there is an extra inducement: the local bus company (Southern Vectis) has fixed up a special ticket for road-rail travel connected with 'breakaway' holidays on the island at off-peak times of the year (since the island is so far south its spring starts early and its autumn goes on longer than the mainland's). This ticket enables you to travel free all over the island's 150 square miles. You pay an all-in amount for the holiday which covers rail fares from your home town to Portsmouth, the ferry from there to the island, accommodation (with breakfast and dinner) and the ticket for unlimited bus travel within the island. At the time of writing a two-day break could cost £30 (more if you came from far afield or wanted a superior hotel; less if you were to take self-catering accommodation and less, of course, for children; also less, pro rata, if you stayed longer). The road-rail day-ticket (or its weekly equivalent) is also available to people not on a breakaway package holiday.

Wherever one goes on bus journeys round the island there are beautiful shorelines and sea views, woodlands, rolling hills, historic buildings or unspoilt towns that still recall the days when the island was a favourite retreat of Queen Victoria and of the Prince of Wales' fashionable yachting set. Much of the island is owned by the National Trust.

Ryde

I arrived at Ryde on a Friday evening and stayed there for the first night. I spent the second night in Shanklin.

As soon as one steps onto the ferry from Portsmouth there is an instant feeling of getting away from it all: the engine throbs, the wake makes a shining swathe in the Solent as the boat sweeps round, and the golden egg of the setting sun vanishes below the horizon leaving behind a pearl-pink sky. There is plenty of interest on this brief voyage – a quick glimpse of *Victory*'s masts as we pull out of Portsmouth, the old forts (Spitbank, Horse's Sand and No Mans Land) that have stood guard in the sea for two centuries, and the rusty *Mary Rose* excavation ship. The *Mary Rose* capsized and sank in 1545 while in action against the French, and her hull is still intact in the mud of the seabed, as are innumerable objects from Henry VIII's time. The marine archaeologists on the excavation ship are bringing all this up to be displayed eventually in a special museum on shore.

The Portsmouth lights twinkled in the twilight behind us and then the spires of Ryde came into sight, above its jumble of sparkling white Regency and Victorian houses piled up steeply above the shore. We moored at the end of the 2,000-foot pier (built in 1814), along which a train whisked us, and within minutes I had arrived at Yelfs Hotel (once a coaching inn) and was sitting down to a dinner of local crab.

Next morning, after wandering briefly among the shops in the Royal Victoria Arcade and the seafront gardens, I watched the passing scene while waiting for my first bus of the day. Across the road from the bus-stop stands the Royal Esplanade Hotel, its facade rich with grapes and hops among lacey cast-iron balconies. From the sandy beach a Hovercraft (like a large and noisy frog) took off across the sea.

The bus clambered up among stucco villas and stone mansions, every turn bringing into view different glimpses of the turquoise Solent below, its forts now tiny specks. Azaleas, camellias and all the other flowers of spring were out. We passed a willow-fringed pool, and there were views of hills inland and, on the other side, vast sandy beaches and a silver sea dotted with tiny sails.

St Helens is a village with a huge green. In summer one can take a ferry from near there to Bembridge harbour, but I stayed on the bus until it reached the centre of Bembridge and then, after fuelling myself with a cup of particularly good coffee at the little Fox's Head restaurant, I slowly walked *back* to the harbour we had just passed (doing it this way meant that I walked downhill, not up).

Bembridge

Bembridge has an old windmill, cottages named for the plants around them (Woodbine, Bay, Fuchsia) and several inns – one built to look like a boat. I visited the little Maritime Museum (it has finds from wrecks, models of ships, and two colossal anchors outside) where I bought a plate with the old saying 'It is better to travel hopefully than to arrive' – good advice for bus riders! I decided to give the more distant lifeboat station a miss. Down by the harbour pleasure boats were moored and the skeleton of a great old hulk was slowly rotting. Round the once-grand memorial fountain of porphyry and granite, just by the bus stop, came a cavalcade of children on ponies.

The bus goes by Whitecliff Bay, near which is a good view of the hilltop obelisk that is a memorial to the first commodore of the Royal Yacht Squadron (founded in 1815), and through Yaverland village with its Jacobean manor house, a route that passes fine Regency and later houses set in beautiful gardens, and cottages or farms of stone and thatch. Cocks strutted in a farmyard, ducks dabbled head-down in a pond, and lambs with black faces and socks frisked in the sunshine. The bus wound its way between hedges and trees lining narrow lanes, slowing to a crawl when we caught up with a solitary horse-rider. Then suddenly the whole sea was before us, bright and shimmering – Sandown Bay.

Sandown

At Sandown I relaxed in a deckchair on the vast sandy beach with a view of distant sandstone cliffs and read *Reptiles on the Rocks*, which I bought at the library where the bus stops. Above the library I had found a frowsty little room, full of sun and dust, that dignifies itself with the name of museum – but what a treasure house it is. Fossilized bits of local crocodiles and Oligocene rhinos, mammoths' teeth, the colossal backbone of an iguanodon and even fossilized pearls were among its hoard. The Isle of Wight is rich in prehistoric finds from 30 million years ago when this part of England was steamy jungle: it is only in the Isle of Wight that rocks from the Oligocene period are exposed.

Shanklin

Sandown runs into Shanklin, with small hotels and guest houses all along the way. I stayed on the bus until it got to the old village on the far side of Shanklin. This is certainly picturesque (all whitewashed walls and thick thatched roofs) but, even out of season, it is very touristy; almost every cottage is now a restaurant. However, the famous chine that leads off it was deserted. 'Chine' is local parlance for a narrow ravine cut deep into the soft sandstone by a stream making its steep descent to the sea. Shanklin's chine runs down from the cliff-top village to the esplanade 150 feet below. On entering at the top, one's senses move into another world of cool, earthy smells from the wet cliffs spangled with ferns, moss, ivy and primroses and of fresh sounds such as the splash of water and the song of birds. The first waterfall drops sheer for 40 feet. Wood or stone bridges cross each turn of the winding stream, and there are rustic arbours at every viewpoint. Towards the end a lookout platform provides a tremendous view over Sandown Bay, the pier, sailing boats, bathing huts and windsurfers scudding quickly over the waves. There are various curiosities along the way such as the marble-lined brine bath with steps, in which many Victorian health-faddists half-boiled themselves in heated sea water.

On leaving the chine I walked beside a hedge of hebe, along the esplanade and past the pier, and then took the lift up the cliff (here Shanklin's best hotels face the south and the sea, with glass verandahs so that one may bask even in winter).

The short, serpentine bus journey up and then down to Ventnor is very lovely. There are streams, duck ponds, thatched stone cottages with sparkling white window frames and doors, or slate-tiled with decorative white bargeboards, and – above all – stunning views back to Sandown Bay, with Shanklin itself a mere toy town on its edge and cattle looking like crumbs on the green billiard cloth of fields far below the road. At the top of the steep hill a horse trough (now planted with tulips) bears the message 'Be kind and merciful to all animals', and one's thoughts turn to the time when these wretched beasts had to haul loads uphill on hot days.

Along the bus route is a little pumping station in a field; there are views of white cliffs and then one looks down onto the roofs and into the gardens of Shanklin. Though the cottages are very crowded together, every one finds room for a rock garden, window boxes or glassed-in porch crammed with pot plants.

Ventnor

I spent a pleasant couple of hours in Ventnor before returning to
Shanklin for the night. Ventnor, like Ryde, clings precariously to
steep slopes that go right down to the sea. Its houses are like the
audience in a Roman amphitheatre looking down upon the
spectacle of the sea. After dawdling pleasurably in Mr Keen's
well-stocked bookshop, I walked down past the cascade and the
pier, and then up to the top of cliffs where teazles and pink
campions grow in profusion. Surf was breaking on the rocks far
below and children's voices floated up from the distant beach.

It was pleasant to stroll in the park where a stream gushed,
ducks dashed and a spaniel paddled. Glass frames were full of
geraniums waiting to be bedded out later. Further along a road of
verandahed, gabled and slated houses (many of them hotels now)
lie the Botanical Gardens. Their tropical plants and palms make it
plain why Ventnor calls itself 'the Madeira of England'. In one
corner is a museum of smuggling.

And so back to Shanklin, where the Hartland Hotel was a real find
– lowest-priced of all the accommodation I'd found so far in
my travels, it was comfortable and had very good food, a
swimming pool and other amenities – and particularly pretty
bedrooms with Chinese-style flowers hand-painted on the walls.
Mine, bow-windowed, overlooked apple trees and the pool;
others had their own verandahs.

Next day, because I was a week too early for the coastal route to
Freshwater that runs during some months only, I took a bus
inland and northwards to Newport (and thence to Freshwater).
The route through leafy, winding lanes was much more enjoyable
in the big-windowed bus than it would have been in a low car,
from which one could not have seen over the hawthorn hedges.
The patchwork of fields (grassy or ploughed), coppices and gorse
heaths was dotted with farms, streams and pleasant houses
surrounded by lawns or magnolia trees in bloom. Godshill, like
old Shanklin, is a once-picturesque village now mainly an enclave
of thatched tea-rooms.

The bus crossed the river Medina and entered Newport, the
island's capital, from which I got another bus westward – passing,
as we went out of the town, the mayor with the mace-bearer and
mace processing to church. The bus ran alongside an attractive
terrace of iron-balconied houses raised up on a bank, a tiny green
with colourful little villas, a roadside brook and the turning that
leads to Carisbrooke Castle, a ¾-mile walk. (This is the Norman

castle where Charles I was imprisoned by the Cromwellians, and where donkeys still work the great wheel that hauls buckets of water up a 160-foot well.) Past the dark mass of Parkhurst Forest the landscape opened up, and then a great expanse of the Solent came into view, lively with the white sails of small boats on the choppy waters.

Yarmouth

At Yarmouth (where there is one of Henry VIII's castles) the bus drew up by the harbour – a forest of small boat masts, their burgees flicked by the wind, with gulls wheeling overhead. A crowd of youngsters got on (standing room only then), filling the bus with their cheerful chatter as it crossed the harbour bridge and went over salt flats with a view of constantly changing sea, now dark, now light, and blue, green and grey in turns. A lighthouse, a huge green, a thatched church and then we were at Freshwater Bay, back on the rocky and dangerous south coast of the island that is so very different from the sheltered north, which has only the Solent between it and mainland England. Tennyson, who lived near here, said the air was 'worth sixpence a pint' – what price the dramatic scenery, I wondered? One can bus even further to fantastic Alum Bay, with its multi-coloured sandstone cliffs and its view of those rocky pinnacles, the Needles (to which boat trips go). This is the place for unusual souvenirs such as glass models filled with patterns in 21 different hues of naturally coloured sand. A chairlift goes down to the beach if you want to gather the sands yourself.

Freshwater Bay

At Freshwater Bay I went to see what six burly young men in orange overalls were doing with their huge inflated powerboat. They turned out to be lifeguards engaged on their weekly practice. Each is a volunteer who pursues trades quite unconnected with the sea during working hours. They even raise the money needed to keep the boat going. It is the sole hope for anyone in trouble along the next 20 miles of treacherous rocky coast, subject to the worst of Channel weather.

The next bus, a double-decker, took a deep breath and staggered up the exceedingly steep hill that leads to a heath, golf links and cliff tops owned by the National Trust. Here there are tremendous views of the sea (looking like shot silk), cliffs (white chalk changing to yellow sandstone), bays, surf and hills. In some respects the scenery reminded me of Cornwall. Inland are downs (tracks show up white where topsoil has been worn down to the chalk), with farms nestling at their feet; the hummocks on the horizon are prehistoric burial mounds.

A friendly passenger pointed out to me the hilltop mansion where J. B. Priestley used to live and enlivened the journey with local gossip. The whole of this ride was picturesque and very typical of the Isle of Wight at its best – flint-capped walls, very pretty cottage gardens, quaint little churches, thatching in progress (from the top of a bus one gets a good view of that), an impressive 16th-century manor house (it originally belonged to Edward VI's tutor) and little inn at Mottistone, a barn perched on mushroom-shaped staddle stones to keep rats out, and a particularly fine farm just before Shorwell.

After passing under a rustic wooden footbridge the road turns inland between banks of wild garlic – always winding, rising and falling. The ploughed fields are pale with chalk. When Carisbrooke Castle came into view, spread out along a hilltop, I realized we were approaching Newport again.

Newport

I cannot say much in favour of Newport on a Sunday except that it is quiet. Or it was, until suddenly the air came alive with the sound of music – trombones, drums and bugles, to be precise; all the youth organizations of the town were parading to church. Fortunately I'd already had a look round the church which, though little more than a century old, has a very beautiful (and colourful) interior. It also has one outstanding memorial, a poignant marble sculpture of the 15-year-old Princess Elizabeth (daughter of Charles I) who died in Carisbrooke Castle. Queen Victoria had this beautiful memorial erected when the girl's lost grave was accidentally discovered by workmen in 1856.

There is much more to be seen in the island. For example, I had no opportunity to visit Osborne House, home of Queen Victoria and largely the creation of Prince Albert, where she died. The rooms are kept exactly as they were in her lifetime, and in the grounds are her bathing machine, the Swiss chalet where the children were given lessons in such useful skills as carpentry and cooking, and a miniature fort built by the ten-year-old Prince Arthur. There are also Roman remains, more mansions and museums, a working watermill, a steam railway, a model village, glass-making studios, nature trails, a working forge and much else.

As I wanted to reach the mainland by hydrofoil to Southampton, I took a bus from Newport to Cowes. We passed the grim walls of Parkhurst Prison, ran alongside the Medina estuary and went past a field full of radar scanners in every size and shape (oddly contrasting with the adjoining field of sheep).

Cowes

Cowes is above all a yachting centre, but the season had scarcely begun and there were few people in its steep, old streets. I wandered in and out of alleyways, onto jetties, along the esplanade (which leads to the castle housing the Royal Yacht Squadron) and under the arcades behind the Fountain Inn. Half the town (East Cowes) lies across the mouth of the river Medina, which is crossed on a 'floating bridge' – a ferry that hauls itself across on huge chains that make a hellish rattle and rumble all the way.

I sat on the esplanade looking back towards the colourful houses piled up on the steep flanks of West Cowes. The waves slapped the sea-wall, buoys bobbed wildly and gulls battled hard against the stiff wind which had flung water and seaweed up onto the promenade. I headed for the ferry, hot tea at the Fountain Inn and a snug crossing back to the mainland, home and bed.

THE SCILLY ISLES

St Mary's

Another island-bussing possibility is on one of the Scilly Isles off Cornwall. The Scillies are only 20 minutes from Penzance by helicopter; and on the main island, St Mary's, it is possible to bus about.

One's first view of the Scillies is of a scatter of rocky islets in the blue sea below, punctuated with lighthouses, for the history of the Scillies is a rollcall of ships wrecked in every century. As the helicopter approaches the main island, St Mary's, it comes in low over a shore of cliffs and coves, great sandy bays and a patchwork of granite outcrops, windswept pines and stone-walled fields.

A bus takes one to Hugh Town within minutes. Though the centre of activity on the island, this is not much more than an overgrown village of fishermen's cottages round a harbour, small hotels, a lifeboat station, a few shops and a particularly good local museum. Another bus departs from Hugh Town several times a day for a circuit round the island (which takes only ½ hour). Its route is inland, but the island is so small that from any stop it is easy to walk to the coast and back, perhaps picking up a bus further along the route.

The island is kept firmly unspoilt and uncrowded, its population a mere thousand or so. Growing narcissi and daffodils is the main activity but, as these are sent to market in bud, the fields are never full of flowers. No matter; the cottage gardens and the wildflowers more than make up for this. I was there in April, when gardens were brilliant not only with red-hot-pokers, jonquils and marigolds but semi-tropical plants, too. Mesembryanthemums poured over the walls.

In the hedgerows were a profusion of flowers. Palm trees, cacti, crassulas and saw-tongued aloes grow wild, and the New Zealand flame tree blazes with scarlet flowers in December. Even the hedges have a tropical look with red-blossomed exallonia, glossy-leaved euonymos and magenta pittosporum (a New Zealand shrub) providing the dense windbreak so necessary in these islands where, mild though the climate is throughout the year, formidable gales can play havoc with the crops. The Scillies' great pride, however, are the enormous blue spires of echeum, some nearly 10 feet high.

The bus route is through narrow lanes as rural as it is possible to find. Every viewpoint is incomparably lovely, and the only sign of human activity is the occasional cottage, a group of wicker lobster pots or some churns of milk awaiting collection by the roadside.

I also had time to join a guided walk with a naturalist, David Hunt, along one of the island's three nature trails (picking wild fennel, samphire and sea spinach as I went: 'food for free'). A linnet rose, singing, into the sky, and through David's telescope we saw a close-up of an oyster-catcher probing the wet sands for molluscs. David identified for us the less familiar wildflowers such as dwarf scurvy-grass – a pale-flowered plant clinging to granite walls that is rich in vitamin C (hence its past value in warding off scurvy). Strange whiskery lichens (a synthesis of fungus and algae) grow in profusion, a sure indication of the purity of the air, for lichens die in a polluted atmosphere but live for hundreds of years in fresh air. I saw some of the first butter-flies of the year – holly blues, speckled woods and peacocks.

The nature trail, marked by planks and stepping stones through a marsh, led us amongst rushing streams and reed beds frequented by frogs to a hide where we watched swallows skimming a pool to drink on the wing. A sedge-warbler, yellow throat pulsating, sang non-stop on a bush declaring his ownership of this territory. David told us that every year these little warblers, returning from their winter in Africa, always make for the same group of bushes. We went on through a copse of sallow willows draped with honeysuckle, past a thicket of another exotic settler, Japanese knotweed, and so onto the road again to catch the bus back into Hugh Town.

The whole Scillies story – archaeological, historical and ecological – is most clearly told in the little museum, which not only displays ancient finds but has produced a really clear exposition of local wildlife. Small details linger in my memory: from the wreck of the famous ship *Association*, sunk in the 17th century, a posy ring (i.e. 'poésie', poetry) was poignantly engraved with the rhyme 'God above Increase our love'; there were smuggler's tongs for retrieving kegs hidden underwater and 78 vases, each with a different fresh-picked local wildflower, clearly labelled.

The Scillies are, of course, an enchanting place to stay for days or even weeks, and between the islands 'bussing' is by boat. As to where to eat (or stay), there is plenty of choice on St Mary's at all price levels. Tregarthen's (where Lord Tennyson wrote 'Enoch Arden') do a particularly good lunch to eat on their terrace for only a couple of pounds or so, and fresh-caught fish is cooked at the Galley, owned by two fishermen brothers. When I return to stay, I shall not make for any of the central and convenient hotels (attractive though many are) but uphill to the uniquely romantic Star Castle, where Prince Charles (later Charles II) stayed while fleeing from the Cromwellians. The small fortress, built like an eight-pointed star, is a maze of zigzagging corridors and odd-angled bedrooms. Even the three guardrooms out on the ramparts are now bedrooms, their musket holes glassed in and their interiors comfortably furnished but otherwise just as they were four centuries ago.

11

THE NEW FOREST

*Southampton – Lyndhurst – Brockenhurst – Lymington
– Beaulieu – Hythe*

It was bluebell time when I found myself in Southampton on business. Though summer was scarcely in, England was enjoying its longest spell of non-stop sunshine for half a century. What better than to tack on an extra day and go bussing in the nearby New Forest (though Bournemouth or even Salisbury are suitable bases instead of Southampton)? Later in the year the roads of this area would be packed with cars and caravans, but as yet there were relatively few visitors around to disturb its peace.

The Forest's 93,000 acres are not all tree-covered. The scenery varies from woodland to heath, farmland to riverside, with small towns and isolated houses along the way. When William the Conqueror hunted there ('he loved the red deer like his own children', wrote a contemporary chronicler rather ambiguously), the heaths and woods must have been even wilder – a veritable jungle of undergrowth. Now not only ponies and some deer graze freely, but cows, donkeys and even pigs. All have owners and are rounded up when required, for under ancient rights 'commoners' are entitled to let their animals feed in the Forest (except where, to protect areas of young trees, wire fences have been put up to keep the animals out by the Verderers who manage the Forest). These animals are one of the many attractions of any drive through the Forest; the bus has to avoid them, not vice versa, when they stray onto the roads, and most are quite unperturbed by the presence of traffic.

Although there are a lot of conifers too, the woodlands through which the buses go are mainly of broad-leaved trees – ancient oaks and great beeches, in particular. I only once caught a glimpse of a herd of roe deer in the gloaming beneath them; these and fallow deer account for the total population of about a thousand (there are only about 30 of the great red deer left). The ponies and cattle are far more numerous, as well as less shy, and are seen everywhere, occasionally turning up among the village shops despite grids and gates intended to keep them out.

The Forest has been designated a National Nature Reserve because it is so rich in rare plants and wildlife. Great care is taken to arrange the recreational facilities (camp sites, car parks and all the rest) in such a way that, despite the millions of visitors every year, the Forest suffers a minimum of disturbance or damage.

Lyndhurst

A bus from Southampton took me to the 'capital' of the New Forest, Lyndhurst – the name means a wood of lime trees – through woodland where dappled sunlight fell onto moss-green trunks and a floor carpeted with rusty leaves. The brilliant light green of new oak leaves contrasted with the softer colour of graceful birches, well-nicknamed 'the ladies of the woods', and an occasional gnarled stump of ancient grey.

At Lyndhurst the Forest's Verderers hold their court to settle any disagreements among the commoners. Their hall, in Queen's House, is said to be very fine, but it was closed when I was there because the entire Queen Anne house was shored up awaiting repair.

I went instead to the nearby church which makes up in beauty what it lacks in antiquity (it was the masterpiece of a Victorian architect, William White, who got the job mainly because he charged less than his more celebrated colleagues). The interior is a colourful pattern of bricks in various reds and yellows, with clusters of dark slate columns topped by capitals carved with Forest foliage. The red timber roof has a dozen huge wooden angels playing on trumpets, lutes and tambourines – in fact, the church is particularly rich in carved figures and heads of Protestant martyrs. There was quite a to-do when the eminent Frederick Leighton offered to paint a fresco, unheard-of since the Reformation. Despite objections to such a 'Papist embellishment', the offer was accepted and there it is: a dozen life-size virgins, wise ones with bright lamps and cheerful faces, foolish ones dejected in the dark. The church has other assets, too, such as

Burne-Jones windows and a clock which, for technical reasons that are beyond me, horologists consider a national treasure.

Behind the building lies a simple grave, easily missed, where 'Alice in Wonderland' is buried, its only decoration the little daisies and birds-eyes which embroider its turf. 'Alice' grew up to become Mrs Reginald Hargreaves and president of a local Women's Institute; she died in 1934.

Before walking down the High Street I called in at Mr Strange's strange shop – dozens of antlers hang from the ceiling, and the huge head of a red deer presides over the counter. Mr Strange is a butcher, and his speciality is the produce of the New Forest, particularly venison. I added to my small baggage a joint and some venison sausages, well worth the effort of carrying them home to London.

Lyndhurst's main street runs downhill, flanked by shops and houses, tile-hung and some with pretty hexagonal chimneys and lattice windows. Wistaria rambled over a porch, and lilac and laburnum brimmed over fences.

'Do you go to Brockenhurst?' I asked the driver of a bus that drew up at the bus-stop. 'If I have to', was the lugubrious answer. The bus whisked through Goose Green and then into the cool of overhanging trees. Brick houses came into sight along with a few half-timbered ones.

Brockenhurst

Brockenhurst village is pleasant, if undistinguished, but it has one or two good eating places including a bistro called Splashes (because it is near the watersplash where the road fords a small, sparkling stream). I sat by the footbridge on a seat hot from the sun, listening to the gurgle of water, a distant woodpigeon and the soft movements of a mare and her foal grazing by the waterside. Every private house in the Forest has a cattle grid at its gate to prevent the ponies from eating the tulips and pansies; level crossings, too, are guarded by grids to keep animals from wandering along the railway lines.

My next objective was the railway station. No, I'd not lost faith in the buses, but I'd heard there was something of interest in the 'down' waiting room – and so there was. It is a collection of autographed photographs of eminent Victorians – Tennyson, Longfellow, Darwin, Browning and others, whose splendid, bewhiskered faces recall a time when great men really looked the part. The pioneer photographer Julia Cameron had lived nearby, and she made the waiting room a present of the portraits because it had been the scene of an emotional reunion with her long-absent son.

The next bus ride went across heath as well as through woodland blazing with gorse (later, red heather would take over). There were occasional thatched cottages, and many solid late-Victorian houses set well back behind their pink rhododendrons or their flowering cherries. We had to slow down and detour round a donkey that was rooted in the road with oak-like permanence, its sides taut and round as a tennis ball, its eyes firmly closed in its indifference to the bus.

Lymington

Lymington is an enchanting town on the estuary of a river named after it. It is entered by a road with an attractive terrace of early Victorian houses, fanlights over the doors and shutters at the windows, leading to the very wide High Street, thronged with market stalls on Saturdays. There are many fine Georgian (and earlier) houses. Some of the most attractive have been taken over – as so often happens – by solicitors for use as offices, including the beautiful Ivy House (curiously named since it is covered by a very ancient Virginia creeper, its stem well over a foot thick).

It took my eyes some minutes to adjust from the brilliant sun to the gloom inside the church. It is an odd mixture: rugged old stone walls on one side contrast with a white pillared and panelled gallery, on the front of which black-and-gold panels chronicle various benefactions. My eye was caught by the Blakiston memorials. When Anne died in 1862 she was 81; her husband had died, aged 45, in 1806. His memorial, for which she presumably chose the words, says, 'To those who knew him the Enumeration of his Virtues would be superfluous: To those who knew him not it might be tedious.' Hers, on the other hand, goes on at length about her virtues. Georgian restraint contrasted with Victorian pomposity?

Many of the shops in the High Street have a pillared frontage. Up above project bay windows or canopied balconies with decorative wrought-ironwork. Between are alleyways with glimpses of green beyond or courtyards with flagstone paths leading to cottages and beds of wallflowers or pansies. Wine merchants and antique shops are numerous, giving way – as the street starts sloping down towards the river – to yacht stores and shops or restaurants with names like Limpets or Shipmates. In the distance, above the trees, rises an obelisk (a memorial to some long-forgotten admiral), precisely placed to provide a focal point as one looks down the High Street.

A cobbled, pedestrian-only street twists its way steeply down, and suddenly I found myself on the quayside (a good place to picnic, incidentally, with cold meats or a quiche bought from the delicatessen on Quay Hill). Most of the moored craft were small yachts, but there were a few fishing boats, and the little black-headed gulls, of which there is a huge colony on this coast, were keeping a sharp eye on them. Further along, hundreds of slender masts stood like a marine coppice against the cloudless blue sky. Young men with high boots and tanned faces were busy doing complicated things with ropes or were perched up in the rigging, which the wind plucked like harp strings.

To return to the High Street I strolled up picturesque Nelson's Place, past the colourful houses of Captain's Row and along Grove Road. Grove Road was surprisingly rural for a street in the centre of town – clover, meadowsweet and dandelion clocks brightened the grassy roadside. There are fine houses along there and the only crinkle-crankle wall I know outside Suffolk, its sinuous brickwork warm to touch, the mellow red tinged with grey lichen. Clumps of pretty toadflax on it were in flower. Further along, the road lived up to its name – a grove of blossoming trees, shrubs and creepers with bees busy on the tiny pink flowers of cotoneaster and butterflies on the lilac or wistaria of the cottage gardens.

My bus swung out of town past cottage gardens with clematis, elderflowers dancing in the breeze, and snow-white washing on a line. At a bus-stop by a stream there was time to enjoy bluebells, new fronds of bracken, pink Herb Robert and campions. I suddenly realized what a very decorative plant the common nettle is, a plant on which we rather pointlessly wage a war that the nettles always win in the end.

The road to Beaulieu crosses Beaulieu Heath, with a view of the Isle of Purbeck to the right (one is nearer the sea than one guesses) across acres of gorse and heather, and of Hatchet pond where anglers wait, ever-hopeful. There are some particularly immaculate examples of the thatcher's skill along the way. The decorative treatment of the roof ridges is a thatcher's trademark, and each has his own pattern. Some add a reed pheasant, owl or peacock to distinguish their work.

Then came the clear, tranquil water of Beaulieu river (among the reed beds that provide the thatch) and the attraction that later will be bringing thousands of cars to spoil these pleasant parts – Lord Montague's colossal motor museum and entertainment grounds. The remains of the Cistercian abbey, founded by King John, are now a mere appendage of all this and can be visited only if you pay to see the rest of the show. I did, but for my taste it was the least interesting thing I did that day. Clearly tens of thousands of people would think otherwise, for it is a top tourist attraction – and, of its kind, it is superbly well done.

Beaulieu

Beaulieu village is extremely beautiful, with superb views of the very lovely river, the abbey walls and rural peace. In the distance great trees crowd down to the river edge, their boughs sweeping low to the sunlit surface of the water. The grass is lush, cows wander right into the quiet village street, the only person in sight is a man slowly walking his Sealyham and the only really busy individual is a coot paddling rapidly by.

The bus climbed up through cool woodland and then across more heath. The imminence of Southampton is hinted at by pylons striding across the landscape and a distant prospect of factory chimneys. Suburban gardens flashed by, bright with azaleas, and then we were at Hythe, an old boat-building town.

Hythe

The ferry to Southampton waits at the end of a long pier built a hundred years ago. A primitive train carries passengers to it, a two-minute journey of jerk, squeak, rock and roll all the way. The train is about 60 years old and may be excused its arthriticky state. Onto the ferry (*Hotspur IV*) streamed businessmen with briefcases, housewives with shopping baskets, schoolboys with their bags – and a girl clutching a large melon. It takes ten minutes to cross the River Test. All kinds of craft pass by or are moored there: naval ships, a car ferry to France, the cruise liner *Oriana*, a fireboat, landing craft and pleasure boats *Solent Queen* and *Island Scene* waiting for day-trippers.

At the other side a long queue was already waiting to board for Hythe. We all streamed off and dispersed to buses that go to the centre of Southampton. I ended my journey where I had begun.

That night on television the New Forest was in the news – drought, sun and breeze had combined to bring devastation, and hundreds of those lovely acres had been consumed in a great forest fire.

12

BUSSING ABOUT IN A NATIONAL PARK

Any bus ride through a National Park is bound to be full of scenic interest, for the National Parks are vast stretches of countryside – mostly wild, but with some farmland – that are protected by law from development that would spoil them.

Bus services are often encouraged in the Parks in order to reduce the amount of car traffic and the necessity for unsightly car parks. More than in many other places, extra bus services may be run specifically to suit the convenience of tourists as much as residents. Many set out from car parks on the perimeter of a National Park in order to encourage motorists to leave their cars outside.

A particularly rugged National Park in the West Country is *Dartmoor* (take along Sir Arthur Conan Doyle's *Hound of the Baskervilles* to read!). Apart from everyday buses around the moor, there are special double-deckers in summer that take you right across from Plymouth to Exeter or Newton Abbot, and some minibuses link up moorland villages between these towns. (Timetables are available from Dartmoor National Park Office, County Hall, Exeter.)

Further northwards is the *Peak District*, rich in beauty spots and stately homes. It is very well covered – extra weekend buses supplement the everyday services connecting with cities such as Stoke-on-Trent, Derby, Chesterfield, Sheffield and Manchester. There's also a scheme for combining cycle hire with bus riding: cycle until you're tired, then take a bus and leave the cycle at a collection point. (Timetables are available from Peak District National Park Office, Aldern House, Baslow Road, Bakewell.) A good base might be Buxton.

The *Yorkshire Dales* have magnificent scenery and buses that run every day through Wensleydale in the north and Wharfedale in the south. (Timetables and the 'Dalesrider' leaflet about scenic routes are available from Yorkshire Dales National Park Office, East Parade, Harrogate.) A suggested base is Richmond.

The coastal area of the *North Yorkshire Moors* is well served by buses, many from Whitby; a few also go across the moors. (Timetables are available from United Automobile Services, Grange Road, Darlington.)

Apart from numerous everyday buses in the *Lake District*, there are small companies operating minibuses over some of the most spectacular passes and alongside the lakes. There is also a special bus linking the Lake District with the Yorkshire Dales. (You can get a bus map and details of operators from Lake District National Park Office, Bank House, High Street, Windermere.) Keswick and Grasmere are central bases from which to set out.

Northumberland's National Park includes a long stretch of the Roman Wall and, in addition to everyday services, there are special Roman Wall buses that stop at the principal forts and other sights, with a taped commentary. Car drivers are encouraged to park and take the bus. (Timetables and leaflets about the Wall and its buses are available from Northumberland National Park, Bede House, All Saints Centre, Newcastle upon Tyne. Timetables of all buses in the park can be acquired from United Automobile Services, Grange Road, Darlington.) Hexham is the town nearest to the middle of the Wall (see Chapter 2).

Apart from the National Parks, certain regions – usually less large and wild – have been designated 'Areas of Outstanding Natural Beauty'; their character too, is protected by law from alterations that would spoil them. Some are largely farmland, but all are as enjoyable as the National Parks. A number are easily reached from big cities and their total acreage is as great as that of the National Parks. They, too, are an excellent choice for a day or more of bussing about. The map on page 140 shows where they are, and several are described in accounts of journeys elsewhere in this book.

EXMOOR
Ilfracombe – Lynton – Lynmouth – Porlock – Minehead

The summer's journey described here skirted the coastline of one of the west country's National Parks, Exmoor. It would take a day to do the trip there and back, perhaps lunching at Minehead on the way out and taking tea at Lynmouth on the way back.

Ilfracombe

Ilfracombe, just outside the National Park, is a good base from which to start. It is a big seaside resort of coves and bays with plenty of hotels or guest houses from which to choose (and plenty of bus routes in addition to the one described). It is built around an old harbour and surrounded by a steep, rocky landscape. When not bussing about, one can take boat trips – in particular, a two-hour journey by steamer to Lundy, the National Trust island. The name means 'puffin isle' in Norse, and among its flowery gorges and castle ruins nest not only some puffins but razorbills, kittiwakes and many other sea birds. The island has its own breed of wild ponies and a colony of seals.

Lynton and Lynmouth

The bus route to Lynton goes through Combe Martin, a village nestling at the mouth of a gorge, its old inns looking out to the surf of the Bristol Channel and the Atlantic beyond. This beautiful coast, a medley of cliffs and coves, is National Trust property and from here right along to Minehead is a coastal footpath with spectacular views all the way. It is easy to walk a bit and bus a bit alternately, for footpath and bus routes repeatedly encounter one another.

If you stay on the bus, it at first goes inland a little way (to Kentisbury Ford on the edge of Exmoor) before descending to the twin towns of Lynton and Lynmouth. Lynton is on a cliff a dizzy 500 feet above Lynmouth, to which one descends by a unique water-operated cliff railway. Lynmouth is the older and more picturesque of the two, with thatched houses around a harbour, but Lynton has a museum of Exmoor curiosities worth visiting before the descent or on the return journey.

Porlock

The woodland road into Somerset is exceedingly steep, with stunning views. Porlock – a village of narrow, winding streets and thatched cottages – lies tucked in among hills. It was once a port but is now a mile inland. Its Ship Inn is a quaint place for a pause (Robert Southey wrote some of his poetry there) and the ancient church, though so tiny, holds a surprise – a 15th-century tomb of unusual magnificence. You can also watch pottery being hand made at Culborne Lodge. But as there are only two buses a day, there may be little time to linger.

Minehead

The bus continues to Minehead, a large and cheerful holiday town spread out around a great, curving bay where at low tide the sea goes far out, leaving a vast expanse of sand. Here, too, is a pottery where visitors are welcome to watch. Quay Town is the old part, rising up above a harbour built in the time of James I. One can return from here to Ilfracombe by steamer unless pressing on by bus to complete the journey at the little port of Watchet, from which Samuel Coleridge's 'Ancient Mariner' set out on his fateful voyage.

All the transport described in this journey (except the steamers) can be travelled on without charge if a family buys beforehand a special 'rambler ticket' which covers one day's unlimited travel for two adults and two children throughout the route – possibly the best bargain of any in this book. The ticket also covers the old steam railway near Minehead.

More bus trips from Ilfracombe

The National Park route described above is only one of many scenic bus trips that can be taken from Ilfracombe. I stayed there nearly a week, going out in different directions each day. I chose the Headlands Hotel, which is ideal for the purpose because it is close to the bus depot (and to the quay from which steamer trips start, too). This was only one of its many virtues. From the outside it looks very ordinary, but its owner was once a manager for a tour-operating company and knows what is needed to make visitors comfortable and content. He employs a good cook. But the hotel's biggest asset is its site – right on the edge of the sea and with a cliff-top garden (and all this for one of the lowest bed-and-breakfast rates of any in this book).

Ilfracombe itself is an unpretentious place with a lot of early Victorian charm in the pink-and-white terraces set high up and the iron-pillared shops down below selling beach hats, kites and suchlike. Its great attraction is its unique shore – rocky promontories, sandy coves, tunnels, inlets and caves. In high summer and at the spring bank holiday it gets overcrowded, but at other times it is easy to find peaceful corners – the tiny cottages and gardens in Britannia Row, for instance, or the less-frequented side of the harbour (a good spot to enjoy the superbly fresh fish-and-chips from Bernie's). Its museum is crammed with treasures, from Victorian knickers to Tibetan prayer wheels, from a piece of the Queen Mother's wedding cake to primitive tooth-pulling gadgets. There is even Granny Scott's red flannel petticoat. (In

1797 Granny spotted French ships approaching. All the men were away fishing, so Granny got the women to put their red petticoats round their shoulders and march up and down so that from a distance they would look like soldiers on parade. The trick worked and the ships turned away.)

One of the oldest inns, the George and Dragon, is a good spot for a fireside lunch when it's chilly. It has slabbed floors, oak benches and rough stone walls. There I sat listening to the latest television soap operas being discussed in broadest Devon accents over darts and real ale or cider by young men with tattooed arms, dark beards and gold rings in their ears – descendants of Drake's men?

Outside the rain ran downhill in streams, and turbulent foam pounded the indifferent rocks. Even the gulls stood around looking chilly and fed up. Fortunately, only one day was like this. The west country is at its best in spring and celebrates with flower festivals then, so that is the best time to go there.

At the end of each day's exploration it was a pleasure to sit at my bedroom window in Ilfracombe watching the setting sun gild the window frame and the grey herring gulls or blackbacks sail close by, effortlessly roller-coasting along the air currents, wheeling as gracefully as a child's kite.

Among bus routes from Ilfracombe which I enjoyed were the following:

To Woolacombe Bay and Mortehoe

Both are close to Ilfracombe. Here one can walk on the spectacular Morte Point, a National Trust headland. The turf (cropped short by roaming sheep and rabbits) is like a tapestry of tiny wildflowers, with unusual slatey rocks breaking through here and there. Great clumps of pink thrift defy the salty winds; gulls have nest holes in cliffs that descend, sheer and dizzying, to the surf below and to the sandy beaches where children probe the mysteries of rock pools.

To Combe Martin, Berrynarbor and Arlington

The bus has to struggle up steep winding streets till the view of Ilfracombe's bay, with white sails billowing and the tiny 14th-century chapel on Lantern Hill, dwindle below. The road goes by heath and headlands, rocks and surf, and banks crowded with the cheerful faces of dog-daisies. Then it leaves the early morning sunlight to plunge into a green tunnel of trees. Berrynarbor is a picturesque cluster of whitewashed cottages and lattice windows, but Combe Martin goes on and on – it is the longest village in England (ten bus-stops long).

The cottage gardens are full of brilliant colour from irises, lupins and marigolds. Beyond, the hilly landscape is like a quilt of green fields until the turning for Arlington is reached. A ten-minute walk along a lane brimming with campion, wild garlic and speedwell (patriotically red, white and blue), and with butterflies brings one to the gate where miaouing peacocks do guard-duty, hopeful of visitors' scraps.

Arlington Court, a Regency house on an estate that had belonged to the Chichesters since Norman times, is not merely beautiful. It is one of those rare stately homes which still feel alive with the personality of their final owners – in this case Miss Rosalie, the last of the Chichesters, who lived there till she died, in her eighties, in 1949. She was a collector of tiny, beautiful things – shells, animals carved in semi-precious stones, ships' models and silver trifles, and they are all still as she left them. Her bedroom is intact. China toothbrush holder, silver button-hook, glove stretcher – all these bring alive a vanished life-style.

Within the very lovely grounds the National Trust has housed its now unsurpassed collection of carriages, where one can discover the difference between a barouche and a brougham, a gig, a phaeton and a victoria. All are kept in immaculate condition by the coachman, Russell Forehead, who previously worked in films – masterminding cavalry scenes in such epics as *The Charge of the Light Brigade* or *Lawrence of Arabia*. One can visit the stables and meet his coachhorses, sniff the leathery smell of the tack room, or be taken for a wagon ride by him among the groves of towering rhododendrons by the lake.

As in most National Trust houses, lunch is both good and inexpensive. Even the butterpats carried the Chichester emblem – a heron – which turns up in garden statuary and carpet patterns, too.

To Hunters Inn

This hostelry is at the heart of what has rightly been called the most romantic scenery in all Devon – the Heddon Valley (preserved by the National Trust) on the edge of Exmoor. Moors, rocky headlands, dizzy heights and distant views, shallow streams, serpentine lanes – the route has just about every picturesque ingredient. From the inn there are riverside walks and a nature trail with a booklet to help one recognize, for example, dippers (little paddling birds), an old lime kiln, oyster-catchers on the shore and various kinds of fern or lichen. Afterwards Devon cider or a Devon cream tea at the inn is a necessity.

To Chambercombe

Just outside Ilfracombe is a medieval manor house with walled water-garden (tadpoles thriving among the water lilies and marsh marigolds), a tiny chapel inside the house and a gruesome legend of wreckers and a body walled up for two centuries. It has a priest's hole and furniture with hidden places to keep jewels. Altogether it is a house full of secrets. There's even a secret about the floors: they look highly polished but are not; their shine comes from the mixing of cider with ash from lime kilns and other (now long forgotten) ingredients. But outside all mysteries vanish.

Further along this same route one can visit the working watermill at Hele, the castle at Watermouth – now housing craft and antique shops and demonstrations of cider- and butter-making – and the caves in Watermouth cove. (If visiting the Manor House allow plenty of time. It is a quarter-hour walk from the bus, one has to wait for a guide, and buses back are infrequent.)

To Lee Bay

This is another picturesque cove, so near Ilfracombe that one can even walk back over the famous Torrs Walk (National Trust), with magnificent coastal scenery. The serpentine road down to Lee runs between high banks typical of Devon which in summer are bright with fuchsias. There are pretty cottages of whitewash and thatch, some draped in wisteria, and walls where ferns, moss and foxgloves grow.

To Barnstaple

(There are two ways to get there; the Combe Martin route is prettier but longer.) This town, twice the size of Ilfracombe, has better shops and, on Fridays, a very lively market. It retains much of its Georgian and early Victorian dignity, and there is plenty to see just strolling around the High Street and Beauport Street with the little lanes in between. Butchers Row is still a row of butchers' shops. In the tiny 17th-century schoolhouse 'for 20 poor maids' one can get a good inexpensive lunch.

The museum in little St Anne's Chapel repays a lingering visit to relish all the insignificant trifles that have somehow survived the years: yellowing handbills to sell 'a genteel cottage' or gather people to celebrate 'the glorious event of the passing of the Reform

Bill' (1832); an eight-year-old's frail sampler of the same year, painstakingly stitched. They have here the guns of the real Tom Faggus (the blacksmith-turned-highwayman immortalized in *Lorna Doone*) which were found, after his hanging, hidden in the thatch of his cottage.

Barnstaple also has a cooperative workshop where a dozen young craft workers can be seen engaged on various skills; a factory producing traditional Barnstaple pots; and an ornate statue of Queen Anne presiding over the quayside colonnade and the bus station.

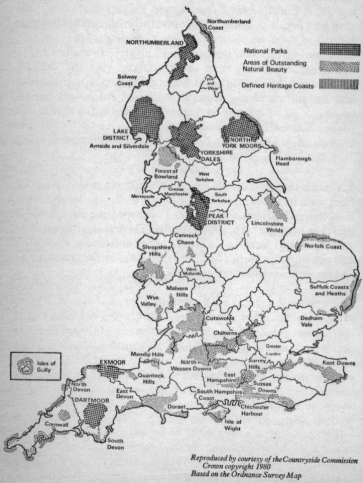

Reproduced by courtesy of the Countryside Commission
Crown copyright 1980
Based on the Ordnance Survey Map

13

ENGLAND'S BIG TOE

St Ives – Land's End – Penzance (and villages between)

In Cornwall I decided to base myself on one place and spend a few days radiating out and back – making loop bus trips like the petals of a daisy and sleeping every night in the same centre (with my family). Instead of avoiding tourist spots, I went into the thick of one and, instead of going out of season, I went in summer.

My base was St Ives in Cornwall. It was seething with summer tourists and I wondered whether the buses would therefore be packed and hot. But there was no need to worry! Though coach tours were booked out for a fortnight ahead and car parks early each day put out 'Full' placards, the buses remained half-empty – airy, comfortable and roomy.

There was a petrol shortage that year and car drivers spent a good deal of their holiday in queues at garages (some queues were miles long) waiting for the few gallons they could get. Meanwhile we on the buses sailed happily by them. We could go to all kinds of beauty spots, on or off the beaten track, and never have to turn away for lack of parking space. Only in Penzance at rush hour were we held up in a traffic jam – but, while the red-faced car drivers fumed, we bus passengers took our ease.

The disadvantage of an in-season bus journey is not, therefore, the crowds – they stick to their cars and coaches – but the fact that one does not experience places in their everyday, real-life wear. Also, then one may come across some of the old traditions that still survive in Cornwall, lost to the rest of England long ago: hurling, an ancient game that was the forerunner of rugby and is still played on the dedication anniversaries of some churches; guise dancing before Christmas (when disguises are worn); or rituals with corn dollies at harvest time.

However, summertime brought two bonuses. In a tourist area like Cornwall the bus company runs some extra services not operated out of season, and those stately homes that open only in summer are all available to visit.

Cornwall is a huge county. My chosen area was Penwith, the big toe of England. It is roughly diamond-shaped, with St Ives, Land's End and Penzance as its best-known centres. Penzance has the most bus services, but even St Ives had more than enough for the few days I was able to stay.

The Western National Bus Company does more to encourage my kind of joy riding than some other bus companies. One can buy a pass which, for one week, entitles the user to go anywhere without having to buy individual bus tickets. A few of its buses have open tops. It also issues leaflets of recommended country and coastal walks (from one mile upwards), noting which bus services will take you to the start and which ones bring you back.

Non-walkers also can find their bussing options much extended by considering a short walk from one bus route to join up with another. Examples are the easy mile downhill from Paul (an interesting church) to Mousehole, or Mousehole to Lamorna Cove along the coast (2½ miles), or Sennen Cove to Land's End (a breathtaking 1¼ miles of cliff-top scenery).

St Ives

The fishing village of St Ives was first 'discovered' in the 19th century by artists such as James Whistler and Walter Sickert, who were attracted not only by its picturesque cottages and steep, cobbled lanes around the bay, but by the very special light. There is said to be more ultra-violet in it than usual, and the sky and sea can certainly be incredibly clear and beautiful at times.

The artists are still there (and writers, too). Many open their studios for visitors to wander in and out, and there seem to be art galleries or craft shops round every corner. A number of the traditionalists exhibit together in a former church, the modernists in a former fish warehouse. In a recently created undercover market behind the famous Sloop Inn busy craftsmen are open to view in workshops producing pottery, leatherwork, silver, enamels and textiles. The building is an excellent example of how modern design can incorporate time-honoured natural materials such as slate, granite and timber. Upstairs is a gull's eye view down into the market from a gallery café serving home-made salads and pastries.

Barbara Hepworth's house (where the sculptor died tragically in a fire a few years ago) has been turned into a permanent gallery for some of her work, while others stand in her rambling, semi-tropical garden. This is right in the heart of St Ives, completely hidden behind 20-foot stone walls. Her studio is full of poignancy: not only are her tools and work clothes still as she left them the day before she died, but half-worked blocks of marble attest to what might have been.

There are lots of pleasant things to do in St Ives, but doing nothing is the pleasantest of all – and, oddly enough, one of the best spots for this pursuit is the bus station. St Ives might well claim to have the best bus station in Britain so far as its site is concerned – it is high on a cliff overlooking the bay and the so-called Island (really a peninsula) which has a tiny ancient chapel, sometimes floodlit, topping its grassy hump. Tradition has it that the chapel stands over the original grave of St Ia or Iva, the 6th-century Irish missionary after whom the town is named. One looks down from the bus station onto the roofs of St Ives, a higgledy-piggledy geometric pattern of ridges and troughs – old slates weathered, sagging and encrusted with lichen; newer ones still shiny enough to turn silver when the sun catches them; and contrasting warm terracotta ridge tiles and chimney stacks. Squeezed between the houses are tiny courtyards crammed with green shrubs or leafy pot plants.

Gulls nest in the angles between chimneys and roofs, preferring this centrally heated accommodation to slumming it on the cliffs. The chimney pots, too, are used by the gulls, who find them ideal lookout posts from which to spot shoals of fish in the bay (like the huers, human lookouts of old).

Tucked into the cliff under the bus station is one of St Ives' nicer cafés, bistro in style but producing the very best of English breakfasts. I know no better start to a day's bussing than one of Tilly's huge breakfasts eaten *al fresco* at a balcony table while watching the birds and boats below and the bright lollipop sunshades beginning to sprout on the sandy beaches.

It's a good spot in which to read the short history of the town by Sparrow and Williams (*About St Ives*), when the places they write about are laid out at your feet. Straight ahead is the stone pier built in 1770 by Smeaton (designer of the Eddystone lighthouse), and one can imagine it heaped in the past with stacks of tin or barrels of salted pilchards for export, or with landed coal and wood. Time and again this harbour was raided by pirates, for until the 18th century all trading was by sea – there were no roads over the moors and the railway did not come until 1877. Farther off is Godrevy lighthouse which inspired Virginia Woolf (who spent memorable holidays in St Ives as a child) to write her novel *To the Lighthouse*.

The steep contours of St Ives have kept it quite small, but every bit of its limited space is used to maximum effect. Houses are built on any rocky surface that will take them and others are crammed in between every whichway. Fish cellars now house shops, and attics restaurants – there are plenty of good cafés and the upstairs ones have the bonus of marvellous views over the sea. Best of all for a platter lunch is the tranquil lounge of the Chy-an-Dour ('house-by-the-sea') Hotel up Treganna Hill: its terraced lawns command a seven-mile panorama of sea and shore. But the restaurants have strong competition from *the* original take-away food, the Cornish pasty – a meat-and-two-veg dinner packaged in pastry, just right for today's bus travellers.

St Ives has much to enjoy: fine gardens, cliff-top walks, the famous Bernard Leach pottery, a lifeboat station open to view, a magnificent 15th-century church with unusual gilded carvings in the roof and others on bench ends, boat trips to watch seals, a fascinating pre-cinema museum of cinematography (Victorian peepshows, optical illusions and magic lanterns) and another of local history. But above all there are the twisting, zigzag lanes, a mapmaker's nightmare, their crazy angles dictated by the rocky outcrops on which the houses jostle one another like seabirds' nests on a cliff. Tourists wander as if in a maze. But one hardly hears a Cornish voice among all the babel of accents in the summer. One must go elsewhere to find the Cornwall of the Cornish.

Land's End via Pendeen

To visit Land's End is an obvious 'must' when in Penwith, and the route from St Ives is superb. It runs along the narrow strip between Penwith's backbone of granite hills and the untamed Atlantic coastline to the north. Nothing lies between those cliffs and America but 3,000 miles of ocean, which has pounded them into one of Britain's harshest winter coastlines – a place of storms, and jagged rocks – and one of its most beautiful in sunny summers.

It was a freak summer that year and, up on the open top of the bus, huddled in my raincoat, I got a taste of Cornwall's savagery during the day's ride. The rain lashed down in torrents, the wind howled, and spray wrapped the granite headlands in invisibility. Nearly all the tourists had gone to earth and the wild, wet solitude was in total contrast to my previous day in St Ives.

It is easy to understand why Cornwall abounds in eerie legends of ghosts and goblins, wizards, mermaids and other harbingers of doom. The Atlantic gales whip the sea into a boiling hell and flatten the crops; cattle huddle miserably in the lee of any shelter they can find. Years of this kind of weather have contorted the gorse permanently into witch-like shapes. Almost no trees grow on this side of Penwith: the salty gales are too much for them. The few stunted ones that do survive are bent and wizened. The wind found the stitch holes of my walking shoes and nipped my toes.

The ruins of an old building or some great prehistoric stone would suddenly spring into sight as the mist cleared, only to vanish again in a second as it swirled back again. Solid shapes appeared and disappeared as lightly as any spectre.

Yet the bus also brushed by high banks gay with pink campion and Herb Robert, celandines, violets and wild garlic flowers, and passed beneath the occasional palm tree – tokens of Cornwall's sunnier side that flourishes despite such extremes of rain and wind. It is these contrasts that give the area its fascination – the bright and the dark, the smiling and the cruel coexisting. One moment the view is of wild, bleak moors and the next of a cottage garden neat as a picture postcard. The barren rocks loom menacingly above; look down and, hidden among small ferns, a tiny stream gurgles.

There are lots of interesting places at which to break one's journey for a couple of hours, for example Gurnard's Head, Morvah or Sennen Cove – especially the last, with its silvery sands and view of Cape Cornwall. For walkers the coast is easy to reach in kindly weather from the bus and there is a coastal path all round it. The National Trust owns many of the headlands with the most spectacular views (a large part of Penwith is protected as an area of oustanding natural beauty). A large-scale Ordnance Survey map, coupled with booklets available locally giving guidance on walks short or long, will indicate any number of good routes.

My choice of stop that day was Pendeen, to visit the working Geevor tin mine, not long opened to the public. This side of Cornwall is littered with the ruins of old tin mines identifiable by gaunt chimneys on the horizon and crumbling walls. Only a few are still alive and well, but Geevor employs 400 workers. Wearing miners' safety helmets, visitors are shown round the surface works (not underground), the winding gear, the ore-crushers and the filtering sheds with one of the miners as a guide. Everywhere water is running – water red with traces of the iron particles that have to be filtered out from the tin particles. Through shed after shed, from one great wooden tray sloping down to another, the particles are rinsed and rinsed again until the two metals gradually separate, the heavier iron eventually sinking away from the thin ribbon of tin that is left. Only four tons a day is thus yielded, but it fetches nearly £8,000 a ton.

The mine has an exceptionally interesting museum attached, telling the mining story from prising flints out of chalk with animal bones in the Stone Age right up to compressed-air drills and electric detonators. Life-size models viewed from dark passageways give one the illusion of being in a mine; miniature models show how the whole complex network of galleries and shafts is at that moment operating half a mile beneath one's feet and for two miles around. Some galleries stretch below the seabed.

Just along the road is Bottalack, peppered with disused mines; the mines' Count House where the miners drew their pay is now a restaurant (Pendeen itself has the Miners' Country Kitchen and a mining museum).

Another stop, involving a mile's walk down a lane rosy with pompoms of thrift, enabled us to visit the Pendeen Watch lighthouse, sited there in 1900 (and converted from oil to electricity in 1926) because so many ships broke up on the nearby rocks. As in all lighthouses, the interior is like the dream homes which polish and paint manufacturers show in TV commercials, all gleaming brasswork and immaculate mahogany with green paint that looks – well, fresh as paint. Notices ask you not to fingermark the metal fittings and I climbed apologetically up the dustless stairs. The lighthouse keeper refers to his responsibilities as 'mostly housework'.

'Well now, me darlings', he begins in true Cornish style as he explains the workings of the great lantern. Prisms of the purest glass so concentrate the light from a 3.5-kilowatt lamp that its beam can be seen nearly 30 miles away unless obscured by fog, in which case a horn with a blast audible for 10 miles comes into operation (so dense are the fogs that, a few days after our visit, two ships collided nearby and sank with the loss of four lives – in *June*).

And so, onward to Land's End, a place on which to turn one's back – a litter of cafés and car parks. Looking fixedly out to sea instead, one should be able to spot two more lighthouses. A dozen of the 92 lighthouses round England and Wales are near Cornwall's deadly shores. But on a day like this, even the weirdly shaped rocks – named Spire, Knight, Kettle-Bottom and Shark's Fin – are hidden in spray.

Before the lighthouse, wrecks were so numerous that the locals made a good living plundering them. The lighthouse on the Longships Rocks was built in 1795; so primitive were conditions inside that the lighthousemen had to cook their meals on the oil lamps themselves. The first tower was too short (stormy waves engulfed the lantern) so in 1875 the present 120-foot tower replaced it. The equally tall one on Wolf Rock, which replaced iron beacons, is a few years older.

Out there beyond the rocks and foam lies, perhaps, Lyonesse, the lost land of so many King Arthur stories. Just here the Atlantic meets the English Channel, and when these two giant waters collide in an exceptional storm, anything is possible: drowned churches and trees, and the shifting of mountainous sand dunes, are realities not legends.

With the wind making it hard not to lean at a 45-degree angle, I soon retreated to the well-upholstered lounge of the Land's End Hotel, an excellent Cornish pasty (5p cheaper than those of the café outside) and, joy of joys, rum-and-shrub, the best remedy for icy toes and nose. Shrub is an alcoholic cordial peculiar to the west country. It has been made (from a concoction of herbs) for at least three centuries, and it is said that its affinity for rum was first noticed when barrels of rum hidden underwater by smugglers got salty and the shrub was added to mask it. Lovage makes another such cordial, often mixed with brandy.

To return via Penzance, taking buses through the southern half of the peninsula, shows how different Penwith is south of its granite backbone. There is a wider area of fertile land sheltered from Atlantic winds, where flowers are grown for the London market – fields of daffodils, irises and tulips at the start of summer. Broccoli, cauliflowers and new potatoes are grown here, too. This side of the coastline has more sandy beaches and sun-trapping coves, more little fishing villages and more trees.

The Cornish hedgerow is basically a dry-stone wall topped with turf which soon attracts wildflowers, gorse and shrubs so that it rapidly becomes a high bank, cutting off the car driver's view – but bus passengers, even on single-deckers, can see over the top. Buses travel slowly enough for one to enjoy and identify the multitude of wildflowers in the banks as one goes along. At one halt I counted over 20 varieties just outside my window.

Few bus rides in Penwith do not pass reminders of Cornwall's great antiquity. Wayside crosses are typically Cornish and usually medieval, put up beside roads that led to churches or perhaps to commemorate someone. Many are stones with disc-shaped tops inscribed with a crucifix or other carvings. But these are comparative newcomers to the scene. Thousands of years before Christ, Stone Age people were building great tombs and temples here made from massive slabs or boulders. Particularly common are long stones (menhirs), of which many can be seen along the bus routes – single upright slabs which may have been primitive tombstones. Though it lacks both index and map, a useful booklet to take along is the Cornish Archaeological Society's guide to these local antiquities – shops and tourist offices sell it for a few pence. It also explains some of the Penwith place names, which are pure Cornish. The language is related to both Welsh and Breton and died out nearly two centuries ago. Crows-an-Wra, a hamlet with a stone cross on this route, means 'the witch's cross'.

There are old churches, too, but few have interesting interiors because Victorian 'improvers' unfortunately ripped out much that gave them character. In many places they are outnumbered by Methodist chapels. Cornwall has always taken religion seriously, even to the extent of rebelling against the Reformation in 1548, and John Wesley repeatedly visited this area during the 1740s. He was indefatigable, riding from hamlet to hamlet over moorland tracks, and made thousands of converts (and a good many enemies). All these chapels sprang up in his wake.

From Penzance (to be explored on a later day) the principal route back to St Ives, via Crowlas, turned out to be neither the prettiest nor even the shortest, but it has more buses and they nip along the main road quickly. This road has attracted to it various entertainments such as the vast outdoor 'Age of Steam' railway exhibition, Lelant's model village and leisure centre, and other well-planned activities for children in particular.

From the top of the bus just outside Penzance one can see helicopters taking off for the 20-minute joy ride to the Scilly Isles. On the other side of the road, over the railway lines, is Mount's Bay with St Michael's Mount and its castle perched 300 feet up (easy to reach on another bus, then by ferry or walking over the cobbled causeway if the tide is out). It is now in the care of the National Trust. Like Mont St Michel off the Normandy coast, the steep mount is an island only at high tide. For centuries it was topped by a priory under the authority of the abbey on Mont St Michel, but in 1425 it became a fortress. Perkin Warbeck, pretender to the English throne (he claimed to be one of the two princes murdered in the Tower of London), used it as his base in 1497. It was held during the Civil Wars by the Royalists, as were most of Cornwall's strongholds. The castle is now a mixture of every architectural style from the 12th century onwards. At the foot of the Mount is its own small harbour and fishing village.

On many bus routes St Michael's Mount suddenly pops into

148

view unexpectedly and each time it looks quite different. It is not just a question of the angle from which one sees it. The sky and sea are always changing, and the castle changes with them.

Another of the advantages of this route is the view of the Hayle estuary before entering St Ives. The Hayle is wide and shallow here, ambling among pools and sand dunes known locally as towans. But once it was deep and tidal for four miles inland, in the days when Bronze Age miners bartered their tin with foreign ships. One of the few havens along the rocky northern shore, it was the landing place for many of St Patrick's missionaries from Ireland, now remembered as saints peculiar to Cornwall and after whom so many Penwith churches are named.

As the bus approaches Carbis Bay the horizon is suddenly bisected by an immense granite needle on a hill, the Knill monument. Knill was an 18th-century customs collector (his house can still be seen in Fore Street, St Ives) who built this 500-foot steeple, now in a grove of rhododendrons, with the intention of being buried inside it at his death. He left money for a ceremony that still takes place every fifth year on St James's Day (25 July), when ten girls and two widows dance round the steeple to a tune played by a fiddler.

Near the finish of this route is an even more welcome sight at the day's end: John Beck's fish-and-chip restaurant at Carbis Bay. The queues outside tell their own story. If this is not the best fish-and-chippery in Britain, it must surely be the best in Cornwall.

It is also possible to leave the bus at St Erth and finish the journey on the very scenic railway line that runs into St Ives along this estuary and the coast.

Zennor and Penzance

Zennor is quickly reached by bus. It nestles just off the main road, in one of the innumerable valleys carved out by streams tumbling some 800 feet down that granite backbone to the Atlantic shore. The church is famous for its mermaid, carved on an ancient bench end. The story goes that she lured a young man, one of the church choir's sweetest singers, to the sea and his death. Very Cornish, too, is the notable eccentric who created Zennor's Wayside Museum, which is something really special – yet mercifully the crowds have not invaded it.

A lifetime ago, a Colonel Hirst happened to notice some curious old implements among a heap of scrap-iron about to be shipped abroad. He decided to buy them. From this chance acquisition began a long pursuit of abandoned tools of vanishing trades and old household utensils. In his garden he displayed and labelled his finds with admirably large, clear explanations, and he threw open the gates to any passer-by who cared to enter without charge.

And what an extraordinary collection it is: there is a wheeled barrow from which water was sold for ½d a bucket; strange tools for gathering fuel from the moors; and an oven like a huge clay pot in which smouldering faggots of wood were placed to heat it and were then removed so that the food could be put in.

Stones, so freely available here, were turned to innumerable uses – smugglers tied their loot to a stone with grooves or holes for the rope and sank it in a pool or the sea. Querns are round stones between which wheat was ground into flour. And what a variety of arm-aching irons for washdays: box-irons, heated by putting a hot coal inside; solid flat-irons; charcoal irons with chimneys; and goffering rollers to pleat frills. Then there are models of fishing and mining cottages and ancient hill forts, tombs and other antiquities. The watermill beside the garden's hurrying stream is also open to view, as is the restored miller's cottage.

After seeing so much, a restorative visit to the nearby Tinners' Arms was obviously necessary. This old pub, with ceiling of varnished boards and big stone hearths, was temporarily the home of D. H. Lawrence until he found High Tregarthen cottage (not far off, downhill between the farms of Tregarthen and Tremedda, which the bus passes).

Zennor Head (National Trust) is only a half-mile walk away but I wanted to see the other Cornwall, the moors inland that are less celebrated than the coast but have a wild beauty of their own. There were several ways to get from Zennor to Penzance across the moors. The road to Morvah and via Madron was tempting – Lanyon Quoit, a 4,000-year-old tomb, the carvings and monuments of Madron church, the ruins of one of the oldest tin mines – but I chose the quicker Newmill route on an open-top bus in order to have more time in Penzance later.

At Penzance (the name means 'holy headland') the bus deposited me near the harbour. The quay leads out over a decrepit bridge to the sailors' end of town. There is a big Aladdin's cave of a shop selling shells from all over the world which takes bookings for shark fishing and other sea trips. Then, round a corner, I came to a yard where monsters loomed: colossal navigation buoys of all shapes and sizes, each with its name painted on it – Knight Errant, Montamopus, Udder Rock, Exe Fairway. As I stared and wondered, a uniformed officer came to see what I wanted and ended by giving me a private tour.

It turned out to be one of the Trinity House depots that look after all the navigation buoys, lighthouses and lightships round England's coasts. Trinity House was chartered by Henry VIII as a semi-religious body charged with responsibility for ensuring safety at sea. It was given a coat-of-arms incorporating four galleons, and its flag is the Red Ensign of the merchant navy with the four Tudor galleons added to it. It was not until 1836, however, that Trinity House took over control of all lighthouses and brought efficiency to a previously haphazard situation.

Although a lot of sophisticated automation now goes into these buoys, some give their warnings as effectively as ever by means of simple devices invented long ago. The doleful moan of buoys like the one at Swithian (listen to it just before the last bus goes, when most visitors have left the miles of sand dunes desolate) is achieved by a giant iron tube like a vast whistle: air is let in or kept out by four rubber balls pushed in and out of sockets by the waves. A loose length of chain, continually swishing, is enough to keep the ironwork free from marine growth.

Only a few yards beyond the Trinity House depot is the Barbican (barbican means a town's outer defence), once a stone fortification, then a warehouse and now imaginatively restored as a crafts centre with workshops, gallery and coffee bar. It was designed by Percy Williams, who created the equally inspired Sloop crafts centre at St Ives.

The rest of the waterfront is promenade. Turning uphill, I soon came to the parish church, set in a particularly tranquil graveyard of lawns, old tombstones and trees in which to sit and watch the sea below. The church itself has an unusual Gothick revival interior dating from 1832 – full of space and light, with a gallery round it and a blue-white-gold colour scheme. The font is made of serpentine, a polished stone peculiar to Cornwall.

Beyond lies Penzance's most beguiling road, Chapel Street. There is so much of interest in this single road that the tourist office (opposite the Guildhall) has, in addition to its leaflet with a complete town trail to follow, one on Chapel Street alone. Antique, craft and book shops are sandwiched between restaurants and historic inns – each with its ghost, minstrel's gallery or what-have-you. Most famous and colourful of all is the Admiral Benbow. The owner, once a diver and collector of bits from wrecks, has written a small book about it. Its interior is crammed with his finds, and painted figureheads guard every corner. It was truly a smugglers' inn, and the exploits of one man who decoyed the customs men away by climbing on the roof and firing from there is well commemorated: look up outside and you will see his effigy clinging to the slates.

Chapel Street also has its Museum of Nautical Art, with a full-size section through an 18th-century man-o'-war as well as models, old ships' carvings, elaborately decorated cannons and treasure recently retrieved from the *Association*, which sank off the Scilly Isles in 1767. Strangest building of all is the Egyptian House, built as a museum about 1835, which looks as if it would be more at home on the Nile than displaying local crafts for sale.

West of Chapel Street lie Georgian houses. Regent Square is particularly attractive, the houses unconventionally laid out around a dog-leg street. By St Mary's Terrace, a gate leads into the very pretty Morrab Gardens, a few sloping acres punctuated with fountain, bandstand and flowering shrubs. Leaving by an opposite gate I found myself facing the entrance to the larger Penlee gardens, which surround the town's museum with tree ferns and other semi-tropical plants.

The museum is unpretentious, but its local exhibits are well displayed. The bird room helped me to identify a number of the plants as well as birds I'd seen from buses, while other rooms explained the fishing and mining history of the area. One display is devoted to the life of Sir Humphrey Davy of miner's lamp fame, who was born in Penzance just over two hundred years ago. His statue dominates Market Jew Street, the big shopping centre that runs down from the handsome domed building of Lloyds Bank (once the Market House).

I went by the library, pausing not only to look at an Armada cannon outside it but to scoop up some bargains in their used book sale. I then went along North Parade, a quiet backwater of terraced Regency houses, slightly faded and with gardens slightly neglected but no less attractive for that.

Every so often one comes across chunks of granite said to be the largest ever cut (Queen Victoria's tomb at Windsor is among the candidates). The 18-foot top step of the Law Courts in the nearby main road also makes this claim. *The Guinness Book of Records* is silent on the subject of granite, but at least where length is concerned Penzance's slab must be hard to beat.

I walked back to the bus station again after a break at the Wharf House, another imaginative conversion by the harbour. Once a warehouse, it is now a very good restaurant and serves teas, too. Its bar has a great window with one of those memorable views of Mounts Bay, and it was only a last-minute dash away from my final bus home that day.

I chose a different bus service this time to return to St Ives, one that trundled up and down small lanes, past almshouses and over streams, winding between little gardens rich in lilac and laburnum. This bit of Penwith is nicknamed the Golden Acres because it is so fertile. We went by Suttons' seed trial grounds – a rainbow of pansies – and by fields full of new potatoes.

Gulval is a picturesque village celebrated for its flowery churchyard and vicarage garden, with interesting monuments in its church. It was a spot worth lingering in (though one can walk down to the main road with its more frequent bus service).

Then the bus strained uphill to Ludgvan with its stone cottages around a tiny triangular village green (not an unusual layout in this part of England). The tumble of mixed flowers in small cottage gardens was as colourful as a kaleidoscope. One more village, Nancledra, sheltered in a valley with an old watermill (now a garage) by its stream. This was a very Cornish route with a little of everything along the way.

Porthcurno, Newlyn and Mousehole

For my third day's trip, after the usual drive to Penzance, I chose a bus route that would take me to some of the sheltered coves and fishing villages within a short distance of Penzance, a particular feature of the south coast of Penwith.

So, out through the western suburbs of Penzance we went. At first the bus was full of shoppers, but they soon alighted leaving only a few of us to jog on past the bowling green. We went past a thatched farmhouse sunk, it seemed, several feet below road level (or had the road risen?) so that only the top half of the front door was visible; along the Esplanade and by the Bolitho Gardens (the Bolithos were – and are – a wealthy banking family of civic benefactors). The bus strained up steep Chywoone Hill to where Adit Lane runs down towards the sea. Adit means the lowest drainage level of a mine, often in a cliff just above sea level, so presumably there were once mine workings below us. We drove through Paul, which has a church with box pews, a barrel ceiling, handsome monuments and the grave of the last speaker of Cornish as a native language (who died in 1777). We passed a garden walled entirely with old tombstones. There are views over the moors and then the bus dips into leafy valleys – down and then up, all the way. The turning to Lamorna Cove runs through a tangle of bent tree trunks thick with ivy, birch saplings and sycamore.

Lamorna has its cove, granite cliffs, jetty and a few cottages and is a good spot to linger in, but I decided to press on inland with the bus. Huge rounded boulders lie half-buried in the fields, looking like the humped backs of whales in the sea. To the left is a ring of 19 great stones, 'the merry maidens', and not far off their two 'pipers', each nearly 15 feet tall. Stone Age and Bronze Age people erected these circles of (originally) 20 stones in a number of places. Their purposes are not now known, so stories grew up to explain them; it was said that people who danced on Sundays were turned to stone. A burial chamber is usually found near each such circle and Tregiffian is no exception.

At a wayside cross the bus turned, passing fields with typical Cornish stiles of stone steps. St Buryan (another cross here) has a shop specializing in things made from serpentine, and a church with a fine interior and a wood screen carved with a notable menagerie of beasts.

A precipitous road snakes its way down the steep sides of St Levan's valley. One can walk into Treen and from there to some of the National Trust's beauty spots on this colourful coast – half a mile to Treen Cliff and the Logan Rock, a mile to Penbarth Cove. 'Logan' means 'moving' and this delicately balanced, 66-ton rock could be rocked with little effort until in 1824 a high-spirited young lieutenant pushed it right off its perch. He had to have it replaced, but it has never been quite the same since.

After miles of countryside Porthcurno took me by surprise, because one's first impression is of the overwhelming presence of the telecommunications industry, which has a training college and other enterprises in this remote spot. At Porthcurno the transatlantic cables enter the sea. But once the bus has parked (for motorists there was not one space left in the huge car park) it is easy to leave all that behind and wander down to the beach – one of the most remote in England, though only an hour from Penzance.

On this beautiful and romantic coast a circular open-air theatre – the Minack – has been carved out of the cliff top where once there was nothing but a depression filled with gorse. The theatre developed gradually over the last 50 years, but it is now superbly equipped. Stage and backdrop are of stone – or, rather, the backdrop is the sea and the sky, for the audience sits with its back to land. It is worth seeing even when no play is being performed.

The same bus service returned me to Newlyn, where a different scene awaited. This is a busy little town with quite a big harbour; a 'meadery' where one can eat as well as enjoy free samples of this very ancient Cornish wine made with honey (the name 'mead' comes from a Cornish word for honey); and fish warehouses at which great juggernauts from France call daily to load up with

154

lobsters. I walked from the bridge spanning the roadside stream as far as the church to find Harveys' warehouse and buy two very big crabs, freshly caught and cooked, for under £1 for the pair. Newlyn was the centre of a celebrated group of artists at the turn of the century, of whom Stanhope Forbes is the best known. They painted the harsh life of the fisherfolk and villagers as it really was in those days, and the quality of the Cornish light and water as it still is. I was lucky to find an exhibition of their works showing at the town's art gallery, collected together from all over the country for a few weeks. The Queen's Hotel always has examples on view.

Mousehole (pronounced Mouse'l), a few minutes away by bus, was called by Dylan Thomas 'the loveliest village in England', and there he spent his honeymoon. He stayed at the Lobster Pot, which is still a delightful spot to choose, its dining room hanging right over the harbour. Mousehole is less lovely than it used to be, because its popularity has brought too much traffic for its narrow and twisting streets – the bus driver's task was about as easy as squeezing toothpaste back into the tube, even though specially narrow buses are provided for the Mousehole service.

A good place to start exploring Mousehole is in the Penlee bar of the Old Coastguard Hotel, dedicated to the nearby Penlee lifeboat. Its walls are covered with mementos and photographs of the local lifeboat's work. The aerial pictures of ships breaking up or gone aground on this treacherous coast sent me back to the RNLI's collecting box in the bar. Britain is the only country in which such a heroic service is manned by volunteers and financed only by what the public gives to support it. Looking at these photographs of local storms, one understands why Mousehole's harbour is almost completely enclosed in granite walls with a gate to close off even its very narrow entrance when the weather is at its worst.

The village is picturesque. It has old cottages, almshouses, cobbled lanes, and an ancient inn with a porch hanging half across the road. From the Cornish Range I bought the tastiest (and cheapest) Cornish pasty yet and ate it sitting on the harbour steps, watching and trying to identify the different kinds of gulls – black-backed, herring, black-headed – and their youngsters, still in the brownish plumage of the first two or three years of life.

On the quay a table bore a collection of sea urchins. The absent diver who was offering them thus for sale (at far less than the shops) trusted one to put the money through the outsize keyhole of his front door, moneybox-style. Sea urchins, which seem to have been designed by the Almighty for the express purpose of making into lamps, are a relative of the starfish, covered when alive with 600 little plates bearing sharp spines that move this way and that as they browse on seaweed. The Cornish call them zarts, or mermaids' eggs.

It is worth the steep climb up the other side of Mousehole not only to see the spectacular view but to visit the bird sanctuary. The Yglesias sisters, having acquired a reputation for the care of injured wild birds, were brought so many that eventually their house and garden were turned into a hospital and convalescent home, particularly for seabirds and the crow family which flourishes in Penwith (magpies, ravens, jackdaws and so forth). Eventually the enterprise grew so big that the RSPCA stepped in to finance it for over twenty years. Then, a few years ago, this support was withdrawn. The sisters, by then in their 80s but undaunted, started a fund-raising campaign that allowed the bird sanctuary to survive – but only just. Its story has been told in a book by one of the sisters. Every year about 1,500 birds are treated, though only half can be given a new lease of life. Many are dying from oil spilled by tankers (after the *Torrey Canyon* disaster, 8,000 birds were brought here). Others have broken wings, broken legs or eye injuries. Some are choking on fish hooks. Orphaned chicks need feeding every half hour round the clock.

I walked through the old-fashioned garden of wallflowers, columbines and forget-me-nots to find a multitude of wire enclosures containing birds on their way to recovery and freedom. It was fascinating to see at close quarters wild sea birds such as divers, not to be found in zoos and too shy to encounter in the wild except through binoculars.

By the time I started on my homeward journey (back to St Ives via Penzance) it was milking time, and the bus had to wait for an unhurrying herd of cows in the lane ahead. The grass on the verges is evidently much sweeter than that of the fields, and the stone walls are ideal for scratching on – if you are a cow, that is – regardless of the Western National Bus Company's timetable. On the cows waddled, unflustered by the growing queue behind. It was pleasant to pause and enjoy the ivy trails on the walls, a solitary palm tree, primroses, violets and new little fronds of bracken bright among the grass: just a very ordinary Cornish evening.

14

A DICKENS TRAIL

*Gravesend – Cobham – Cooling – Higham – Chalk –
Strood – Rochester – Chatham*

A good choice of book to take when bussing about in Dickens
country would be *Great Expectations, Pickwick Papers* or *Edwin
Drood*. The last is particularly full of references to the area. This
part of Kent played a large part in Dickens' life. He spent his
childhood in Chatham (1816-21), honeymooned in Chalk (1836)
and died in Higham (1870). He wanted to be buried here rather
than in the glory of Westminster Abbey.

Gravesend he knew well, travelling regularly from its station to
London during the 1860s, but he had no great liking for it
('Muggleton' in *Pickwick Papers* was based on Gravesend),
though its waterfront inns, Town Pier restaurant, old fort,
covered market, lanes on Windmill Hill and church where the
Indian princess Pocahontas was buried in the 17th century are all
worth visiting (see Chapter 5). (The local library has produced a
leaflet on 'Dickens in Gravesham', the name for Gravesend and
its surroundings.)

Cobham

A bus from Gravesend takes only a half hour through a beautiful
area with fields of daffodils in spring to reach a village he liked
much more – Cobham, named after an ancient family. Here the
old, timbered Leather Bottle Inn is full of Dickens mementos. It,
too, appears in *Pickwick* along with the church (famous for its
brasses), adjoining medieval almshouses and the great park of
Cobham Hall, a Tudor mansion that is now a girls' school and is
sometimes open to the public.

A ¼-hour's ride back as far as Chalk enables one to pick up
another bus for a ¾-hour journey in the opposite direction

through very different scenery. Instead of woods, marshes stretch towards the North Sea on a little-frequented peninsula between the Thames and Medway estuaries. There are glimpses of ships passing or, in autumn, migrant wading birds arriving. The first chapter of *Great Expectations* describes this wild place:

> . . . Ours was the marsh country, down by the river, within, as the river wound, twenty miles of the sea. My first most vivid and broad impression of the identity of things seems to me to have been gained on a memorable raw afternoon towards evening . . . the dark flat wilderness intersected with dykes and mounds and gates, with scattered cattle feeding on it . . . the low leaden line beyond was the river . . . the distant savage lair from which the wind was rushing was the sea . . .

But in May the scene was different. At the start of the ride, after the domesticated gardens lay flat fields hedged with hawthorn or with long rows of towering poplars protecting the blossoming apple orchards from east winds off the North Sea. Some fields were green with wheat, others brilliant yellow (full of rape, grown for the oil-rich seeds). Ploughed, baked earth alternated with pastures where young lambs grazed. The honeyed smell of meadowsweet was in the air. There were scattered farmhouses, weatherboarded or tile-hung, some with handsome Georgian doors or windows. In every cottage garden wallflowers were growing abundantly.

At Higham the road crosses the railway, and alongside it are reeds and the vestiges of the canal that ran along there long before the railway was built in Dickens' time. The canal went through a long tunnel in the chalk hills and one can see its entrance still, with the railway line disappearing into it, below the brow of the hill where four oast-houses stand. Its purpose was to provide sailing barges with a short cut between the Thames and Medway estuaries, but tidal delays made it a longer route and so it fell into disuse.

Further on, towards the marshes, a great container ship seemed to slide among the fields (an optical illusion – the Thames on which it sails is hidden from view). Birds sing, butterflies flutter and there is a cloudless blue sky above the chalky tracks that lead off to the marshes. This is one of the few wildernesses left near London, though it is under constant threat of exploitation for oil refineries or even as a dumping ground for London's refuse. One has only to look across the Thames to what has happened to the Essex shore, a mass of chemical tanks, to see how serious a threat this is.

When Dickens took his long, solitary walks around this area, smock windmills were his landmarks – several dozen dotted the peninsula (one was still working until about 40 years ago). Now electric pylons stand out on the skyline.

Cliffe is a village of weatherboarded houses, much neglected, and a very splendid 13th-century church. Once, as its name suggests, it was on the edge of the estuary, but silt built up the miles of marshes that now separate it from the water.

Cooling

At Cooling (which has the spectacular, moated ruins of an ancient castle with a fine crenellated gateway) the road zigzags until it comes to the church and graveyard that inspired the dramatic opening to *Great Expectations*, where Pip is seized by the escaped convict. You can see the sad little row of a dozen tiny graves that were of Pip's brothers and sisters in the story. A church (probably the first was wooden) has been here since the 9th century, continuously used by worshippers until now. But, after a thousand years, the old building is now locked and unused.

The castle stands in an isolated spot which has, in fact, quite a history. Celts, Romans and Saxons in turn lived there. The village was then given to a relative of William the Conqueror, whose widow (described as the richest woman in England) later sold it to the Cobhams, a family of lawyers, in the middle of the 13th century. The Cobhams played an active part in state affairs and as a result were given permission to put up the moated castle in 1381.

It was in due course inherited by Joan Cobham, who married a Lollard leader, Sir John Oldcastle. He was executed in 1417 for his adherence to John Wyclif, and the local church was then forbidden by the Pope to hold services. But Puritanism lived on, and when Mary Tudor tried in 1553 to impose Catholicism again, Sir Thomas Wyatt (who was connected to the Cobhams by marriage) led a rebellion against her.

What happened to cause the partial demolition of the castle no one knows. Possibly Cromwell was responsible, for he certainly had a go at it in 1643 (the Cobhams had remained loyal to the crown). In the 18th century the castle was sold. The family who owned it by about 1760 were the Comports, who built a house within it (still there, but much altered), and Comport children lie in those tiny graves in the churchyard. Now it belongs to the trustees of Rochester Bridge and is leased to a private occupant.

The castle's turbulent history is now over. Roses ramble on its ragstone walls, there are bulrushes and water lilies in the moat, and rooks fly through the arrow slits.

159

(For anyone not in a hurry, the bus continues to High Halstow where there is a nature reserve containing Europe's biggest heronry, active in the spring. From High Halstow one can take a bus straight to Rochester, skipping Gad's Hill.

Chalk

Alternatively, take the bus back from the castle and get off at Forge Lane, Chalk, where the picturesque original of Jo Gargery's forge (Pip's early home) still stands, a tumbledown, weather-boarded cottage with yellow roses rambling above faded blue shutters. More disputably, a cottage nearby bears a plaque stating it is where Dickens spent his honeymoon (he wrote part of *Pickwick* while honeymooning in Chalk and the landlady of this cottage, Mrs Craddock, appears in the book); however, there is no conclusive proof.

Buses from Chalk to Rochester are frequent and quick. They pass by Dickens' last home, the 18th-century house at Higham called Gad's Hill Place (now a girls' school, not open to the public). It stands opposite the Falstaff Inn, where he used to take an active part in the local cricket club meetings (the inn has a very good buffet). A tunnel under the road, its entrances still just visible among the ivy, linked his front garden with another where for many years he had a big chalet sent to him in prefabricated parts by a Swiss admirer. In this he used to write, and that is what he was doing on the day he died. It can now be seen outside the Dickens Centre in Rochester.

Strood and Rochester

Go on through Strood (its old Crispin and Crispianus Inn, one of Dickens' favourite haunts, is described in *The Uncommercial Traveller*) and then over one of Rochester's triple bridges to alight and walk along the High Street, lined with old buildings, tearooms, inns, antique and bookshops. The Tourist Information Centre is there and, among much else, it has a leaflet explaining all the Dickens' place references to be seen in or near the High Street, such as:

Royal Victoria & Bull coaching inn (mentioned in *Pickwick* and
    Great Expectations)

Guildhall: 18th-century rooms and museum (*Great Expectations*)

Corn Exchange: spectacular clock (*Uncommercial Traveller*)

College Gate and Gatehouse tearooms (*Edwin Drood*)

Watts Charity: old hostel, sometimes open (*Seven Poor
    Travellers*)

Nos. 150-154 (Uncle Pumblechook's shop in *Great Expectations*)
The Dickens Centre: 15 rooms recreating scenes from the books
and from his life (the Nun's House in *Edwin Drood*)

The Norman castle and the Norman cathedral, Minor Canons
Row and what was once a monastery vineyard – all these occur in
Edwin Drood and other books. Many of the names Dickens used in
his stories can be deciphered on tombstones around the cathedral.
Restoration House (where Charles II stayed on his way back to
the throne) became Miss Havisham's house in *Great Expectations*.

Chatham

Rochester and Chatham are almost one now: a few minutes on a
bus and Chatham centre is reached. Dickens' father worked in the
old part of the naval dockyard on the river, where Nelson's *Victory*
had been built (guided tours on weekdays). The modest family
home at 11 Ordnance Terrace is still standing, near the railway
station (it may be turned into another Dickens museum), and
Fort Pitt fields is where the famous duel in *Pickwick* took place.
High over the town are the 'Great Lines' – walls, moats and
crumbling forts strung along the hills, mostly built during the
invasion scares of Napoleonic times.

There is much more to see in the Medway towns. Dickens
doubtless knew the Huguenot community (they have their own
square in Rochester still, called La Providence), the huge sailing
barges (once river cargo ships, a few dozen are now preserved and
sailed for pleasure or in races), the Tudor seamen's hospital
founded by Sir John Hawkins, and the summer shipboard 'court'
and cruise of the mayor.

Between May and August are held a Dickens festival, a
street fair, 'Navy Days' at the docks and a regatta. This is Royal
Engineers' country, too, and their museum at Brompton Barracks
on the edge of Chatham is far more interesting than most
regimental museums – with a splendid statue of General Gordon
on a betasselled camel outside. Threading through everything are
the winds of the Medway, semi-industrial but well worth a boat
trip (book at the Sun Inn).

The area is certainly worth an overnight stop, but it is not well
endowed with hotels. The friendly Cedar Hotel (near the Crispin
and Crispianus) is the nicest.

Note: As this book was going to press, I learned that the Cliffe –
Cooling – High Halstow service may be reduced in 1981. Check
with the East Kent Maidstone bus company.

15

IN APPLE-BLOSSOM TIME

Maidstone – Hadlow – Tonbridge – Tunbridge Wells
– Matfield – Maidstone

This is a journey for late springtime, but to be sure of doing it when the pink blossom is at its best, first phone the South Eastern Tourist Board (see Appendix B) to ask whether it is fully out yet. There are many possible routes. Mine took in historic towns, many pretty villages, and miles of orchards (and hop fields) in between. It can be done in a day but deserves two.

Maidstone

I started at Maidstone, where the remains of the 14th-century archbishop's palace and the church (one of the greatest and finest of that period) stand by the river among beautiful gardens. The archbishop's stables now house an impressive collection of historic carriages, well worth a visit, and the gatehouse contains a Tourist Information Centre which can provide details of much else, including river trips. From here there are two bus routes to Tunbridge Wells, each taking about 1¼ hours, so that one can go out one way and return another.

The bus that goes via Tonbridge at first runs through the Medway valley, with occasional glimpses of medieval church towers and an ancient bridge at West Farleigh. Mereworth is memorable for its church – an unusual one to find in the countryside, copied from 18th-century London churches (its steeple imitates that of St Martin's-in-the-Fields). Hadlow's landmark can be seen for miles: an octagonal Gothick 'folly' tower nearly 200 feet high, built by a landowner who used it (the story goes) to keep watch on his errant wife. In fact, it was built in 1838 by an eccentric called William May whose *folie de grandeur* expressed itself in this attempt to outdo Beckford's great tower at Fonthill. It is not as tall, but at least it is still there (Beckford's tower collapsed).

Hadlow

I stopped off at Hadlow to investigate further. Through an ornate arch, romantically creeper-covered like some haunted ruin from a Tennyson poem, one can walk into grounds where modern houses are discreetly hidden among the conifers and bamboos. The tower itself is now a home, too (a Danish artist lives there), and its florid pinnacles can be admired only from a discreet distance. Its great height dwarfs the simple tower of the nearby church, at the end of a picturesque cobbled lane (Church Road) and a brick path through the graveyard. Two very small boys were hunting for something among the sunlit tombstones. 'Have you seen God?' the younger one asked me. This was not out of concern for my soul, it turned out – they were taking literally the proclamation on the church notice board that 'He who seeks God will find him here'. What *can* be found there is the very elaborate mausoleum of William May, the folly-builder, sadly in need of rescue from weeds and decay. Parts of the church are Saxon. In its shady interior the scent of lilies hung heavily on the cool air as I wandered round followed by the two small boys, who were then debating the whereabouts of heaven.

Hadlow, though only 30 miles from London, is a country village still, with a history that goes back thousands of years. It was one of the first Stone Age settlements in Kent, and it claims to be the birthplace of the printer William Caxton. It has survived many changes and hazards (including bombs in the Second World War). As the bus moved on it passed first a derelict brewery and then a flourishing agricultural college – as one way of life passes, another arises.

Tonbridge

Tonbridge is an ancient town, but not particularly attractive now. The Saxons built a fortress on the mound by the river, and then the Normans used it for the same purpose. The ruins are medieval with the addition of an 18th-century mansion and attractive gardens. The High Street and Bordyke have a few timbered and Georgian buildings and down an alley is an old church said to have brilliant modern stained glass – but I found the door locked because of vandals. So was that of the chapel in Tonbridge School: the sundial outside says 'Keep innocency, Do the Thing that is Right', but the school authorities evidently put more faith in locks than in exhortations.

One can eat at inns or at The Winch; better still, picnic in the castle grounds or sit, as I did, by the river, watching a brood of 16 tiny fluffy ducklings paddling determinedly against the tide. A new block of offices has been designed with sensitivity to blend into the waterfront scene and there is a walkway beside the river.

Back on a bus and along a main road that rides high on a ridge, I found fine views. Agreeable, unassuming houses lead to a wide, tree-lined avenue that descends to Southborough. There are lacy iron verandahs above the shops and early Victorian houses set well back from the road. A minute later we were in Tunbridge Wells.

Tunbridge Wells

I made straight for my hotel, the Wellington, which is outside the centre and right by the famous Wellington Rocks on the common – an extraordinary formation, rounded yet craggy and deeply fissured. The hotel, full of portraits and mementos of the Duke, is all that one might expect of a Tunbridge Wells hotel in the grand Regency manner (though the bill was fortunately not equally grand): crimson velvet, solid mahogany, classical pillars and crystal chandeliers.

Early next morning I walked down into town across the common. The sunshine was on my face, birds were singing, dogs of every pedigree were taking their masters for walks. The white smoke trail of a plane bisected the clear blue sky, and the sun highlighted the fresh green of newly unfolded chestnut leaves.

Tunbridge Wells, all ups and downs, had its heyday as a spa in the 18th century. Between stately avenues, squares and crescents are intriguing tiled footpaths with picturesque cottages. The official guide includes a plan enabling one to thread a way through the town and hardly ever walk along a road. From the start many of the houses were built as visitors' lodgings, and there are still bed-and-breakfast rooms to be had in, for instance, picturesque Bedford Terrace, near the famous Pantiles where the therapeutic spring is.

The water from the cool spring tastes faintly rusty. It bubbles up into marble basins a few feet lower than the paving stones, and an attendant with a dipper fills a glass for you to sip as you view the Pantiles before setting off to window-shop there. Named for the red roof tiles originally used (in contrast to the rest of the slate-roofed town), the street is a pedestrian promenade sheltered by a row of trees down the middle and by a colonnade in front of small shops selling antiques, hand-made chocolates, leather goods, books and suchlike. Some shops have wrought ironwork, bay windows or weatherboarding above, with hanging lanterns or clocks. Steps go up and down; at a lower level are houses in fondant colours, Assembly Rooms where Victoria stayed while still a child-princess, a Corn Exchange topped by an overweight Ceres flourishing her sickle, and a muster of antique shops. 'Here health and social pleasures reign . . .' begins an 18th-century ode to the town. Both still do.

As the Stuarts were regular visitors to the Wells, it is not surprising that the parish church was dedicated to Charles I, martyr but not a saint. By comparison with most Kentish churches this is a parvenu – less than 300 years old – but a very handsome one; its elaborately domed and garlanded plaster ceiling is a work of art.

Both church and Pantiles lie at the south end of the High Street, which curves as it ascends north to Mount Pleasant Road, a wide shopping street with museum and Tourist Information Centre near the top. To the right lie the beautiful Calverley Gardens and Crescent Road, along which one is surprised by Calverley Park Crescent. Its houses have their plain backs facing the road, and only if one walks round to the other side is the almost Bath-like elegance of the crescent revealed: slender white columns supporting delicately railed verandahs, and pretty half-moon gardens. There were deep pink camellias blooming against a warm stone wall when I was there.

The journey back to Maidstone starts through a very green route, with mansions concealed behind high hedges of cypress, laurel or holly, drooping larches and thickets of venerable trees. The bus goes past the greens and almshouses of Pembury, on through ploughed fields, by oast houses and great barns, and past views of sheep grazing.

Matfield

I broke my journey at Matfield, tempted by the tables in the sunshine outside the Wheelwright's Arms, a pretty weatherboarded inn with roses climbing round the windows and hanging baskets of flowers at the timbered porches. Matfield has a huge green. I walked across it enjoying the smell of mown grass and the tiny daisies spangling the turf. A large fish suddenly leapt in the small pond.

Among many attractive houses fringing the green is a formal mansion, its date declared on the old rainwater heads as 1728. 'Mind the Time' warns the ornamental, one-handed clock above its stables – good advice when there is a bus to be caught – so I did not linger much longer by the cottages, the quaint butcher's shop or the Cherry Tree tearooms.

From here on the orchards multiplied, some with lambs under the trees, and the hop fields; with them the oast houses became more frequent, too – at Beltring there is a congregation of 30 in one group. We crossed one stream after another, rose high up for distant views and plunged down again. More barns, old wagons, white horses (there really do seem to be a great many white horses in Kent, and they are the county emblem, seen adorning village signs).

At Nettlestead Green one can buy English wine (and see grapes growing in late summer) at Cherry Hill Vineyard, which was the first one to start up (in 1966) since the Middle Ages.

The journey was nearing an end. After Teston there is a tranquil view of one of the Medway's lovely bridges, the sharp spike of a church spire announcing the village of Barming, and then within minutes the bus is into the environs of busy Maidstone. Yet even there spring and nature have their way: my last memory is of a bird nesting within the broken glass cover of a tall streetlamp – 'mod cons' preferable to the hazards of life in the wild?

16

1066 AND ALL THAT

*Eastbourne – Pevensey – Hastings – Battle – Ninfield
– Hailsham – Lewes – Eastbourne*

A day on the buses makes a change when, during a seaside family
holiday, swimming, sunbathing and sandcastles begin to lose
their appeal. Eastbourne is one of the pleasantest seaside resorts I
know (and comfortable York House Hotel, facing the sea, has a
particularly friendly staff and atmosphere). Eastbourne also has
the bonus of being on the coast where English history started – or,
at least, where most history books like to start – in 1066. So, for
the high spot of an Eastbourne holiday, I worked out a bus
trail following in the steps of the Normans, along the shore
and inland through the hills of the Sussex Weald. 'The
Fortifications of East Sussex', a well-illustrated booklet
published by the County Council, does much to bring alive the
battles of long ago.

Pevensey

Pevensey Bay, lined with miles of shingle, is only a few minutes by
bus from Eastbourne. The spot on this bay where William
beached his Norman ships and waded ashore that stormy
September is hard to recreate in one's imagination, for the bay is
now crowded with bungalows (and two Martello towers). In any
case, the shoreline has moved south over the centuries as the
Atlantic seas have piled silt on it, so it is better to stay on the bus. It
goes on to Pevensey Castle.

On landing William had found the remains of a ten-acre
Roman fort, the greatest of many built to keep the Saxon tribes
from landing 1600 years ago, and he made use of it. He dug ditches
inside the old walls as an additional defence for his camp. Later he
handed the place over to his brother to fortify properly with a

great keep. This castle – where the Roman walls, ditches and keep are still to be seen – continued in use right up to the Second World War. The remains of gun emplacements and lookouts, camouflaged to look like ruins, are still there.

The castle stands on a mound that was once virtually surrounded by sea (the '-ey' in Pevensey is Saxon for island). One can clearly imagine this when approaching by bus, for it stands up high above the land over which the bus runs (once sea where ships sailed). It looked dramatically bright when I saw it against a sombre, rain-laden sky, with the downs dark behind. Before the waters receded, a little port had grown up outside the castle, and some of its old buildings still survive – the 14th-century Mint House (the Normans started minting coins at Pevensey), the Court House and the 13th-century church. At the adjoining village of Westham is a church of even greater antiquity and grandeur, said to have been the first the Normans built in England.

The first part of the bus ride to Hastings is over clay marshes (they were under the sea in 1066) called the Pevensey Levels. The Haven river and the rippling drainage dykes were fringed with reeds; black-and-white Friesian cows grazed beside them as well as sheep that looked picture-book white because they were newly shorn. Calves scattered and ran at our approach, grass still hanging from their mouths. Graceful willows bordered the road until the bus got to the 15th-century Lamb Inn, climbed a hill with sea views and then entered the outskirts of Bexhill. This is the more attractive side of the town, and the bus travels along a surburban avenue where instead of hedges or fences there are roses all the way, their scent drifting into the bus. At Bexhill when the tide is low it is possible to see the remains of drowned forest exposed, a reminder that once land linked England with France. The further side of the resort is a boring suburb, but it is soon followed by St Leonards, where there are still many elegant streets from the 1820s when the town was first laid out (Warrior Square is particularly fine); it is virtually part of Hastings now.

Hastings

Hastings (described in Chapter 6) commemorates its place in the story of the Norman Conquest with a great 'Conqueror's Stone' by the pier. When William left Pevensey he marched to Hastings, and on its hilltop he erected a fort of prefabricated wooden parts shipped from Normandy. Later he had a stone castle built there, of which fragments still remain. It was not here, however, that the famous 'Battle of Hastings' took place but at Senlac (Norman for 'sandy lake') six miles inland, on a hill where King Harold had drawn up his foot soldiers to await the onslaught of the Norman cavalry. The place is now known as Battle. (Hastings commemorates the battle every October with torchlight processions and other junketings; a leaflet is obtainable from the town's information centre, 'Department 1066').

The Hastings castle remains (there is a lift up to them not far from the bus station) are impressive fragments of what was once a place of considerable pomp. The Norman kings used this, their first castle in England, whenever travelling between their two kingdoms in England and France. There was a church inside it and a college for priests of which Thomas Becket was once the dean. The mound on which it stood was created from the sandstone hewn out to make the flanking ditch – a massive task, depicted in the Bayeux tapestry.

That famous tapestry inspired another effort in recent years, by the Royal School of Needlework, whose 250-foot panorama of English history hangs in the town hall next to the bus station. While parents settle down to Tusker beer at the Town Crier pub next door, children may enjoy this vast picture strip, but I thought it a pity so much effort should not have had the benefit of a good artist to design the figures, choose less garish colours and give the faces more character. There is a good model of the Battle of Hastings showing exactly how the opposing armies encountered one another. The town hall itself is a piece of high Victoriana with stained glass, font-like plant containers and so forth. The outside adjoining the bus station is decorated high up with colourful panels depicting local history – and a couple of lively red devils.

Battle

The bus to Battle climbs out between verandahed and bay-windowed houses to a road with views across fields and into wooded valleys. I got off at the edge of Battle to lunch at the copper-topped bar of the ancient Chequers Inn, and then walked into the town centre along a road which has the abbey's immense, buttressed wall of stone on one side and pretty cottages on the other. Among these is the medieval house where, when Henry VIII broke up all the monasteries, the Abbot of Battle retired to live (it is now a bookshop). Nearby is the church which, among much else of interest, has an alabaster tomb on which the figures of Edward VI's tutor and his wife are gilded and painted in heraldic colours.

169

Battle Abbey was built by Benedictine monks from Normandy on the battle site. Although in ruins, the remaining stonework includes some fine examples of Norman craftsmanship. Not far off, the exact spot where King Harold died is marked by a monument presented by the French people in 1902; William himself commemorated his heroic enemy with a high altar on this spot, within a church that has long vanished. At what is now the Pilgrims' Rest restaurant monks used to dispense alms to poor travellers.

The town museum explains, with models, how the battle was fought. It also houses a replica of the Bayeux tapestry, in which can be found illustrations of horses being disembarked at Pevensey ('Pevensesae'), the fort being built at Hastings ('Hastenga'), and finally the death of Harold and flight of the English.

The museum also contains the historical bric-à-brac that gives most local museums their particular charm – as miscellaneous as a mighty axe head unearthed on the battlefield, deadly cock-fighting spurs and some 2oz coins that weighed heavy in the pocket in 1797. Worth two pence, they were almost immediately discontinued because their weight made them so unpopular.

Of more substance is the display explaining the Sussex iron industry, which flourished at many small sites in the Wealden forest from Roman times until 1820. One fine example of Sussex ironwork is a magnificent fireback in the old building that houses the Tourist Information Centre and a display of local crafts. The centre has a free leaflet about the town with the aid of which I found a footpath leading through fields at the back of the houses.

A punnet of strawberries added to the pleasure of the short ride into the hills of the Weald to Ninfield. Up and down went the road between beeches and sweet chestnuts and through a grove of huge rhododendrons in bloom. It was a beautiful route, winding this way and that, woodland alternating with golden fields of barley or occasional cottages with red roses splashed against white walls. Once or twice the skeleton fingers of a dead elm clawed at the sky, but in every other particular the countryside pulsed with life.

Ninfield

At Ninfield the need to change bus routes gave me time to stroll along an obscure path. Starting opposite the bus-stop, it led through woods and by hidden cottages to the modest church which has one or two unusual features – a minstrel's gallery and, below it, the mechanism of the clock on the weatherboarded turret above, ticking steadily away behind glass. Up in the turret is a solitary 14th-century bell, and in the churchyard a vast convoluted yew looks almost as old. The church road leads to a clump of Scots pines, their fircones strewn all over the ground. Beneath the tree is a rather odd example of Sussex ironwork: the village stocks has four leg holes, one very much bigger than the other three. Just here, William raised his standard on the eve of the great battle.

The road to Hailsham lies through a landscape of tranquil prosperity with great farms and barns, stone walls bearded with moss, ancient inns and weatherboarded cottages. The delphiniums stood as erect and blue as stained-glass saints, bracken was as high as the hedges and water lilies spread their waxy petals wide. Views were panoramic whenever the secret shades of the woodlands opened up: at this time of year, dense foliage screens much of what can be seen earlier. Many of the medieval houses along the way are now restaurants; the picturesque old forge was long ago turned (like so many others) into a garage when motors replaced horses.

The most interesting village on the way is Herstmonceux, a Norman name, and if you want a gardening basket, this is the place to buy one. Herstmonceux is the centre of traditional Sussex trug-making ('trog' is a Saxon word meaning boat), and the baskets are made of overlapping willow boards like a boat.

Hailsham

Guidebooks tend to dismiss Hailsham as dull, but there are some ancient buildings and distinguished shop fronts as well as a pleasant churchyard with brick-paved paths and an avenue of variegated hollies clipped into neat little lollipop trees. Hailsham, which has a great market of three acres, used also to have the doubtful distinction of making ropes for the hangman.

From there it is a short run back to Eastbourne. However, anyone who preferred to stay overnight at Hailsham could go direct from there to Lewes next day. (This ride takes one through rich farmland and across streams, with views from its highest point across to Firle Beacon, a 700-foot landmark on the South Downs. Time and energy permitting, Ringmer's church is worth a visit. On the way to it is a tortoise, embodied in the village sign, known as Timothy; his mortal remains are now in London's Natural History Museum. Timothy belonged to the aunt of the naturalist Gilbert White, who wrote about him in his *Natural*

171

I returned to Eastbourne for the night, bussing along roads with verges 'painted all with variable flowers' and past attractive small houses, patches of woodland or open country. Polegate's windmill peeps over the top of suburban bungalows and their trim gardens, with Combe Hill (once an Iron Age stronghold) beyond; within minutes Eastbourne is in view again.

Next day I went to Lewes via Newhaven. This is one of the most beautiful bus routes I have found, and a double-decker gives one a superb view. The bus climbed out of Eastbourne between attractive old and not-so-old houses, flint walls and timbered inns (Eastbourne's excellent little art gallery lies on this road, set in a pretty garden, and the old church). Ahead lay the wooded downs, densely green as spinach purée, except where a chalk cliff stood out stark white. Ash and sycamore tapped at the windows, through which the fresh morning breeze streamed in. Looking backwards, I saw the great bay far off and bright as silver, with the golf course forming a bowl of shaven turf between it and the road.

Across vast acres of windswept wheat and barley the view receded into a far blue distance. Villages came and went, with flint walls and leafy lanes, until we reached one of England's beauty spots – the broad valley of the river Cuckmere, which glides in lazy S-bends through the water meadows. It is wide, shallow and brilliantly blue, with cows dozing on its banks.

Onward the hedges were full of flowers, and poppies brightened the cornfields until, past Seaford, the once salty marshes heralded our approach to Newhaven. Soon its ships came into view. The tide was out leaving only a thin brown current in the estuary, and on the great timber posts in its banks the brown bladderwrack hung like frilly knickers.

The bus to Lewes goes inland from here, not from the town centre, travelling through the big level valley which the river Ouse has carved out between the hills – a region of marshland drained by brooks and dykes. It was in this river that Virginia Woolf (who lived at Rodmell) drowned. The wind was now very lively and people were struggling against it, heads down or clutching their hats. Even the gulls were battling hard, up among the splendid scenery of the sky.

Lewes

After William was crowned he rapidly started building castles to keep his conquered subjects under control and his continental enemies out. The English had seen nothing like them before –

immense stone structures, almost impregnable. He allowed his nobles to build their own castles, too, in return for pledging their service to him. The usual plan involved an outer wall enclosing a bailey (courtyard) filled with huts where the garrison lived and where animals could be kept in time of siege, with a tall keep on a mound in the middle (the lord's dwelling place) into which all could retreat if the outer walls were breached by an enemy. There was such a castle at Eastbourne but it has vanished.

The one at Lewes, a very early example, still stands, built to an unusual design with two mounds and keeps. (The mounds were built from blocks of chalk). Outside the wall of the bailey a great, dry moat was added, with a sturdy gatehouse to protect the entrance. Houses soon clustered around the castle and, in the 13th century, these too were enclosed within town walls of which fragments remain on the west side. From the battlements of the one remaining keep is a view down into the old lanes and twittens (alleys) or across to the Downs, the sea, chalk pits and a memorial to Protestant martyrs burnt at the stake in Lewes on Mary Tudor's orders. Lewes to this day celebrates Guy Fawkes Day with anti-Papist demonstrations.

William's son-in-law Warenne sited the castle to protect a strategic gap in the South Downs through which the River Ouse passes. At the same time he built St Anne's Church and a priory (which, like Battle Abbey, was later demolished on the orders of Henry VIII). Its ruins can still be seen (walk down cobbled Keere Street), and its hospitium, a hostel for travellers, is now a church in which Warenne and the Conqueror's daughter are buried. It stands in Southover High Street, one of the most attractive streets in Lewes, which also contains a museum of Sussex crafts, particularly ironwork (Sussex trees fed the iron furnaces of England centuries before the coke-smelters of the north took over). The museum is in a timbered house that once belonged to Anne of Cleves, fourth wife of Henry VIII. Southover Grange, where the diarist John Evelyn grew up, has pleasant gardens open to the public. Back towards the bus station and over the river just beyond it lies Cliffe High Street, with quaint timbered houses overhanging the narrow road and Harvey's, the local brewery.

The return from Lewes to Eastbourne on an express bus follows an attractive route through an area of outstanding natural beauty. The bus lumbers out through narrow streets with flint walls and houses that are half-timbered, weatherboarded or faced with coloured stucco; it passes over the river and near the old brewery. Then comes a vast panorama of meadows and hills. We passed flint barns, monumental oaks, briar roses and honeysuckle in hedges, as well as cottage gardens thronged with lupins, a river (the Cuckmere again) with yellow water lilies and ducks swimming softly down, and Windover Hill, rising high. If you change buses at Polegate, this gives a chance to visit the milling museum in the 1817 windmill, two sails of which dropped off one day (narrowly missing me!). They're back on again now, rather more securely fixed. And so to Eastbourne once again.

17

THE LAKE DISTRICT

Windermere – Wrynose Pass – Hardknott Pass –
Coniston – Windermere

The Lake District and its bus services are unique. Strictly speaking, the area would be better called the Mountain District for, huge and numerous though the lakes are, the mountains take up most of the space. Necessarily, therefore, roads are relatively few, but buses run on virtually all of them. This means you can go almost anywhere by bus – along lake shores, through valleys and up mountain passes. There is one private bus company which even goes up and down gradients that make some car drivers blench. And just about every one of these roads has spectacular views: no one need depend on advice about which bus service to pick for a scenic ride, as all are good.

The Lake District surely needs no description here; its beauties are world-famous. Of all our National Parks it is the most outstanding, but this naturally brings tourists by the million. The many walkers soon disperse into the hills, but in July and August car drivers can be a menace when they crowd the narrow lanes and little towns. It's not much fun for them, either: stone walls and 'no parking' signs prevent them from pausing where they wish. The case for bussing about is therefore a particularly strong one in this area.

Anyone planning to bus in the Lake District may well find that their hotel or hostel has an excellent binder called 'How to Explore the Lake District without a Car', which has been supplied by a local group of the Friends of the Earth. In it will be all you need in the way of bus maps, details of cheap-rate tickets, timetables and much else. Libraries and National Trust information centres also have these binders. (Incidentally, Friends of the Earth tell me that the best base from which to go bussing is Ambleside, followed by Windermere, Grasmere and Keswick in that order.)

If, however, you need to assemble all these useful things for yourself, here is a list of what to obtain. First of all, get bus timetables and route maps from the two major bus companies in the Lake District (Ribble and Cumberland; for addresses see Appendix A). There is also a private company called Mountain Goat which runs some very unusual services. Its minibuses, run on propane gas not petrol, can get to all sorts of places high up in the mountains (one of these journeys is described later in this chapter). The little seats are not comfortable for the long of leg or the broad of bottom, but some of the routes are so exceptional that it is worth putting up with this for a couple of hours or so. Some Mountain Goat buses run on regular routes (timetables are available from the company at Victoria Street, Windermere); others do special excursions, details of which are also obtainable. It is necessary to book seats on their buses.

The local Friends of the Earth (3 Wansfell Holme, Windermere) can send you a typed outline for a day's bussing between Kendal and Keswick. They have worked out a programme which shows how stretches of riding on a Ribble bus can alternate with a trip on a lake steamer, dropping in on one or another of Wordsworth's homes, or a visit to Brockhole (this is a 'must' early in any Lake District holiday, for it is a first-rate centre which illuminates the history, wildlife, recreations and every other aspect of the district).

The Friends of the Earth have another sheet called 'In the Steps of Wordsworth' which gives details of how to get to most of the places associated with the poet, using buses (with or without occasional walks at some points). The routes pass through particularly fine scenery.

Then there is the Fellrunner, a bus manned by volunteers. It goes from Penrith to villages in the very lovely Eden Valley – different routes on different days. (Details are available from Mrs G. Beitch at 5 Salkeld Road, Langwathby.)

One really vital bit of paper to acquire is the public transport map published by the Lake District National Park (Bank House, High Street, Windermere), which shows the routes of all the buses so far mentioned, one or two others belonging to very small firms, and the Post Buses (see Chapter 19). The map also shows rail and boat services that connect with the buses.

Finally, 'Explore Cumbrian Heritage' is a booklet produced in conjunction with the National Trust, illustrating and describing stately homes and other sights accessible by bus, with times of buses that go to them. (This is obtainable from the Ribble or Cumberland bus companies.)

Where accommodation is concerned the Lake District offers a bewildering choice, from dozens of youth hostels to really luxurious hotels. Like all tourist boards, the Cumbria Tourist Board (see Appendix B) has a 'Where to Stay' book that lists hundreds of alternatives.

Alternatively (and this is what I did) one can find a room in a carefully chosen farmhouse through Sue Butcher's farm booking service (her address is Littlewood Farm, Staveley, Kendal). Ask for her list of farmhouses on bus routes. I had a very pleasant few days at 17th-century Natland Mill Beck dairy farm, Kendal, where for a few pounds I had an almost luxurious room with 300-year-old built-in cupboards and an electric blanket (the best of ancient and modern), log fire, colour TV and delicious breakfasts with home-made bread.

I went to the Lake District in June–perhaps not the best time, for the daffodils that inspired Wordsworth start in late March (phone Windermere 4444 to find out when and where to see them), while it is not until October that the spectacular russet bracken colours the hills. Nevertheless, June anywhere has great charm. It is the month of briar roses, strawberries, cream teas and village fêtes; of new-mown hay and new-shorn sheep looking oddly skinny; of foals and calves, ducklings and cygnets; of poppies in corn, dog-daisies on the banks, and honeysuckle in hedges. Thistledown is idly afloat and industrious bees are on the wing. 'The fields breathe sweet' in June, and it is a good time to travel about (even if wind and water are frisky and the sun coquettish) because it falls between the May bank holiday rush and the July-August school holiday pressures.

This, above all months, is one in which to take picnics and a pocket-sized book to identify wildflowers (see 'Bookshelf'), particularly in the Lake District where so many grow. When bussing about, it is the easiest thing to ask the driver to drop you off in any pretty area you see and then to hail a later bus as it comes by (not the kind of liberty you can take with a coach or a train).

June can, however, turn showery – though usually not for long – and in any mountainous area a pocket mac is necessary. Inside the Mountain Goat minibus we were snug enough, however, and what started as a grey day brightened later.

Windermere

The little bus set out from Windermere through a road fringed with larches and rowans, past Brockhole and the Stagshaw Gardens of the National Trust and past cows grazing among the ruins of a Roman fort. Houses were of grey stone with slate roofs or else whitewashed; over dry-stone walls, velvety with moss, hung clusters of elderflowers or the ruby trusses of rhododendrons. Through water meadows a shallow river wound its stony way and every so often the soft turf was thrust aside by rocky outcrops or rose up in mounds where the glaciers of the Ice Age had deposited their debris. This is a landscape of immense antiquity. We passed a slate factory, where great slabs – green or blue-grey – waited to be sliced in an old bobbin mill no longer needed by the once thriving woollen industry. The mill got its power from water, and just beyond can be seen the foaming source of that energy, Skelwith Force.

As we climbed into the hills roving sheep watched us curiously – the Jacobs, with multiple horns and black-and-white fleece, and the dark, shaggy Herdwicks, an oddity for they have fewer ribs than other sheep and are unique in their willingness to eat bracken. John Peel's 'coat so grey' (*not* gay) was made of Herdwick wool, and he hunted among these mountains.

Jack, our driver, paused beyond the gunpowder mill, now a hotel, to let us see . . . a sewage works. Or rather, to not-see it, for the whole point is that clever landscaping completely conceals what might have been an eyesore. Jack was a connoisseur of sewage works: 'There's another very nice one at Grasmere', he told us with relish. Even new buildings have to be faced with local stone to preserve the integrity of lakeland architecture, and a brick house is a rarity.

The bus toiled upwards. Beech trees met overhead, tiny ferns sprouted from the walls and foxgloves thronged the verges. Beyond the Three Shires Inn a pillar stands where once Lancashire met Cumberland and Westmorland (before bureaucracy erased the ancient boundaries). There was a tarn fringed with yellow irises, and pied wagtails flicked their tails nearby. Tarn is a Norse word for a pool; when the Viking raiders settled in Cumbria they brought their own vocabulary, and it still lives on in local place names such as thwaite for clearing, beck for stream, gill for ravine and so on.

Wrynose Pass

'Extreme caution' warned a road sign; we were entering Wrynose

Pass. Jack pointed up to a distant spot, once a Stone Age factory with a thriving export trade. There immense numbers of stone axe heads were hewn, taken to the seashore to be polished with sand and then bartered with traders from Normandy. The huge heaps of spoil up there show that the craftsmen operated a very strict quality-control system.

The mountain got steeper, its rocky side deeply grooved by a swift, silver thread of a stream rushing this way and that. Elsewhere more water spread wide like a shimmering cloak over great boulders. Here were fell sheep, black-faced and horned. Looking back, I saw that tarn again – but by this time it was just a bright dewdrop lying within the green bowl of hills far below us.

As we went still higher, the vegetation changed. White cotton-flowers and reeds grew in the boggy ground and lichen crusted the rocks. Clouds floated serenely behind a grimly jagged skyline. Far down, clumps of trees looked like mere tufts of moss, and the road we had just traversed was no more than a thin cord of brown idly dropped by some giant hand on a green velvet cloth. The tarn, perpetually changing, was a sliver of cold steel.

At last we reached the top, a place of wilderness and beauty. But was it unspoilt? Hardly. Some lout had discarded a cola tin and sweet packet in one of the little streams and, as if that were not enough, suddenly a TV crew arrived to film some publicity stunt of the Mountain Goat company. The lovely solitude was ravaged.

Hardknott Pass

Our bus pressed onward and down. Ahead of us lay a great valley, with road and river zigzagging through it like a couple stepping out some complicated dance together. This led us to Hardknott Pass, a 1-in-3 gradient with acute bends all the way – the shortest, steepest pass in all Europe. Cars regularly get stuck there, and even Jack (not helped by a cow ambling in front) ground to a halt, backed down and took a fresh run up. A sheep gazed in amazement at our performance while within the bus there was general sympathy for the laden, armoured legionaries who once marched this way – for beyond lies a Roman fort that is one of the most outstanding sites in Roman Britain, not just unusually well preserved but in a commanding position with magnificent views (someone called it a fortress in the air). Built in the time of Emperor Hadrian (of the Wall), the garrison consisted of Slavs who comforted themselves in this chilly exile with hot baths and central heating – the bath house is still there to be seen.

The head of the pass is a good place for a break. I sat by a tiny rivulet almost hidden in the wiry grass, watching a water boatman skim the surface and the pebbles shining bright below the little trickle. I could see the source of the small stream high in the mountain above me and follow its course for miles down below me, as it wound its way to a river and thus to a far distant ocean. A marvellous landscape: rocks jagged and fissured, lichen almost fluorescent green and bracken luxuriant.

All the way down were hairpin bends, leading to Eskdale and more pastoral scenes with buttercups, speedwell and foxgloves; there were wagtails again, birch trees, whitewashed farms and a group of back-packing youth-hostellers. Up in the hillside is a huge red scar where once iron was mined and railroaded to the coast (the old line is still there, with steam locomotives now pulling carriages of tourists).

Coniston

The journey continued up and down all the way through crags and bracken, a panorama of great peaks. Sheep were not yet sheared, their fleeces hanging shaggy and beginning to fall off naturally. The River Ulpha was strewn with mighty boulders and walls were made of colossal stones. A great slide of 'spoil' spilled down where once slate used to be quarried. Humpback stone bridges were succeeded by picturesque cottages with honey-suckle growing up their stone walls and lanes pink with foxgloves, briar roses and campion. We had a god-like view (backwards and down) of the immense sands of Morecambe Bay, miles away, and another of dense, sombre Drysdale Forest (far ahead and high up). There were a few patches of early heather brightening the roadside and then Coniston's shining surface came into view with cottages that still have the old spinning galleries once common in lakeland, and a slate memorial to Donald Campbell who died while attempting to make a new water-speed record on the lake. We made a brief pause to see the now celebrated *Gondola* steamboat, 120 years old (rescued by the National Trust from a watery grave and restored to all her former glory with bright paint and gilt), and so we returned to our starting point at Windermere. Of all the bus rides in this book, this was one of the most memorable, and it was made even more interesting by Hunter Davies' lively paperback *A Walk Around the Lakes* (Hamlyn). Even he took buses occasionally. He quotes another walker, Alfred Wainwright (whose fell-walkers' guides are now internationally famous): 'The slower the bus the better I like it. There's nothing more restful than a stopping bus.'

18

REAL ALE TRAIL
YORKSHIRE DALES

Skipton – Grassington – Aysgarth – Hawes – Richmond

There is no breathalyzer to face after drinking if your transport is a bus, and as CAMRA (the Campaign for Real Ale) publishes a *Good Beer Guide* describing hundreds of pubs where real ales are to be found, this makes the planning of a day's inn-to-inn bus route pretty simple. (CAMRA's address is 34 Alma Road, St Albans, Herts.) Most of its 150 local branches publish guides to their own areas, though some are more informative than others.

CAMRA has made a lot of headway in its efforts to persuade publicans to stock beers made by the traditional methods and not just mass-produced keg beer.

CAMRA defines real ale as beer which (after being brewed from unadulterated hops, malted barley and yeast) is kept in vented casks in the pub's cellar and dispensed by means of a tap or pump, not by gas pressure. Some is made by the big companies but most is from small local breweries distributing only within their own neighbourhood. This makes the exploring of unfamiliar territory particularly interesting for real ale enthusiasts.

Yorkshire is one county that has always taken its beer seriously, and here a 'real ale trail' through areas of scenic beauty is full of scope. In addition to the normal opening hours (see end of this chapter), pubs in towns with markets often stay open throughout the afternoon on market days. The local branches of CAMRA have combined to produce an excellent guide to North Yorkshire inns, and with its help I picked a Sunday route for early summer through the Dales National Park starting at Skipton (easily reached from Manchester, Bradford or Leeds, for example) and going up Wharfedale to Hawes in Wensleydale and thence through Swaledale to Richmond (from which it is not difficult to get back by bus via Scotch Corner to Leeds again). So combined with travelling through three of the loveliest dales and passing some very attractive villages, one has a choice of more local ales than could possibly be sampled, allowing for the limitations of opening hours as well as one's own physical capacity. But avoid high summer and bank holidays, when crowds are attracted to the Dales, and winter or weekdays when some of the buses do not run.

The scenery is very varied – luxuriant grass, dry-stone walls, picturesque woodlands, turbulent streams and waterfalls (often aptly named 'forces'), rolling hills in front of rolling clouds, grey stone cottages, vivid village greens, gaunt crags and zigzagging ascents and descents. Wildness, isolation and drama contrast with the charm and dignity of gentler slopes with dairy farms.

Skipton

Skipton has long been the centre of the southern Dales, for coaching roads and canal met there. Some medieval buildings still survive the ravages of progress, including Lord Clifford's castle (which is completely intact, with parts still inhabited) and the church which has an outstanding roof and rood-screen. Market stalls are set up in the broad High Street on most days, and old wharves and warehouses line the canal banks. In the corn mill folk museum, working exhibits recreate the occupations of the past. Look out for Stainforth's Celebrated Pork Pie Shop, canal boat trips and many interesting little shops through archways or up alleys – especially near the mill bridge by the church. A good place to stay overnight is the Unicorn Inn, an old beer house by the bus depot which has been beautifully converted into elegant bedrooms with every comfort (colour TV, sofa, tea-making and so forth); not far from it are good restaurants and the Craven bookshop (with very modest prices).

The River Wharfe and its dale are claimed to be the most beautiful in England. Leaving Skipton, we soon overtook a bright-coloured throng of cyclists, legs going like pistons up the hill, and climbed higher towards a bright blue sky. The sun shining through the sycamores made a lively pattern on the road. In the fields bales of hay were stacked, and Swaledale sheep (black-faced and curly-horned) and shaggy, long-horned cattle watched us go by. The wet summer, which had meant late (or lost) harvests, had also made the grass richly green.

Early in the journey we passed pretty Cracoe (a small forest of red-hot pokers peeping above mossy dry-stone walls). Then came one of the loveliest villages anywhere, peaceful Linton, which has both a packhorse bridge and a clapper bridge (made of huge slabs of stone) over the stream that runs right through it, as well as a picturesque inn smothered in yellow roses and Nelly Moser clematis. Linton's big surprise is Fountaine's Hospital, almshouses designed in the grand manner by Vanbrugh in 1720 with cupola, pediments and urns.

Grassington

Next was Grassington, built around a tiny cobbled square on a hillside. It is a prosperous little town with good shops, a folk museum in a cottage, tearoom with crackling fire, and alleyways gay with flowers. This was a good place at which to take a break, where the beauty of the river contrasts with the stark hills around and every cottage is bright with pansies, petunias, lobelias or marigolds.

Even on Sundays some shops stay open, including that of 'the toffee smith' who should surely be in *The Guinness Book of Records* for the variety of toffee he makes. I also found the blacksmith at work and, on sale, pebbles beautifully painted with birds – his blacksmith-son is a gifted wildlife artist in his spare time. Opposite the bus depot is a National Park information centre with many useful booklets that interpret all there is to see in the Dales.

The view along the road through the hills is beautiful whichever way you look. Far off are blue mountains, a changing cloudscape, a patchwork of fields (green, yellow and gold) and rugged heights. Nearby the verges are blue with cranesbills or yellow with buttercups. Slatey stones thrust through turf, mullioned windows decorate old stone houses and the river is wide, shallow and clear. As we pressed on, the bus overtook a white-haired couple pedalling steadily on a tandem bicycle and two young back-packers with a collie.

We drove by a trout farm and then almost underneath the overhanging Kilnsey Crag, a gaunt grey challenge to rock-climbers (though they are discouraged from climbing when buses are passing beneath the crag). A stream was bright with yellow-and white-flowered water plants. We went on to pretty Kettlewell with its old stone bridge and grey houses, and then the road left the river and began to climb beyond Buckden, beautifully sited and with panoramic views along the way. Picturesque white-washed inns, great stone barns, waterfalls and rocky outcrops added variety to the scene, and through the window occasionally came pleasant country smells of hay, catmint, wild aniseed or wild garlic.

Aysgarth

At the head of the dale, where the descent begins, is a tremendous expanse stretching gently downward to Aysgarth. It is worth getting off before the bus enters the village (alight at Palmer Flatt Hotel) to walk down to the 400-year-old Aysgarth bridge and the famous series of waterfalls – shallow cataracts that are very beautiful (especially after a wet season). The water cascades in a white, roaring froth, forming pools and eddies among which young men in thighboots perch (with their fishing rods) on midstream rocks of pinkish stone tinged green by algae. A solitary tern swooped to compete with them for any fish that might have been going.

Nearby is a carriage museum in an old textile mill, and further on is another National Park interpretation centre, housed in what were once railway buildings. The disused track (on an embankment) makes a pleasant walk with an 'Aysgarth Trail' leaflet (not very well designed) to explain the distinctive scenery. The basic rock of the Dales is 300 million years old. Seas covered it and left deposits that became softer rocks of various kinds which eroded or weathered away at different rates. That is why there is such a great variety of landscape, soil and vegetation. Humans have added their variations: small fields are of medieval origin, large ones date from the time of the 18th-century enclosures of common grazing lands. Even the dry-stone walls vary in pattern, as do the shapes of the stone stiles set into them, though all are made on a similar principle – that is, two inward-sloping walls of big, carefully chosen stones (no cement), with rubble sandwiched in between, and a lid of large flat stones on top to bind both walls together and keep the rain out. Wire fences didn't come in until about a century ago; fortunately, the National Park authorities have seen to it that within their boundaries these have not ousted the old craft of dry-stone walling. The old wooden five-bar gates are vanishing though, for most are too narrow to admit modern farm machines. Even their first successors, of strip metal, are now 'antiques', for gates of cheap tubular metal have in turn superseded them.

The onward bus follows a road that rises and falls, with exceptional views at every turn. As it continues uphill it passes through Bainbridge, a village around a big green (complete with stocks), where the river flows down over flat steps of rock.

Throughout the winter a horn is sounded at 9 pm to guide any traveller lost in the fells. The sunny morning had given way to a grey, misty afternoon with ominously dark clouds, a hint of how necessary that horn might be on a really bad night.

Hawes

Finally we reached Hawes, where the famous Wensleydale cheese is made (a perfect complement to Yorkshire ale), where sheep are brought to market, and where back-packing ramblers stride in from their marathon treks along the Pennine Way. This is now the highest market town in England. A cascade rushes among its streets of stone houses at one end of the town and Hardraw Force, the highest waterfall in the country, is about 1¼ miles' walk away. I was told that you get to it through the Green Dragon inn and can walk right behind the 100-foot fall of water (or clamber up and wade across the top of it). In Hawes itself you can watch rope being made, or read on the wall of a cottage dated 1668 the confident stone inscription, 'God being with us, who can be against us'.

The next ride is one which the local bus company considers its *pièce de résistance*, ideal on a summer evening. From Hawes the bus does a swift ascent to mountaineer its way through the Buttertubs Pass to get from Wensleydale to Swaledale. Some of this spectacular moorland road runs at a 1-in-4 gradient, passing through a gorge and then narrowing and zigzagging as it descends. There is an alpine tang to the air. The 'buttertubs' are seven curiously shaped holes in the limestone rock by the roadside, some of them 100 feet deep.

Beyond lies the very pretty village of Thwaite. Then comes tiny Keld, a lovely stone village among the hills right at the head of Swaledale.

Keld, once a Viking settlement, is a place of tiny, narrow lanes lined with foxgloves and bracken. There the bus turns back and retraces its route through Thwaite. In peaceful Thwaite, however, the biggest traffic jam in the Dales had built up. Two herds of sheep were being driven in for shearing. Shepherds in gumboots and cloth caps waved their sticks and shouted; sheepdogs ran hither and yon; the sheep bawled their indignation. We waited – and waited. Eventually the mêlée sorted itself out.

The road zigzagged down to Gunnerside, at the foot of a gorge, which has views of old lead mines (their tracks and tips) on the steep hills. All along this route the river Swale ripples or cascades its way down the rugged dale – so very different a valley from Wensleydale and the road keeps crossing and recrossing it by old stone bridges.

The final stretch lay through woodland and fields, with a great ridge ahead on which trees clung precariously to the vertical rock face. The road wound its way through a glade with the occasional glint of water from the river Swale still faithfully running nearly alongside the road.

Richmond

The end of the journey was Richmond, a town of great charm built on a rock which is almost surrounded by a loop of the Swale. Curfew is still rung each night at 8 pm.

I stayed at the quiet Frenchgate Hotel, where the rooms and garden are pretty and the food good.

A Norman castle perches on a sheer precipice and in the town below is the second oldest theatre in England, built in 1788 and still in use. Altogether Richmond is outstanding among small towns – cobbled Georgian streets, twisting wynds (alleys), old inns, interesting shops, the largest cobbled market square in the country (with a church and an enormous 18th-century obelisk in the middle) – a place in which to linger. The Green Howards have their regimental museum in this church (the parish church is outside the town walls); horse races are held on a course two centuries old; and within easy walking distance are the ruins of Easby Abbey in a beautiful riverside setting.

The houses are made either of rugged limestone, hard and rough-textured, or of sandstone which, being softer, can be sawn smooth and fine. Some sandstone slabbed roofs remain but often the weight brought collapse, so a variety of lighter tiles or slates replaced them including rippling pantiles, originally from Holland.

An excellent local booklet called 'A Look at Richmond' explains as much as one wants to know about the architecture and history. The best walk of all was at the foot of the castle, where a path winds round high above the river foaming noisily below, under a lovely Georgian bridge and over stones (riverbed pebbles were used to cobble the market square). Out of the massive stones that make the castle walls, looming dizzily above, grew more than a dozen self-seeded country flowers. Seats are placed in angles of the walls to catch the morning sun, and there I sat to enjoy the view, the wildflowers and the activities of a curlew and other birds.

As to the ale-tasting aspect of the tour, there is no shortage of good inns at which to pause along the way and sample the local brews, many of them CAMRA-approved. Taylor's (a small family firm) produces distinctively hoppy milds and bitters. Cameron's make a bitter described as 'one of Britain's great beers', as well as the heavier Strongarm. Tetley's bitter or dark mild are widely sold. Theakston's have made a reputation with Old Pekulier, strong and sweet, but they brew a light mild, too. Webster's sweetish bitter and hoppy mild are recommended. Marston's bitter has supporters, but it is not to everyone's liking. Finally, there is strong Bass from Burton (CAMRA don't recommend the Tadcaster Bass).

I am indebted to CAMRA for help in compiling the following list of recommended inns.

Skipton

(11 am-3 pm, 5.30-10.30 or 11 pm on Friday and Saturday, and in summer. Open till 4 pm on Mondays, farmers' day)

Of the ten CAMRA-approved drinking places, here is a selection:

Black Horse 17th-century building, its yard now a market. (Taylor and Younger) Meals, snacks.
Devonshire Vaults Under 18th-century hotel. (Tetley)
Castle Inn Stone pub by castle. (Tetley) Outdoor drinking, snacks.
Chew's Bar One room, with fire. (Bass) Snacks.
Craven Heifer On road to Grassington. Open fire, farm pub. (Bass) Outdoor drinking, snacks.

Cracoe

(Hours as for Skipton, no farmers' day)

Devonshire Arms Stone floors. (Younger) Snacks.

Grassington

(11 am-3 pm, 5.30-10.30 or 11 pm on Friday and Saturday, and in summer)

Black Horse (Theakston) Outdoor drinking.
Foresters' Arms (Tetley) Snacks.

Kettlewell

(Hours as for Grassington)

Bluebell Hotel Old stone building. (Theakston) Meals, snacks.

Buckden

(Hours as for Grassington)

Buck Inn 18th-century hotel. (Theakston, Younger) Meals, snacks.

Thoralby

(11 am-3 pm, 6-10.30 or 11 pm on Friday and Saturday)

George Inn Georgian. (Webster) Snacks.

West Burton

(11 am-3 pm, 5.30-10.30 or 11 pm on Friday and Saturday)

Fox and Hounds Typical village pub. (Cameron) Snacks.

Hawes

(11 am-3 pm, 5.30-10.30 or 11 pm on Friday and Saturday. Open all afternoon on Tuesdays, market day)

Board Hotel (Marston) Outdoor drinking.
Crown (Theakston) Outdoor drinking.
Fountain Hotel (Theakston) Meals, snacks.

Gunnerside

(11 am-3 pm, 6-10.30 or 11 pm on Friday and Saturday)

King's Head Small bar with hand pumps. (Cameron)

Richmond

(11 am-3 pm, 6-10.30 or 11 pm on Friday and Saturday)

Bishop Blaize Hotel (Cameron) Snacks.
Buck Inn (Bass) Snacks.
Holly Hill Stone pub, beamed interior, ales from jug.
  (Theakston) Snacks, outdoor drinking.
Turf Hotel Georgian inn, racing connection. (Bass) Snacks.

MORE ABOUT THE DALES

The three dales I travelled through on this journey are only a
sample. (I did the whole trip one Sunday but wished I had spent at

least two or three days over it.) There are all the other dales, too, and the West Yorkshire Road Car Company (see Appendix A) has a 'Dales Bus' folder describing some of the possibilities – including alternating walks and bus rides. One of the most beautiful and least frequented of the dales is outside the National Park – Nidderdale (it starts roughly halfway between Skipton and Ripon) and I went there later.

Nidderdale

The West Yorkshire buses go up the dale only at the weekend; the invaluable Burton Coach Company (phone Harrogate 711312) runs four bus trips from Pateley Bridge on Fridays, four on other weekdays during term times, and extra ones on those Wednesdays when the Women's Institute has its meetings! This is a real community service geared to the lives of Dales people, and tourists like me need to plan their trips to suit local habits.

Nidderdale has unique attractions. At several places the river Nid was long ago dammed to make a series of great reservoirs for distant cities. These now form a 'Lake District' of great beauty, and the multitude of birds (some very rare migrants) brings ornithologists from all over the world. About 200 different species have been recorded. Then there is the wildly romantic, or romantically wild, How Stean gorge where a stream cascades into a jagged cleft 70 feet deep. (In the modest café at the top, I encountered something even less expected: a superlatively iced 80th-birthday cake on the point of being delivered to Clarence House, London, for the Queen Mother! The café proprietor is a patissière of distinction.) And right at the head of Nidderdale is arguably the most spectacular churchyard in England, in the village of Middlemoor, with views to rival those of Cumbria's Lake District. There was not a tourist, except myself, to be seen that day.

Not the least attraction of Nidderdale is what now counts as one of my favourite hotels, the Yorke Arms at Ramsgill, which (along with perfect food, comfort, antiquity and scenery) has exactly the right kind of welcome, warm without synthetic charm. Some other hotels on bus routes through the dale or near Pateley Bridge include Grassfields and two little inns, the Flying Dutchman and the Royal Oak – the last two are at Summerbridge and Dacre Banks, not in the dale itself. Nidderdale is a place to remember and is well worth the trouble of catching those idiosyncratic local buses.

MORE IDEAS FOR BUS RIDES
TRIPS WITH A THEME

Bussing around in pursuit of a particular enthusiasm can give added interest to a trip. Take your favourite author, for example, and work out a route in his or her particular area: Hardy's Dorset or Jane Austen's Hampshire are good examples. A biography or the author's own writings are an obvious choice of books for the journey. Or go in pursuit of a particular period of history or architecture: East Anglia is a rich hunting-ground for medieval churches, Kent is strong on castles – and there are plenty of good books on architecture and history to take with you. Keen on gardening? Each year a guide is published to private gardens open to the public at certain seasons, listed county by county; or you could make for the tulip fields of Lincolnshire in the spring, or for fruit-growing counties like Worcestershire or Kent in blossom-time. Opportunities for browsing in antique shops are legion if you bus among small country towns almost anywhere. A route along the East Anglian coast is likely to be of special interest to bird enthusiasts, particularly at the time of the autumn migrations.

Many of my journeys had a theme such as these. In all cases, the suggested routes are very suitable for day-trips taken either from home or from one's holiday resort, or for a weekend or mid-week break of a few days (especially out of the peak holiday season). But many could make a mini-holiday in themselves, taken at a leisurely pace with lots of stops: there can be no better way to pass two or three days in the country.

Here are over two dozen more ideas for bus journeys in pursuit of particular enthusiasms.

Shore forts

All round the south-east and south coasts is evidence of the preoccupation with invasion that has worried the English for two thousand years or more. There are remains to be seen of everything from Roman defences along what they called the Saxon shore right up to the 'pill boxes' of the Second World War. Henry VIII's forts alone, or the anti-Napoleon defences, provide enough interest for such a journey – starting and ending wherever you please, from Kent to Cornwall. The Stationery Office (HMSO) produce a useful booklet on Henry VIII's coastal defences (16th century), and others on, for instance, Roman fortifications. Most of these remains are in the care of the Department of the Environment, who issue a season ticket covering unlimited visits to all their monuments.

Canals

England is still networked with what were once busy trade links – the artificial waterways. Some are neglected except by ducks and anglers, some are used only by pleasure craft, and a few still work for a living; all are interesting to look at from passing buses, which often run alongside or cross and recross them. With the aid of the map included in a free leaflet, 'Make the Most of your Waterways' (from the British Waterways Board, Melbury House, London NW1 6JX), planning a canal-side bus trip is easy, and there are plenty of small books to explain the canal scene which are also sold by the Waterways Board.

Local dishes

A gourmet might enjoy seeking out lunch and dinner in places renowned for their local specialities, planning bus trips with good meals in mind. The 'Bookshelf' at the end of this book mentions guides to recommended eating places, but for anyone intent on trying regional specialities the one to get is *A Taste of England*, published by the English Tourist Board. There is no county without something of its own to offer.

Castles

Some counties are richer than others in castles, because history has dictated where massive defences were most needed to repel attack. These counties include Kent, obviously, because it was vulnerable to invasion from France, and the east coast for similar reasons. To the north the threat came from the Scots, and to the west from the marauding Welsh. Northumbria is a great place for castle-hunters.

Stately homes

Though a great many stately homes are open to the public, if you are making an out-of-season journey some may be closed then. To plan such a trip, send for the brochure 'Historic Houses Open in the Winter' (from the British Tourist Authority, see Appendix B for address), which tells you what the possibilities are, county by county, between November and March. Unfortunately it does not say which buses go to which house: you will have to phone the house or a nearby Tourist Information Centre to find out.

Kings and queens

Tracing the relics – buildings, tombs, sites and other monuments – associated with the monarchy over the last thousand years is a game that can be played in almost any part of England. The book *Royal Britain* includes ideas for nearly 40 possible tours around places of royal interest; although compiled mainly for the car-driver, it can be used when putting together a bus tour (available from the British Tourist Authority, see Appendix B).

The sea coast

No one in England is very far from the sea, and it takes very little planning to set off on a series of buses around the coast – with occasional detours inland when there is a break in the continuity of coastal buses. Among many books about the shoreline is the Automobile Association's *Around Britain's Seaside* (available from bookshops), which describes the scenery of 6,000 miles of coast and over a hundred resorts.

Forests

Whether you want a stroll among trees, a picnic, or just to be in the shade on a hot day, woodlands are full of delight, and it is the policy of the Forestry Commission to encourage their use for pleasure. The Commission (25 Savile Row, London W1) issues a series of free maps (very clear) showing where forests are to be found, with information about what you will discover when you get there. Many have special way-marked walks, short or long; information or refreshment kiosks; even observation hides from which to view wildlife. When writing for a 'See Your Forests Map', state which part of England you want. The maps do not tell you which buses go to each forest, so you will need to look at a bus map alongside the forest map to work this out for yourself. Among other books on the subject, *The Forests of England* by P. J. N. Havins is a particularly good guide to the history, wildlife and scenery of the woodlands.

Festivals

The number of towns, or localities, which now have annual festivals (of music, drama or other arts) is so great that an annual directory of them all is published: *Festivals in Britain* (Letts). A holiday booked at a festival centre could be combined with bussing about in the neighbourhood for a contrast with sitting in concert halls or theatres. For example, the Elgar Festival is held in his home town of Malvern. Bus trips in the surrounding, very lovely, Malvern Hills (which Elgar loved) would make an ideal complement to hearing his music.

Literary pilgrimages

After becoming absorbed in a particular writer's books, a deepening interest often leads one to read an autobiography, criticisms of the works or a biography; with this comes an urge to see the places where the author lived or set the stories. Examples of regions particularly associated with specific writers are:

Bedfordshire: John Bunyan (Bedford and Elstow)
Buckinghamshire: John Milton (Chalfont St Giles); Thomas Gray (Stoke Poges)
Cambridgeshire: Rupert Brooke (Grantchester and King's College, Cambridge)
Cheshire: Mrs Gaskell (Knutsford)
Cornwall: Daphne du Maurier (Fowey)
Dorset: Thomas Hardy (Dorchester and most of the county); Jane Austen (Lyme Regis)
Hampshire: Jane Austen (Chawton)
Hertfordshire: George Bernard Shaw (Ayot St Lawrence)
Kent: Charles Dickens (see Chapter 14; also Broadstairs)
Lake District: William Wordsworth (Cockermouth, Hawkshead and Grasmere)
Shropshire: A. E. Housman (Ludlow)
Exmoor: Richard Blackmore, author of *Lorna Doone*
Somerset: Jane Austen (Bath)
Staffordshire: Arnold Bennett (the Potteries)
Sussex: Henry James (Rye)
Thames Valley: Jerome K. Jerome

Warwickshire: Shakespeare (see Chapter 3); George Eliot
    (Nuneaton)
Yorkshire: The Brontës (Haworth); George Gissing
    (Wakefield)
Any of these might be visited by bus, carrying one of the
author's books for reading on the way. One can do the same sort of
thing where landscape artists are concerned: visit 'Constable
Country' in Suffolk, for example, or Samuel Palmer's Sussex.

Architectural trips

These are legion. In a sense all trips are architectural, since
buildings are everywhere, but obviously different localities have
different things to show – from the splendour of medieval
church-building in East Anglia or the Cotswolds, for example, to
the exuberance of early Victorian seaside architecture along the
south coast. How architectural style relates to the geology of
England is vividly shown when the buses move from one county
to another on a long trip and the appearance of houses changes. A
small book that illuminates the subject is *The Stones of England*
(Bedford Square Press). Another pocket-size book, *Discovering
Timber-Framed Buildings*, concentrates on half-timbered houses,
their methods of construction and the differing styles of each
region (Shire).

Roman roads

We are still travelling along many of these. Using the
'Discovering' book on the subject (Shire) as a guide, one could bus
the whole length of a Roman road today. After centuries of use,
such roads are studded with relics from every period of history
over the past 2,000 years, even if only in the name of some ancient
inn or an occasional milestone set up in coaching days.

On the track of smugglers

Many coastal regions to the south and east have a history of
smuggling (there are references to this in the Isle of Wight tour,
for instance; see Chapter 10). Not only on the coast but inland are
places with smuggling connections – houses with tunnels, caves
or potholes used by smugglers and so forth. For instance, not only
Rye and Dymchurch on the Kent coast have relics to show and
stories to tell, but also country villages like Hawkhurst and
Goudhurst. Jeremy Errand's book *Secret Passages and Hiding
Places* has a lot on the subject.

Windmills and watermills

Post mills had bodies that revolved; then came smock mills (only the wooden top revolved, and the base was of brick); and finally tower mills were introduced (all-brick with a rotating cap at the top). Some have been restored and may even, in a few cases, be seen working – watermills likewise. Kent alone has about 30. Whereabouts and opening times can be obtained from local tourist boards (see Appendix B).

Garden tours

Pick the right time of year for these, depending on whether the gardens you want to visit are celebrated for their spring bulbs, summer roses or autumn tints. There are the gardens of stately homes (many run by the National Trust), botanical gardens in some cities, private gardens opened occasionally to the public (for directories, see 'Bookshelf') and horticultural gardens owned by the Royal Horticultural Society, National Rose Society, etc. In addition, in some counties (particularly in the south) nurserymen's grounds are open to the public; municipal parks often reach a very high standard; and the market-gardening areas are a pleasure to see at appropriate seasons – the lavender fields of Norfolk, near Kings Lynn, and the bulb fields of Lincolnshire, near Spalding, for example. Spalding has a spectacular tulip parade each May and organizes other events (leaflet available from Springfields, Spalding, Lincolnshire). The Thames and Chilterns Tourist Board (address in Appendix B) has a particularly good 'Visit a Garden' leaflet with several suggested trails in their region.

Craftworkers

A very large number of rural industries can be watched – one of the most interesting of free entertainments! – with no obligation to buy, though that temptation may prove irresistible. Pottery and weaving are the most widely available, but a huge variety of other objects are still being made by hand. You can see replica pistols and armour being put together, animals being stuffed or rocking-horses made. Less esoteric are basketry and rushwork, boats, bookbinding, bricks, candles, clocks, corn-dollies, embroidery, furniture, glass, jewellery, leatherwork, models, musical instruments, perfume, pressed flower pictures, spinning wheels and wrought iron. These are all examples from the county-by-county guide to craftworkers who welcome visitors, published by the Council for Small Industries in Rural Areas (35 Camp Road, London SW19 4UP).

From source to sea

If you live near a river you may have wondered where it comes from, and goes to, in the course of its wanderings. A trip full of surprises might be concocted by following it – as closely as possible – until it joins the sea. The likelihood is that there will be stretches of it which no bus (or road) reaches, but in all probability you will be able to see a good deal as the buses cross and recross it, perhaps over bridges that are in themselves of historic interest (a bridge-spotter's tour? – children could enjoy 'collecting' all the different types there are, perhaps with the help of the little *Discovering Bridges* book published by Shire).

Antique hunting

Browsing in one antique shop after another has become a national sport, particularly among those with a passion for collecting in one form or another. Most country towns on bus routes have something to offer, but to plan a bus tour systematically it may be worth sending for lists of antique shops in the area in which you are interested. Listed under counties, there will be an indication of each dealer's specialization. (Send a large stamped addressed envelope to the British Antique Dealers Association at 20 Rutland Gate, London SW7 or the London and Provincial Antique Dealers Association, 112 Brompton Road, London SW3 for lists of their members. A comprehensive directory of all dealers is sold by the Antique Collectors Club, 5 Church Street, Woodbridge, Suffolk.) In addition, country towns often have antiques fairs, when dealers from many towns gather to show their wares in a hotel or other venue for a few days. The English Tourist Board (see Appendix B) includes these in its calendar of forthcoming events. Some towns also have weekly antiques markets, or 'flea markets'. Two well-produced local guides are obtainable from the East Anglia Tourist Board (see Appendix B) and the Cotswold Antique Dealers Association (c/o P. Rowan, High Street, Blockley, Gloucestershire). Cheltenham's tourist centre has one, too.

Special occasions

The English Tourist Board's calendar of events covers all kinds of gatherings which might inspire a bus journey. Apart from conventional exhibitions and sports events, it includes sales of fell ponies and Clydesdale horses, sheepdog trials, trotting races, demonstrations of wildflower painting, a steam-engine gathering, a vintage air show, military parades, a torchlight procession, carnivals, a regatta and old ceremonies such as rush-bearing. These were only a small fraction of what was listed for just one locality (the Lake District) recently. Many of the events, incidentally, are free.

History relived

Anyone interested in a particular period of history (or of archaeology) could enjoy a bus journey that illuminated it, planning a route to take in as many relevant sights as possible. If the Romans or the Normans are your choice, the English Tourist Board (see Appendix B) has booklets on both, showing what is where and relating each to its historical context. A Civil War trail is described in another good booklet from the Thames and Chilterns Tourist Board (see Appendix B).

Nature reserves

These tend to be off the beaten track, for obvious reasons, but the Nature Conservancy Council (which manages quite a number of them) tells me the following are accessible by bus – enquire locally about others not belonging to the NCC.

Studland Heath and sand dunes (Dorset): bus from Bournemouth or Swanage

Ebbor Gorge (Somerset): bus from Wells (alight at Wookey Hole; 20-minute walk)

Yarner Wood (Devon): bus from Exeter, Plymouth, Newton Abbot or Okehampton (alight at Bovey Tracey; 30-minute walk) The National Park mini-bus goes nearer but only in summer.

Rostherne Mere Observatory (Cheshire): bus from Manchester or Chester (alight at Bucklow; 15-minute walk) There is an infrequent bus from Knutsford and Altrincham right to Rostherne. Permit needed.

Ainsdale sand dunes (Merseyside): bus from Formby

In each case, a booklet explaining what is to be seen can be obtained for 10p or less from the Nature Conservancy Council (19 Belgrave Square, London SW1X 8PY). It is wise to enquire whether there is currently any limitation on access before you set off.

Wine tasting

A hundred or more vineyards have started up in southern England in recent times, and one could plan a bus tour around a wine-tasting route, visiting those that welcome visitors. For a free pictorial map showing where all England's modern vineyards are, write to the English Vineyards Association, Cricks Green, Felsted, Essex. There are now even more acres of grape vines than there were in the Middle Ages.

Post buses and philatelists

Some rural areas have small red vehicles that are both mail vans and carriers of passengers. They usually start from a town post office and call at small village sub-offices, often going to places that have no other bus – really off-the-beaten-track rides. Stamp collectors in particular seek them out because they often use postage stamps on tickets, with a special mark of cancellation, and special pictorial postcards. There are, at the time of writing, about two or three in each of the following: Cumbria, Lincolnshire, Northumberland, Kent, Surrey, Sussex, Berkshire, Hampshire (including Isle of Wight) and Oxfordshire. Their timetables can be had from post offices.

The English Tourist Board (see Appendix B) publishes a booklet called 'A Guide to Philatelic England'. A stamp-collector could use this to plan a bus tour calling on places where there are stamp dealers, philatelic counters, stamp museums or such collectable items as cachets and railway letter-stamps to be found.

Exploring the South Downs

For the vigorous minority, there is the 80-mile hilltop walk known as the South Downs Way, through spectacular scenery all the way from Hampshire to East Sussex. The less hearty majority can still enjoy the Way, however, by doing stretches of it in small bits – taking one bus to the chosen starting point and catching another at the end of an hour or two's walk (perhaps staying overnight at a different south coast resort or country town each day). This may sound complicated, but it is in fact quite easy to do if you get the free leaflet 'South Downs Way: Public Transport Guide' from the Southdown Bus Company (see Appendix A). It includes a clear map with details of relevant buses and their frequency. A booklet describing what is to be seen along the Way, and an accommodation list, is published by the Countryside Commission (John Dower House, Crescent Place, Cheltenham) and bookshops sell a guide to it published by HMSO.

Photography

Virtually any bus route is a gift to the amateur photographer. I have one of those slim, handbag-size cameras with built-in flash and telescopic lens – easy to carry when one is travelling light, and well suited to photographing anything from wildflowers (better than picking them) to medieval carvings inside a church, a baker at work by the oven or a foal suckling from its mother. These are the sights that the picture-postcards don't record, but they are the very stuff of which journeys round England are made.

BUS PLUS

Foot and pedal

People taking a walk after parking their car must return to it. Bus passengers have more freedom – they can leave one bus at point A and pick up another at point B after an agreeable stroll between the two. Several bus companies have leaflets giving details of scenic walks where this is possible. For people who like to alternate walking with bussing in this way, there is also a list of three-dozen scenic footpaths, of eight miles and upwards, in a free booklet called 'Recreational Paths', which tells where to get leaflets or guidebooks to these paths and contains details of connecting buses. This comes from the Countryside Commission (John Dower House, Crescent Place, Cheltenham) who also have a free booklet describing a hundred country parks, woodlands or other open places that are often within bus ride of towns.

Alternating bus and cycle schemes are described on page 133.

Bed and banquet

Overseas visitors in particular seem to enjoy stepping back in time, sleeping in a four-poster bed and attending a banquet in medieval or Tudor style – often complete with minstrels, wenches, jesters and archery or other combats.

The following towns mentioned in this book have hotels with four-posters: Berkhamsted (Swan), Brentwood (Moat House), Burford (Cotswold Gateway, Golden Ball), Bembridge (Highbury), Cirencester (King's Head, Black Horse), Hawes (Rookhurst Guest House), Lynton (Alford House, Crown, Rockvale, Seawood), Minehead (Woodbridge), St Albans (Noke Hotel, St Michael's Manor), St Ives (Master Roberts), Shanklin (Culver Lodge, Hartland Hotel), Stamford (George), Stratford (Falcon, Haytor, Grosvenor House), Skipton (Snaygill Guesthouse) and Ventnor (Rocklands).

Banquets are organized at Burford (Golden Ball), Grantham (Angel), Rye (George), Stratford-on-Avon (Welcombe, Falcon) and in some Kent castles: Leeds, Allington and Chilham.

A 'GOOD BUS GUIDE'

No one should know better than the bus companies themselves which are their most attractive routes for joy riding. In the course of writing this book I wrote inviting the principal companies to nominate their best journeys by ordinary bus (not special excursions or coach tours). The recommendations from those that replied are set out below – coupled with my thanks for their help. (A map showing the territory each company covers can be found in Appendix A, together with the addresses to which to write for timetables or other information.) I particularly asked for suggestions for day-trips out of the bigger towns and cities, and any useful free leaflets they produced. A number of these are covered by the Explorer ticket (see back of this book).

Bristol

This company has printed seven 'Holiday Bus Hops' leaflets, one for each of the following towns: Swindon, Wells and Glastonbury, Gloucester, Bath, Stroud, Bristol and Cheltenham. Each one lists half-a-dozen places to visit (briefly saying what is of interest there), the service numbers of the buses, and how long the journeys take.

They also run (during summer) a special open-top bus that tours Bristol, another between Bream Down and Burnham-on-Sea, and one from Uphill which goes along the seafront at Weston-Super-Mare through Kewstoke Woods to Sand Bay.

Crosville

In a leaflet called 'Information for Visitors to Chester', the company (which operates in the north-west) describes in some detail about two dozen interesting places to get to by bus – giving the numbers of the buses to catch and the time the journeys take. They also told me that the bus which goes to Manchester via Northwich is worth taking because it runs through the Delamere Forest, while another, going to Newcastle-under-Lyme via

Crewe, provides an interesting ride through the Cheshire countryside.

People living in Manchester can get to the edge of the Peak National Park quite easily by taking the bus to Macclesfield or the one serving the Congleton area. (Crosville also run buses into North Wales.)

Apart from Crosville's own leaflets, a useful guide called 'Out and About in Cheshire' gives information about access by buses. It can be bought from the Countryside and Recreation Division of Cheshire County Council, County Hall, Chester.

Cumberland

'Enjoy Lakeland' is the name of a leaflet with a map showing the best bus routes to places of interest throughout the Lake District. The company particularly recommends the following scenic routes:

Whitehaven – Seascale – Millom (coast road with magnificent views of Ennerdale, Eskdale and the sea)

Whitehaven – Carlisle (industrial and rural mixture)

Whitehaven – Workington – Cockermouth – Keswick (Bassenthwaite Lake and hills)

Maryport – Silloth – Wigton (outstandingly beautiful views of Solway Firth, the Lake District and farming country)

Cockermouth – Loweswater – Buttermere (typical Lake District scenery)

Keswick – Seatoller (into the heart of mountains and lakes; a short journey)

Keswick – Ambleside (up into the hills)

East Midland

There are lots of good bus rides in this area. Derbyshire, the gateway to the Peak District National Park, has routes that take in marvellous scenery and such interesting towns as Buxton, Castleton, Macclesfield, Matlock and Matlock Bath. The Lincoln-Manchester ride is a memorable one across England – it goes through Chesterfield and lovely villages like Baslow, Eyam and Tideswell. In Nottinghamshire lies Sherwood Forest, with country parks and an attractive visitor centre, all served by buses from Mansfield, Nottingham, Retford, Sheffield or Worksop.

Eastern Counties

This company (which operates in Norfolk and Suffolk) has numerous leaflets on 'Days Out from' various places: Yarmouth,

Southwold, Cromer, Norwich and Kings Lynn, for instance. Each describes pleasant places to visit and gives timetables of buses. There are also 'Walkabout' and 'Explorer' leaflets and two about special summer buses, called the 'Suffolk Coastliner' and 'North Norfolk Coastliner', with similar particulars. The first route runs between Felixstowe and Yarmouth and the second between Yarmouth and Kings Lynn.

Eastern National

This company (which operates in Essex) singled out for me eight routes that run through scenic areas, as follows:

Southend – South Woodham – Danbury Common – Maldon

Chelmsford – Thaxted – Debden Green – Saffron Walden

Chelmsford – Danbury Park – Danbury Common – Little Baddon

Colchester – Dedham – and on to Constable Country (East Bergholt and Flatford) on summer Sundays only

Colchester – Colne Valley – Halstead

Colchester – Colchester Zoo – Maldon

Maldon – Burnham-on-Crouch (or Maldon – Bradwell-on-Sea) through the Dengie marshes

Braintree – Finchingfield – Great Bardfield

East Yorkshire

This company named three routes out of Hull: to Goole, past the Humber Bridge site and on through small villages; to Aldbrough Cliffs (spectacular coastal erosion), through farming country; and to Scarborough, a long route through Wolds farming country and old market towns, with opportunities to visit on the way the historic buildings of Beverley or the hustle-bustle of holiday camps between Filey and Scarborough, according to taste. (Another scenic route from Scarborough goes to Malton. This is run by Hardwicks Services, Westwood Coach Station, Scarborough.)

Others they suggest as scenically interesting are:

York – Dunnington Gate – Helmsley – Stanford Bridge – Driffield *or* York – Pocklington – Warter – Driffield; *or* York – Market Weighton – Beverley – Middleton –North Dalton – Driffield

Driffield – Sledmere – Malton

Driffield – Langtoft – Bridlington – Scarborough

They produce a leaflet with map and bus service numbers covering most of the above routes, called 'A Day Out and About

Hants and Dorset

Here are their recommendations:

Southampton to Winchester and Guildford, or Romsey (see also Chapter 11)

Salisbury to any of the following: Stonehenge, through Woodford Valley to Amesbury (unspoilt countryside); through Bourne Valley to Tidworth (unspoilt countryside); to Shaftesbury (very scenic) (see also Chapter 8)

Bournemouth to Poole, Dorchester and Weymouth (delightful scenery and many interesting stops – Bere Regis, Tolpuddle, Athelhampton House and, just off the route, Maiden Castle earthworks)

Bournemouth to Fordingbridge and Salisbury (pleasant countryside, interesting villages – Breamore House and its museums are just off the route, and by taking a second bus one can get to Rockbourne's Roman villa)

Bournemouth to Burley, Lyndhurst and Southampton (through the New Forest)

Bournemouth, Blandford and Shaftesbury (some superb scenery, passing prehistoric hill forts. Both Wimborne and Blandford are worth a stop)

Bournemouth to Swanage, crossing Poole Harbour on the chain ferry (runs through wild heath and sand dunes, past a superb beach, and over the Purbeck Hills. Studland is a delightful village to visit)

Poole to Swanage, crossing the edge of unspoilt Dorset Heath (Wareham and Corfe Castle are worth exploring, up in the Purbeck Hills are spectacular views of land and sea, and the famous Blue Pool is just off the route)

Lincolnshire

The Lincoln – Grimsby route passes over the Wolds with their splendid views and through the beautiful village of Tealby. Lincoln – Skegness is another Wolds ride, going through the two little market towns of Horncastle and Spilsby. The Lincoln – Mablethorpe route passes through another Wolds market town, Louth, with a specially fine church. Boston – Woodhall Spa is a Fens ride. The company has a 'What to see by Lincolnshire' leaflet.

The Viking Way is a long-distance footpath through fine scenery. Each stretch of it has a descriptive leaflet, and for each section there is another leaflet with times of buses which can take you to the start or from the finish of each walk.

London Country

They have booklets about 'London's Town and Countryside', the Rambler's Bus (Surrey Weald) and the Lee Valley Leisure Bus (Essex), though the future of the Lee Valley bus was in some doubt at the time of writing.

Midland Red

This company is very willing to work out itineraries for joy riders: phone the public relations department (see Appendix A). Parts of its area are very beautiful, with places like Stratford-on-Avon, Leamington, Warwick, Evesham and the Malvern hills. It is about to publish its own guide to the Stratford-on-Avon area, and it has special leaflets for youth hostellers.

Oxford – South Midland

Scenic routes and places of interest reached by their buses are described in two leaflets, 'Explore the County by Bus' and 'Oxford to Windsor' (the latter includes bus times). For Oxford to Stratford-on-Avon, see Chapter 3.

Potteries Motor Traction

This bus company's area is mostly industrial but one can get by bus from Stoke-on-Trent to Buxton and the Peak District. Another good ride is across north Shropshire, through Market Drayton to Shrewsbury.

They also recommend bussing to the following places of interest: Uttoxeter, Stafford, Crewe, Sandbach and Congleton. There is a rural route between Uttoxeter and Cheadle (Staffordshire) which goes past the famous pleasure gardens of Alton Towers.

Ribble

This company (which operates in Cumbria) has produced a particularly helpful 12-page booklet in conjunction with the National Trust. Called 'Explore Cumbrian Heritage', it describes and illustrates all the stately homes and other Lakeland sights that can be reached by bus, and gives bus timetables for buses within the Lake District. The area is, of course, easily reached from Carlisle.

Southdown

Having the South Downs and other beauty spots in their area, this company sells a 40-page booklet describing walks which begin and end at bus stops – most of them take about two hours. They can be reached by bus from south-coast towns or from such places as Petersfield, Haslemere, Midhurst, Arundel, Horsham, Haywards Heath, East Grinstead, etc.

There is a special 'rambler' bus on Sundays, with a cheap all-day ticket, which travels through the South Downs north of Arundel with – in addition to fine scenery – stops at a Roman villa, an industrial history museum, nature reserves, a mill and so on.

Trent

They recommend the following routes:

Nottingham – Mansfield – Chesterfield
Nottingham – Worksop – Doncaster
Derby – Belper – Crich – Wirksworth – Matlock
Nottingham – Tuxford – Retford (see Chapter 2)

In addition, the company runs a summer weekend service, described in their 'Peak Pathfinder' leaflet, of buses that go through the wild and beautiful Peak National Park, running from Derby to Buxton. The leaflet also gives the numbers of other bus services that go through a little of the Park as part of their normal routes. Another special bus, on summer Sundays, goes from Derby to Kedlestone Hall (leaflet available).

Most useful of all is their 16-page 'Trent Tripper' booklet, which is an A-Z guide to places of interest throughout their area, coupled with details of bus services that reach them (including times).

United Automobile

This company operates in the north-east; their Holy Island leaflet describes a service that goes from Berwick to this fascinating isle, its castle and sea-birds. The bus runs along the wonderful Northumbrian coast, with beaches, castles and harbours most of the way. The island is two miles off the coast, and the bus reaches it along a causeway exposed only at low tide – so the bus's comings and goings are determined by the tides, but there is enough time to explore the island, its castle and priory ruins.

Another bus, from Newcastle to Carlisle, runs near the Roman Wall. At the Once Brewed information centre one can pick up a smaller bus which goes to the most interesting sights on the Wall, and which has a tape-recorded commentary (in midsummer). (A leaflet on all the bus services of the Wall can be had from the Tynedale Tourist Information Centre, Manor Office, Hexham, Northumberland.)

United Counties

Several of the long routes pass through pretty countryside: Aylesbury to Bedford, Northampton to Cambridge, Northampton to Oxford, Kettering to Peterborough.

West Riding

Although most of this company's territory is industrial, it recommends the Wakefield-Doncaster route through pretty villages like Wragby and Badsworth, passing the entrance to Nostell Priory (National Trust), and also the York – Belby – Doncaster and Selby – Hemmingborough – Howden routes.

West Yorkshire

This company has so many scenic routes that the choice is tremendous. The following are a few suggestions. For a more detailed list, with service numbers, write to the company (see Appendix A) and ask for their Dales leaflet.

A holiday in the Vale of York

York – Wetherby – Knaresborough – Aldborough – Ripon – Thirsk – Northallerton – Borrowby – Easingwold – York (or, after Northallerton, Stokesley – Helmsley – Thirsk – York). The Northallerton – Borrowby buses run only twice a week.

Circular tours from York

York – Boroughbridge – Knaresborough – Harrogate – Wetherby – York

York – Thirsk – Pickering – Malton – Driffield – Pocklington – York

Using some less frequent services: York – Driffield – Beverley – Market Weighton – Holme-on-Spalding-Moor – Selby – South Milford – Tadcaster – York

York – Foston – Sherriff Hutton – York

Circular tour from Skipton

(Saturdays) Skipton – Grassington – Pateley Bridge – Middlesmoor – Pateley Bridge – Harrogate – Otley – Ilkley – Skipton

Circular tour from Leeds

Leeds – Wetherby – Knaresborough – Ripon – Ripley – Pateley Bridge – Harrogate – Otley – Leeds

Cross-country journey

Kendal – Ingleton – Skipton – Grassington – Pateley Bridge – Harrogate – Ripon – Pickering – Whitby (or, after Skipton, Hawes – Ripon, but only on summer Tuesdays, or Leyburn – Ripon, but only on summer Fridays). Grassington – Pateley Bridge buses run only on Saturdays

Tours from Keighley

Keighley – Bingley – Denholme – Oxenhope and back. On Saturdays, after Denholme, Halifax – Todmorden – Oxenhope – Haworth – Keighley

Keighley – Colne – Skipton – Grassington – Kettlewell – Buckden and back

Leeds (or Bradford) to the Dales

Summer weekend services to Hawes and Keld; then Keld – Richmond

Coast and Dales holiday

Whitby – Scarborough – Bridlington – Driffield – York – Wetherby – Knaresborough – Ripon – Bedale – Leyburn

Western National

This company produces leaflets covering the Dartmoor bus services (with map and timetables) and 'South Devon by Bus from Torbay' – an A–Z of interesting places with the numbers of bus services that go to them, journey times, etc. (See also Chapter 12.) The journey from Exeter to Bournemouth (out of their area) is a very good route, too.

Yorkshire Traction

'Take a Countryside Bus Ride' is a 16-page booklet about South Yorkshire. The first half gives detailed information about country walks that begin and end at bus-stops. The second half is a selection of places of interest, with information on buses that go to them from Barnsley, Doncaster, etc. (with timetables).

More good routes are listed in the Explorer Ticket leaflets and in a set of four called 'Just the Ticket' from the Thames and Chilterns Tourist Board (see Appendix B).

City Bus Companies

As explained elsewhere in this book, the majority of bus services in England are run by about two dozen companies operating under the auspices of the National Bus Company – although as this book went to press a new Act had just been passed by Parliament, intended to encourage more operators to start up outside the NBC network.

There already exist a number of small private operators, however. The times of their buses are often given at the back of the timetable books issued by the big companies, but other information is often obtainable from local councils. For example, one very scenic area hardly covered by any of the NBC companies is the Cotswolds, and a book of timetables, covering all the little local operators, is issued by Gloucestershire County Council, Shire Hall, Gloucester. In addition there are post buses, described on page 198.

Similarly, though the major companies referred to in this book have big cities as their termini, the buses that run *within* each city's area do not belong to these companies: they are run by the local council or by a local transport executive. The following have their own transport departments: London, Birmingham and Coventry, Merseyside, Greater Manchester, West Yorkshire, South Yorkshire, Tyne and Wear and about three dozen smaller towns. In some cases, a city's area extends some way into the countryside, so it may be worth enquiring whether its buses do go out into areas of scenic interest.

Just one example is **Sheffield** (South Yorkshire). From the heart of this great industrial city one can very quickly get to the following places of interest: Rivelin Dams (beautiful, almost Alpine scenery around two reservoirs with views along the valley and a nature trail); Low and High Bradfield (villages in a superb valley); Grindleford – Bakewell (climbs up to heather moors, and a National Trust estate where sheepdog trials are held in late summer; interesting buildings along the way); Bamford – Snake Inn (magnificent panoramas along Hope and Derwent valleys; Robin Hood, Jane Eyre and 'Dam Busters' associations – and much else); and Castleton (also along the Hope Valley; castle, caverns and 'Blue John' mines to visit). The City of Sheffield produces a mass of colourful leaflets about all these places, obtainable free from the Publicity Office, Town Hall, Sheffield, S1 2HH.

When I was last in Sheffield, I spent a day doing a circular tour (using three different bus services) which took in Castleton, with time for a visit to one of its spectacular caves, and Bakewell – including a browse in its outstandingly good wildlife bookshop and a genuine Bakewell 'pudding' (as the famous tart is known locally) for tea. The ride was through spectacular Peak District scenery and picturesque villages – and all this is within a short distance of Britain's great steel-making city. (And, incidentally, South Yorkshire boasts the cheapest bus fares in Britain.)

I recently visited another big city which no one seems to think of as anything but industrial: the great port of **Hull**. Once again, the local buses soon whisk one out into the countryside. Although the scenery here is not spectacular (it is very flat, except when one heads into the Yorkshire Wolds), the buses take one to sights that are quite exceptional. I spent hours in Beverley: even if it did not have its superb Minster, it would be a town to remember for its lovely square and a church of exceptional beauty, almost as rich in carvings as the Minster itself. Near Hull there are stately homes, too: Burton Agnes Hall, for example, where – in particularly beautiful Tudor rooms – a large collection of Impressionist paintings is housed so that one can enjoy them in a way quite impossible in the famous but overcrowded galleries of London. And not far off is a coastline with some celebrated spots for bird-watching (as well as seaside resorts). A useful list of a dozen places to visit around Hull (with the numbers and frequency of buses) is obtainable, together with bus timetables, from the Public Relations Office, 77 Lowgate, Hull. Tourists from Europe whizz in and out of the port or pause only for a shopping spree in the city, overlooking all the historic attractions in and around it.

Another bus runs from **Sunderland** to Beamish Open Air Museum, taking in on its way a wildfowl trust, the first rail bridge in the world, a transport museum in a historic rail station, two castles, a scenic cliff and Washington Old Hall (where George Washington's ancestors lived).

If you want to travel on a vintage bus, you can get one from Beamish Open Air Museum in Durham to Tanfield steam railway on summer Sundays.

In the case of the biggest city of all, write to London Transport (Broadway, London SW1) for 'A Day in London's Countryside'. This describes how to get out of the city by Underground and the interesting places you can then explore by LT buses.

Town Trails

This book has been primarily about rural rides. Nevertheless, town buses deserve a mention, too. Bus rides in towns suffer from the usual disadvantages of traffic jams and overcrowded streets, but even so, a good way to get to know a town in outline, so to speak, before exploring on foot is to circulate around its more interesting parts on a bus.

The problem is to know *which* bus service goes round interesting areas of towns – a stranger can easily get on the wrong one and be whisked off to some industrial suburb by mistake. Some bus companies, however, run special buses in summer to take visitors round the most interesting parts. (One example is Colchester, see page 112. Others are Lincoln and Bristol, and the latter has horse-drawn buses. Some provide commentaries as you go along.)

Very few bus companies have had the imagination to think out a 'bus trail' as the Maidstone and District Company has in respect of the ancient port of Faversham. They got the local conservation society to produce for them a pictorial leaflet about one of their routes, the 676, which (starting at the railway station) goes by old almshouses, a pond, a creek, woods containing the ruins of an 18th-century gunpowder factory, the former fishmarket and a number of other local landmarks. It is an hour's enjoyment for the price of a bus ticket.

A phone call to the bus company operating in the town of your choice should elicit information about the best bus to take for a tour of this kind, but you will probably have to provide your own guidebook for commentary on the things to be seen (the local Tourist Information Centre may be able to provide something suitable, usually free).

Special Routes and Buses

Finally, more leaflets from other sources, two being about rather unusual bus routes. The first is about a bus that goes on summer Sundays where no car is allowed – **Goyt Valley**, in the Peak National Park. Car drivers are required to park and get on the mini-bus if they want to see this very lovely and unspoilt valley. In addition to the free leaflet explaining the scheme, an attractive 16-page booklet on the history, wildlife and landscape of the valley is sold by the Peak National Park, Aldern House, Baslon Road, Bakewell, Derbyshire.

The second comes from the **Horncastle** Bus Club, a bunch of enthusiasts who run their own bus service across the Lincolnshire Wolds, one of England's least frequented beauty spots. Only two main roads go through these hills and wooded valleys – and, since 1975, no commercial buses. Local people got together to remedy the situation and started to run buses themselves. Members pay a quarterly subscription and travel free; others are charged fares, and the deficit is made up by various fund-raising activities and a small subsidy from the local council. The club also sells an excellent 32-page booklet describing the interesting places to be seen all along the route, which runs through villages between Louth and Horncastle (this is obtainable, with further details about the bus service, from the club at 40 Southlands Avenue, Louth, Lincolnshire LN11 8EW).

I decided to sample the Horncastle Bus Club's route. I crossed the Humber by ferry (by the time this book is published, the new bridge may be open – the largest suspension bridge in the world). I made my way to Louth, a charming, unspoilt market town, and followed the devious route to Horncastle – devious because the bus winds this way and that to pick up passengers from outlying villages. There were marvellous views even though the hills are not very high.

I have described this Lincolnshire community-run bus in some detail because it is the only one whose route I have travelled, but there are other community buses. The Penrith one was mentioned in Chapter 17. Others run in the following areas: Aldborough (Norfolk), Bassetlaw (Nottinghamshire), Breckland (Norfolk), Cuckmere (Sussex), Hailsham (Sussex), Holt (Norfolk), Lilbourne (Staffordshire), Rother (Sussex), Soar (Leicestershire) and Coleridge (Devon). It is very likely that lots more will start up soon because, as previously mentioned, the Transport Act 1980 gives much greater freedom to private individuals to run bus services.

Anyone interested in getting community buses going can obtain a free leaflet from the National Bus Company (see Appendix A) or read *A Guide to Community Transport* (HMSO) or *Rural Rides* (National Consumer Council, 18 Queen Anne's Gate, London SW1).

Two other booklets on joy riding by bus are produced by volunteers (the Nottingham Transport Group, 17 Humber Road, Beeston NG9 2EJ). One is called 'Rural Rides in Old Herefordshire' and the other, 'Beer, Boots and Buses', is full of ideas for sampling country pubs around Nottingham.

BOOKSHELF

Since travelling light is the essence of bus journeying, one wants to carry only a minimum. Paperback guidebooks good for the purpose are *The Blue Guide to England* (Benn, £7) for the whole country. Up-to-date and comprehensive (covering villages as well as towns), it has maps and coloured town plans showing where bus stations are as well as 'sights' (and it refers to buses in the text). It not only describes places but gives opening hours.

The *Red Guides* (Ward Lock, some under £2 each) have similar virtues, but – a bad omission – too few maps and plans. Each book covers one particular region. The following are available: Lake District, Cornwall, Cotswolds and Shakespeare Country, Devon, Dorset and Wiltshire, Northumbria, South-East Coast, Thames and Chilterns, Wye, Hereford and Worcester, Yorkshire, Bournemouth and New Forest, Dartmoor, Isle of Wight, Norfolk and the Broads, and the Peak District.

The best *maps* to carry are either the 'Leisure Maps' sold by regional tourist boards (under £1, scale 3 miles to 1 inch); the RAC series sold in shops; or the Ordnance Survey's new 'Tourist' maps or, less detailed, their 'Route-masters'. All are exceptionally clear in design, with scenic areas or sights conspicuously marked.

For a greater understanding of what one sees through the bus window, the following are a few useful pocket-sized books: *The Making of the English Landscape* by W. G. Hoskins (Penguin); *The Countryside in Spring, Summer, Autumn, Winter* by A. E. Ellis (four colourful Jarrold paperbacks); *Trees and Bushes* by Vedel and Lange (Methuen); the new 'Gem' (Collins) series – on wildflowers, etc. But the list is endless – books on woodlands, moors or estuaries, rivers and coasts, the farming scene – as infinite as England's own variety is the range of interesting books about it. Usually one can find locally small booklets explaining special features of the county in which one is travelling – such aspects of the landscape as, say, the old tin mines of Cornwall or the Broads in Norfolk.

I usually take my own paperback *Kings and Queens* (Pan) to give me quickly the context of historic buildings and sites that I visit. Of the many books explaining inn signs, the one in the 'Discovering' series (Shire) is easiest to carry.

Shell's guidebooks (from various publishers) are excellent. Though too heavy to carry around, the *Shell Guide to England*, *Shell Book of Rural Britain* and *Shell Book of English Villages* would all be invaluable for finding out about off-the-beaten-track places along one's bus routes or for understanding what is seen on the way. There has been a spate of hefty books about villages lately, and another clear and beautifully produced one is the *Book of British Villages* (Drive Publications).

Joy riding on buses gives one a close view of hedges, of course. Two books that add to the enjoyment and interpretation of them are *The Hedgerow Book* by Ron Wilson (David and Charles) and, with pretty drawings, *Hedgerow* by John T. White (Ash and Grant).

Other books I have found particularly useful at home, to plan a journey beforehand, include: *Gardens Open to the Public* (annual), which gives dates on which hundreds of private gardens (all described) are occasionally open to the public in aid of charity. The gardens are listed county by county; nearby bus services are named (from the National Gardens Scheme, 57 Lower Belgrave Square, London SW1). *Gardens to Visit*, a similar but smaller annual directory, costs 25p from the Gardeners Sunday Organization (White Witches, Claygate Road, Dorking). *Visit an English Garden* (from the English Tourist Board, address in Appendix B) lists gardens regularly open, with buses.

Literary Landscapes of the British Isles by D. Daiches and J. Flower (Paddington Press) is a large hardback that is invaluable for discovering which writers once lived in a certain area, or for planning a 'literary trail' to follow. For other special interests, there are plenty of books to choose from. For example, an enthusiast for archaeology would find useful *A Guide to Roman Remains in Britain* by R. Wilson (Constable), while cathedral and castle-hunters might like to have *Cathedrals of England* by A. Clifton-Taylor (Thames & Hudson, paperback) or *English Cathedrals* by J. Harvey (Batsford, paperback) and *English Castles* by R. A. Brown (Batsford). The Department of the Environment (through the Stationery Office) produces lots of good things on castles and suchlike. There are plenty of popular books on looking at architecture (churches, houses, villages). A particularly sumptuous one is called *Life in The English Country House* by Mark Girouard (Penguin).

The National Trust Guide is a hefty volume describing and illustrating all the NT properties. The Trust (42 Queen Anne's Gate, London SW1) also has a smaller paperback giving the opening hours, nearest buses and so forth. This is useful because NT opening days and hours are erratic, and many properties close in winter. There is also *The National Trust Atlas*, which maps the whole country and shows not only Trust properties but every viewpoint, church or what-have-you that is worth a visit.

Two annuals, *Museums and Galleries* and *Historic Houses, Castles and Gardens* (ABC Historic Publications), give brief descriptions, opening hours and information on buses. The English Tourist Board (see Appendix B) has a regular calendar of forthcoming events in each region (for weekly market days, see bus timetables or guidebooks). Zoos, bird gardens and wildlife parks are covered in the *Penguin Guide to British Zoos*.

There is now a proliferation of guides to eating places. For restaurants consult Michelin's *Red Guide*, the Consumer Association's *Good Food Guide* and Egon Ronay's various directories, which between them cover not only restaurants but also pubs, transport cafés and (in *Just a Bite*) even tearooms and other inexpensive eating houses. The English Tourist Board's guide, *A Taste of England*, tells you where to get traditional dishes. Letts publish *The Best of British Pubs*.

As for hotels, there is an Egon Ronay Guide (now including a special section on low-cost hotels); the British Tourist Authority's *Commended Country Hotels, Guest Houses and Restaurants* and also its *Stay at an Inn*. Consumer Association publishes *The Good Hotel Guide*. The hotels in such guides are in a limited number of places and they may have no guidance to offer on areas you are interested in, so scrutinize them carefully before buying. You may find they feature only expensive places.

For more modest accommodation the AA, the Ramblers Association and the English Tourist Board all have directories of selected bed-and-breakfast places – not only guest houses but farms and small inns. Youth hostels (no age limit) are an alternative (details from YHA, Trevelyan House, St Albans AL1 2DY). Although commercial, the following guides published by

David Murdoch are useful in locating low-cost accommodation: *Bed and Breakfast* and *England's Best Holidays*.

The South East England Tourist Board (see Appendix B) has a particularly good annual list of 'bargain offers' from small hotels outside the summer season. I've tried six of their recommendations and have found their choices very good indeed.

An annual subscription to *In Britain*, a splendid and colourful magazine from the British Tourist Authority, would provide endless inspiration for areas to explore by bus.

Finally, don't ignore secondhand books, even if they are out of date. They can sometimes be more illuminating than their glossy modern successors. Just as this book was going to press, I picked up (for a mere £2) an 80-year-old volume called *Shakespeare's Avon from Source to Severn* (with delightful pen drawings on every page), which has inspired me to start planning yet another bus journey, when I intend to follow this hundred-mile river as closely as buses permit from Naseby in Northamptonshire to Tewkesbury in Gloucestershire, comparing what I see with the way it was when that book was published in 1901, when not even a horse-drawn bus disturbed the rural peace.

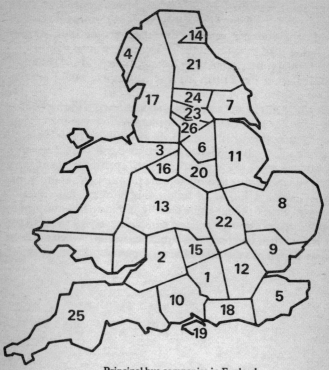

Principal bus companies in England
(numbers refer to the alphabetical list in Appendix A)
Reproduced by courtesy of the National Bus Company

APPENDIX A

PRINCIPAL BUS COMPANIES IN ENGLAND

(For areas in which they operate, see the map opposite. The following county councils also issue bus timetables covering all the bus companies in their county: Durham, Northumberland, Devon, Cornwall, Lincolnshire, Essex and Gloucestershire.)

1 Alder Valley
Thames Valley and Aldershot Omnibus Co Ltd, 3 Thorn Walk, Reading RG1 7AX
Tel. (0734) 54046

2 Bristol
Bristol Omnibus Co Ltd
Berkeley House, Lawrence Hill, Bristol BS5 0DZ
Tel. (0272) 558211

3 Crosville
Crosville Motor Services Ltd
Crane Wharf, Chester CH1 3SQ
Tel. (0244) 315400

4 Cumberland
Cumberland Motor Services Ltd
PO Box 17, Tangier Street, Whitehaven, Cumbria
CA28 7XF
Tel. (0946) 63222/7

5 East Kent
Maidstone
East Kent Road Car Co Ltd/Maidstone & District Motor Services Ltd, Station Road West, Canterbury, Kent CT2 8AL
Tel. (0227) 66151

6 East Midland
Mansfield
East Midland Motor Services Ltd/Mansfield District Traction Co Ltd
New Street, Chesterfield, Derbyshire S40 2LQ
Tel. (0246) 77451

7 East Yorkshire
East Yorkshire Motor Services Ltd 252 Anlaby Road, Hull HU3 2RS
Tel. (0482) 27142

8 Eastern Counties
Eastern Counties Omnibus Co Ltd PO Box No 10,
79 Thorpe Road,
Norwich NR1 1UB
Tel. (0603) 60421

9 Eastern National
Eastern National Omnibus Co Ltd New Writtle Street, Chelmsford, Essex CM2 0SD
Tel. (0245) 56151

10 Hants & Dorset
Gosport & Fareham
Hant and Dorset Motor Services Ltd/Gosport & Fareham Omnibus Co, The Square, Bournemouth, Hants BH2 5AB
Tel. (0202) 23371

11 **Lincolnshire Road Car
Co Ltd**
PO Box 15, St Mark Street,
Lincoln LN5 7BB
Tel. (0522) 22255

12 **London Country**
London Country Bus Services
Ltd, Lesbourne Road, Reigate,
Surrey RH2 7LE
Tel. (073 72) 42411

13 **Midland Red**
Midland Red Omnibus Co Ltd
Midland House, 1 Vernon Road,
Edgbaston, Birmingham
B16 9SJ
Tel. (021) 454 4808

14 **Northern**
Northern General Transport Co
Ltd 117 Queen Street, Gateshead
NE8 2UA
Tel. (0632) 605144

15 **Oxford – South Midland**
City of Oxford Motor Services
Ltd 395 Cowley Road, Oxford
OX4 2DJ
Tel. (0865) 774611

16 **PMT**
Potteries Motor Traction Co Ltd
Woodhouse Street, Stoke-on-
Trent ST4 1EQ
Tel. (0782) 48811

17 **Ribble**
Ribble Motor Services Ltd
Frenchwood Avenue, Preston,
Lancs PR1 4LU
Tel. (0772) 54754

18 **Southdown**
Southdown Motor Services Ltd
Southdown House, Freshfield
Road, Brighton BN2 2BW
Tel. (0273) 606711

19 **Southern Vectis**
Southern Vectis Omnibus Co
Ltd Nelson Road, Newport, Isle
of Wight PO30 1RD
Tel. (098 352) 2456

20 **Trent**
Trent Motor Traction Co Ltd.
PO Box No 35, Uttoxeter
New Road, Derby DE3 3NJ
Tel. (0332) 43201

21 **United Automobile**
United Automobile Services Ltd
United House, Grange Road,
Darlington, Co Durham
DL1 5NL
Tel. (0325) 65252

22 **United Counties**
United Counties Omnibus Co
Ltd, Bedford Road,
Northampton NN1 5NN
Tel. (0604) 35661

23 **West Riding
Yorkshire Woollen**
West Riding Automobile Co
Ltd/Yorkshire Woollen District
Transport Co Ltd, Barnsley
Road, Wakefield, WF1 5JX
Tel. (0924) 75521

24 **West Yorkshire**
West Yorkshire Road Car Co Ltd
PO Box No 24, East Parade,
Harrogate, Yorkshire HG1 5LS
Tel. (0423) 66061

25 **Western National
Devon General**
Western National Omnibus Co
Ltd/Devon General Omnibus &
Touring Co Ltd National House,
Queen Street, Exeter EX4 3TF
Tel. (0392) 74191

26 **Yorkshire Traction**
Yorkshire Traction Co Ltd
Upper Sheffield Road, Barnsley,
South Yorkshire S70 4PP
Tel. (0226) 82476

The regional bus companies listed above are all subsidiaries of the
National Bus Company (25 New Street Square, London EC4A
3AP). Enquiries about services should be made to local
companies.

Overseas visitors can get a lot of help from their branches of the British Tourist Authority including a list of guidebooks, accommodation directories and maps purchasable from the BTA, and details of the 'Open to View' ticket giving admission to country houses. Overseas offices are listed below.

Argentina
Av. Córdoba 645 P. 2°
1054 Buenos Aires
Tel. 392-9955

Australia
171 Clarence Street
Sydney N.S.W. 2000
Tel. 29-8627

Belgium
23 Place Rogierplein
1000 Brussels
Tel. 02/218.67.70

Brazil
Avenida Ipiranga 318-A, 12° Andar,
conj. 1201, 01046 São Paulo-SP
Tel. 257-1834

Canada
151 Bloor Street West
Suite 460
Toronto, Ontario M5S IT3
Tel. (416) 925-6326

Denmark
Møntergade 3, DK-1116
Copenhagen K.
Tel. (01) 12 07 93

France
6 Place Vendôme
75001 Paris
Tel. 296 47 60

Germany
Neue Mainzer Str. 22
6000 Frankfurt a.M.
Tel. (0611) 23 64 28

Holland
Leidseplein 23, Amsterdam
Postal address:
Leidseplein 5 (5e etage),
1017 PR Amsterdam
Tel. (020) 23 46 67

Italy
Via S. Eufemia 5
00187 Rome
Tel. 678 4998 or 5548

Japan
Tokyo Club Building
3-2-6 Kasumigaseki
Chiyoda-ku, Tokyo 100
Tel. 581-3603 or 3604

Mexico
Rio Tiber 103 – 6 piso
Mexico 5 D.F.
Tel. 511.39.27 or 514.93.56

New Zealand
Box 3655, Wellington

Norway
Marieboes gt 11
Oslo 1
Tel. (02) 41 18 49

South Africa
Union Castle Building
36 Loveday Street
PO Box 6256
2000 Johannesburg
Tel. 838 1881

Spain
Torre de Madrid 6/4
Plaza de España, Madrid 13
Tel. 241 13 96 or 248 65 91

Sweden
Malmskillnadsg 42, 1st floor
Postal address: Box 7293
S-103 90 Stockholm
Tel. 08-21 24 44

Switzerland
Limmatquai 78
8001 Zurich
Tel. 0147 42 77/97

USA
680 Fifth Avenue
New York, NY 10019
Tel. (212) 581-4700

612 South Flower Street
Los Angeles, CA 90017
Tel. (213) 623-8196

John Hancock Center (Suite 3320)
875 North Michigan Avenue
Chicago, IL 60611
Tel. (312) 787-0490

APPENDIX B

TOURIST BOARDS

British Tourist Authority
Queen's House,
64 St James's Street,
London SW1 A 1NF
Tel. (01) 499 9325

English Tourist Board
4 Grosvenor Gardens,
London SW1W 0DU
Tel. (01) 730 3400

Cumbria Tourist Board
Ellerthwaite, Windermere
LA23 2AQ
Tel. Windermere (096 62) 4444
Written and telephone enquiries
only.

East Anglia Tourist Board
14 Museum Street,
Ipswich IP1 1HU
Tel. Ipswich (0473) 214211

East Anglia Tourist Board
Bailgate, Lincoln LN1 3AR
Tel. Lincoln (0522) 31521
Written and telephone enquiries
only.

**Heart of England
Tourist Board**
PO Box 15,
Worcester WR1 2JT
Tel. Worcester (0905) 29511
Written and telephone enquiries
only.

**Isle of Wight Tourist
Board**
21 High Street, Newport,
Isle of Wight PO30 1JS
Tel. Newport (098 381) 4343/4

London Tourist Board
26 Grosvenor Gardens,
London SW1W 0DU
Tel. 01-730 0791

North West Tourist Board
Last Drop Village, Bromley Cross,
Bolton BL7 9PZ
Tel. Bolton (0204) 591511
Written and telephone enquiries only.

Northumbria Tourist Board
9 Osborne Terrace
Newcastle upon Tyne NE2 1NT
Tel. Newcastle upon Tyne
(0632) 817744

**South East England
Tourist Board**
Cheviot House, 4-6 Monson Road,
Tunbridge Wells TN1 1NH
Tel. Tunbridge Wells (0892) 33066

Southern Tourist Board
The Old Town Hall, Leigh Road,
Eastleigh, Nr Southampton
SO5 4DE
Tel. Eastleigh (0703) 616027

**Thames and Chilterns
Tourist Board**
8 The Market Place,
Abingdon OX14 3HG
Tel. Abingdon (0235) 22711

West Country Tourist Board
Trinity Court, Southernhay East,
Exeter EX1 1QS
Tel. Exeter (0392) 76351

**Yorkshire and Humberside
Tourist Board**
312 Tadcaster Road,
York YO2 2HF
Tel. York (0904) 707961

NORTHUMBRIA

CUMBRIA

YORKSHIRE
AND
HUMBERSIDE

NORTH
WEST

EAST
MIDLANDS

HEART
OF
ENGLAND

EAST
ANGLIA

THAMES
AND
CHILTERNS

LONDON

WEST COUNTRY

SOUTH
OF
ENGLAND

SOUTH EAST

Regional tourist boards in England
Reproduced by courtesy of the English Tourist Board

Having discovered the fascinating range of ideas for bus trips suggested throughout this book, you'll probably need no encouragement to start 'bussing about'! But just in case, the publishers of this book have struck a deal with the National Bus Company that will give you two half-price days out by bus.

At the bottom of this page are vouchers for the purchase of two of the new NBC **Day Explorer** tickets – at half price! These new tickets are available for travel on many buses run by most of the NBC subsidiaries up and down the country (see Appendix A for a map and a list of names and addresses).

Day Explorer tickets take you on days out from many main population centres and resorts to some marvellous places: there are **Day Explorer** routes into specially chosen parts of the countryside, to stately homes, to the seaside, to museums, to zoos.

Pick up your local 'Day Explorer' leaflet and find out more!

Day Explorer tickets are available for families, individual adults or children, and with these vouchers you can halve the cost of a day out to just £1.50 for the family (instead of £3), or £1 (instead of £2) for one adult, or 50p (instead of £1) for a child or old-age pensioner. The Family ticket covers two adults and two children.

So just cut out the vouchers below and present them at a local office of a participating National Bus Company subsidiary, along with the rest of the cash you need for your tickets. Once you've got your tickets, it's entirely up to you when and where to travel, because the **Day Explorer** ticket is made valid by you whenever you want to use it!

Happy bussing!

DAY EXPLORER ½ PRICE VOUCHER

This voucher entitles the holder to purchase one NBC 'Day Explorer' bus ticket at either half the Family, Adult or Senior Citizen rate.

It should be presented with cash equivalent at a local office of one of the participating NBC subsidiary bus companies.

NO CASH VALUE – SUBJECT TO USUAL CONDITIONS
Valid until 31 December 1982

DAY EXPLORER ½ PRICE VOUCHER

This voucher entitles the holder to purchase one NBC 'Day Explorer' bus ticket at either half the Family, Adult or Senior Citizen rate.

It should be presented with cash equivalent at a local office of one of the participating NBC subsidiary bus companies.

NO CASH VALUE – SUBJECT TO USUAL CONDITIONS
Valid until 31 December 1982

Also in Hamlyn Paperbacks

Hunter Davies

A WALK AROUND THE LAKES

'This is the most readable book on the Lake District I have found.' VIVIAN BIRD in the BIRMINGHAM POST

'Mr Davies escorts you on a Boswellian talk-and-walk, peopling the lakes and fells with all the local noteworthies, alive or recorded . . . a book worthy of its kinship with both Wordsworth the poet and Wainwright the fell wanderer.' THE OBSERVER

'Hunter Davies, with his persistent curiosity, is an ideal travelling companion: enthusiastic and thoroughly nosey. *A Walk Around the Lakes* . . . is a continual discovery and a delight.' EVENING STANDARD, LONDON

' . . . enormously interesting and entertaining. It must go to the top of the list for anyone taking an interest in the Lake District . . . even if you've never been there it makes excellent reading.' THE LADY